CHAPTER ONE

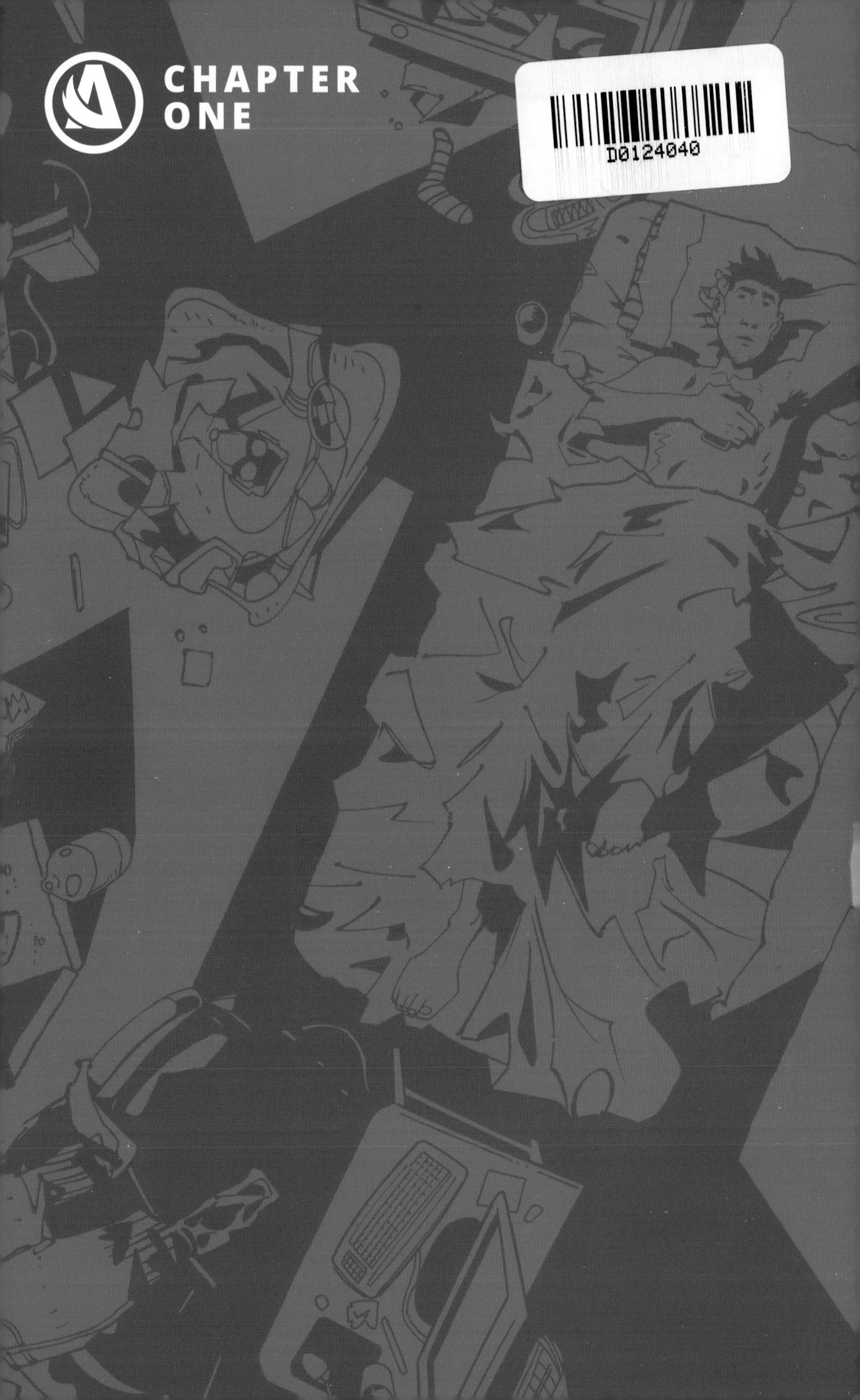

POP QUIZ

written by **JOE CASEY**
penciled by **DAMION SCOTT**
inked by **ROBERT CAMPANELLA** with **MOSH STUDIOS**
lettered by **AW'S DC HOPKINS**
colored by **SIGMUND TORRE** with **MOSH STUDIOS**

JOSEPH ILLIDGE • senior editor
DESIREE RODRIGUEZ and **AXEL BORDELON** • editorial assistants
cover by **DAMION SCOTT**, **ROBERT CAMPANELLA**,
and **SIGMUND TORRE**

LION FORGE

ISBN: 978-1-941302-75-0

Library of Congress Control Number: 2018934987

10 9 8 7 6 5 4 3 2 1

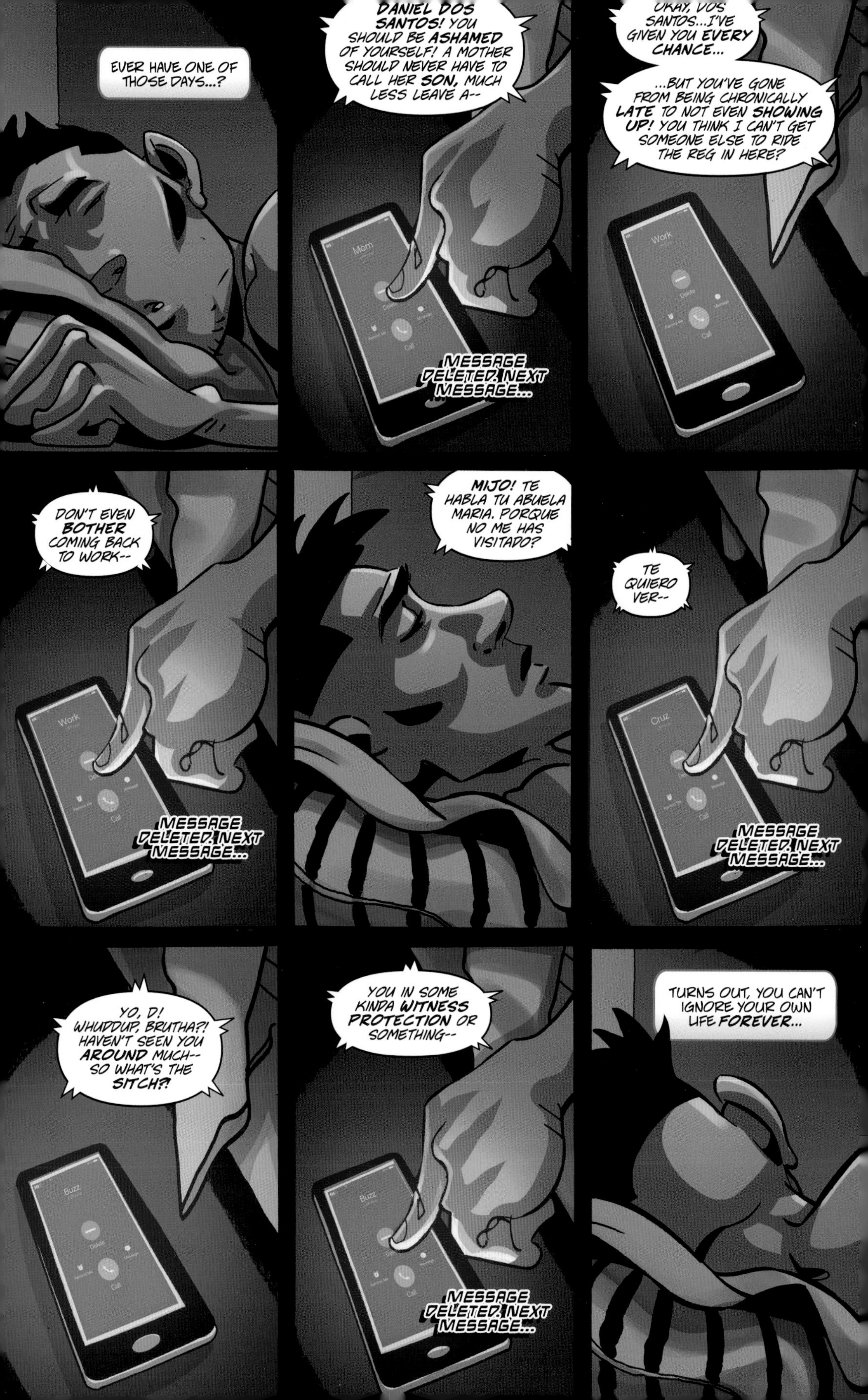
EVER HAVE ONE OF THOSE DAYS...?
DANIEL DOS SANTOS! YOU SHOULD BE ASHAMED OF YOURSELF! A MOTHER SHOULD NEVER HAVE TO CALL HER SON, MUCH LESS LEAVE A--
Mom
Delete
Message
Remind Me
Call
MESSAGE DELETED. NEXT MESSAGE...
OKAY, DOS SANTOS...I'VE GIVEN YOU EVERY CHANCE...
...BUT YOU'VE GONE FROM BEING CHRONICALLY LATE TO NOT EVEN SHOWING UP! YOU THINK I CAN'T GET SOMEONE ELSE TO RIDE THE REG IN HERE?
Work
Delete
Message
Remind Me
Call
DON'T EVEN BOTHER COMING BACK TO WORK--
Work
Call
MESSAGE DELETED. NEXT MESSAGE...
MIJO! TE HABLA TU ABUELA MARIA. PORQUE NO ME HAS VISITADO?
TE QUIERO VER--
Cruz
Call
MESSAGE DELETED. NEXT MESSAGE...
YO, D! WHUDDUP, BRUTHA?! HAVEN'T SEEN YOU AROUND MUCH-- SO WHAT'S THE SITCH?!
Buzz
Delete
Message
Remind Me
Call
YOU IN SOME KINDA WITNESS PROTECTION OR SOMETHING--
Buzz
Call
MESSAGE DELETED. NEXT MESSAGE...
TURNS OUT, YOU CAN'T IGNORE YOUR OWN LIFE FOREVER...

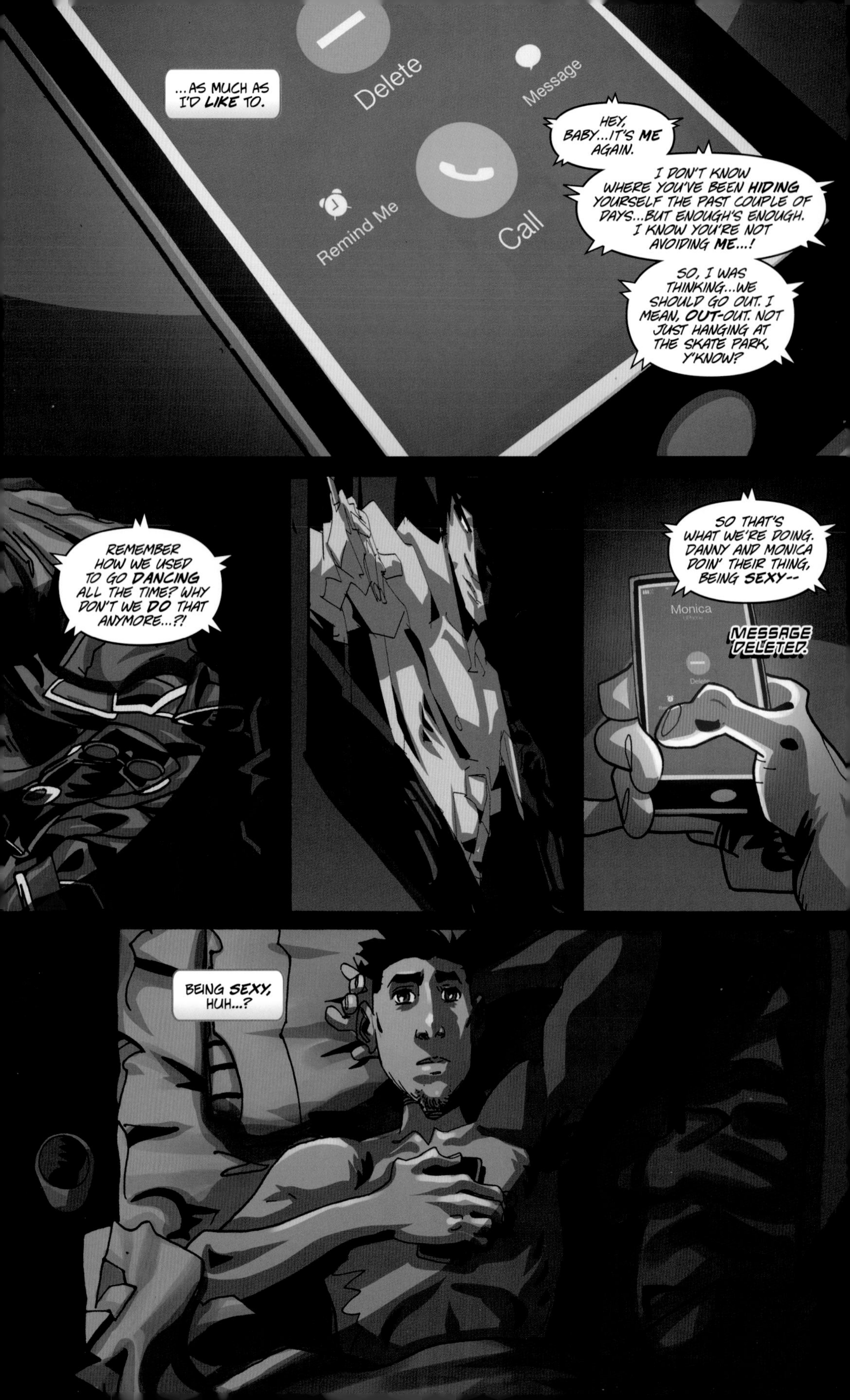

...AS MUCH AS I'D LIKE TO.
Delete
Message
Remind Me
Call
HEY, BABY...IT'S ME AGAIN.
I DON'T KNOW WHERE YOU'VE BEEN HIDING YOURSELF THE PAST COUPLE OF DAYS...BUT ENOUGH'S ENOUGH. I KNOW YOU'RE NOT AVOIDING ME...!
SO, I WAS THINKING...WE SHOULD GO OUT. I MEAN, OUT-OUT. NOT JUST HANGING AT THE SKATE PARK, Y'KNOW?
REMEMBER HOW WE USED TO GO DANCING ALL THE TIME? WHY DON'T WE DO THAT ANYMORE...?!
SO THAT'S WHAT WE'RE DOING. DANNY AND MONICA DOIN' THEIR THING, BEING SEXY--
Monica
MESSAGE DELETED.
BEING SEXY, HUH...?

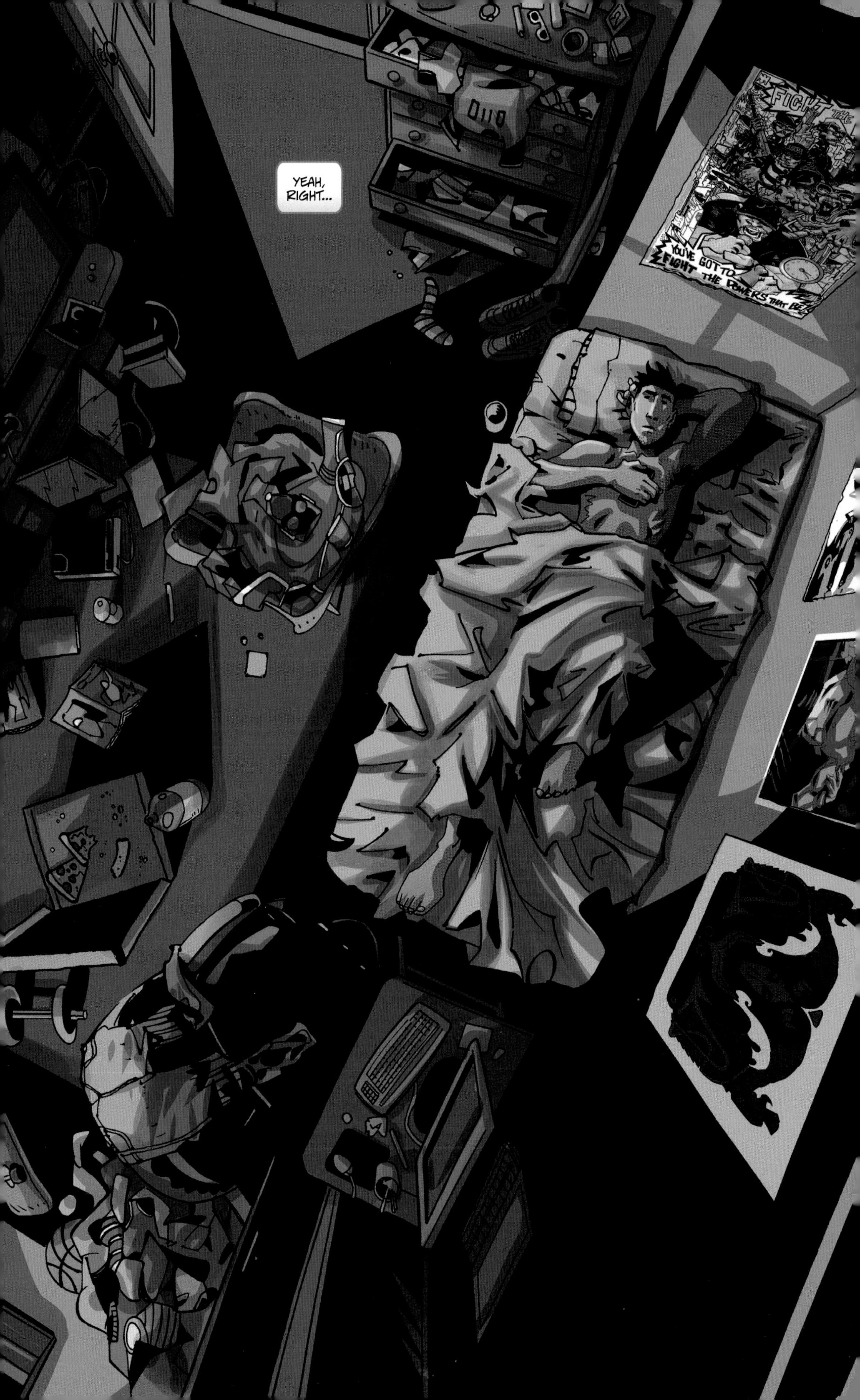
YEAH, RIGHT...
FIGHT THE
YOU'VE GOT TO FIGHT THE POWERS THAT BE

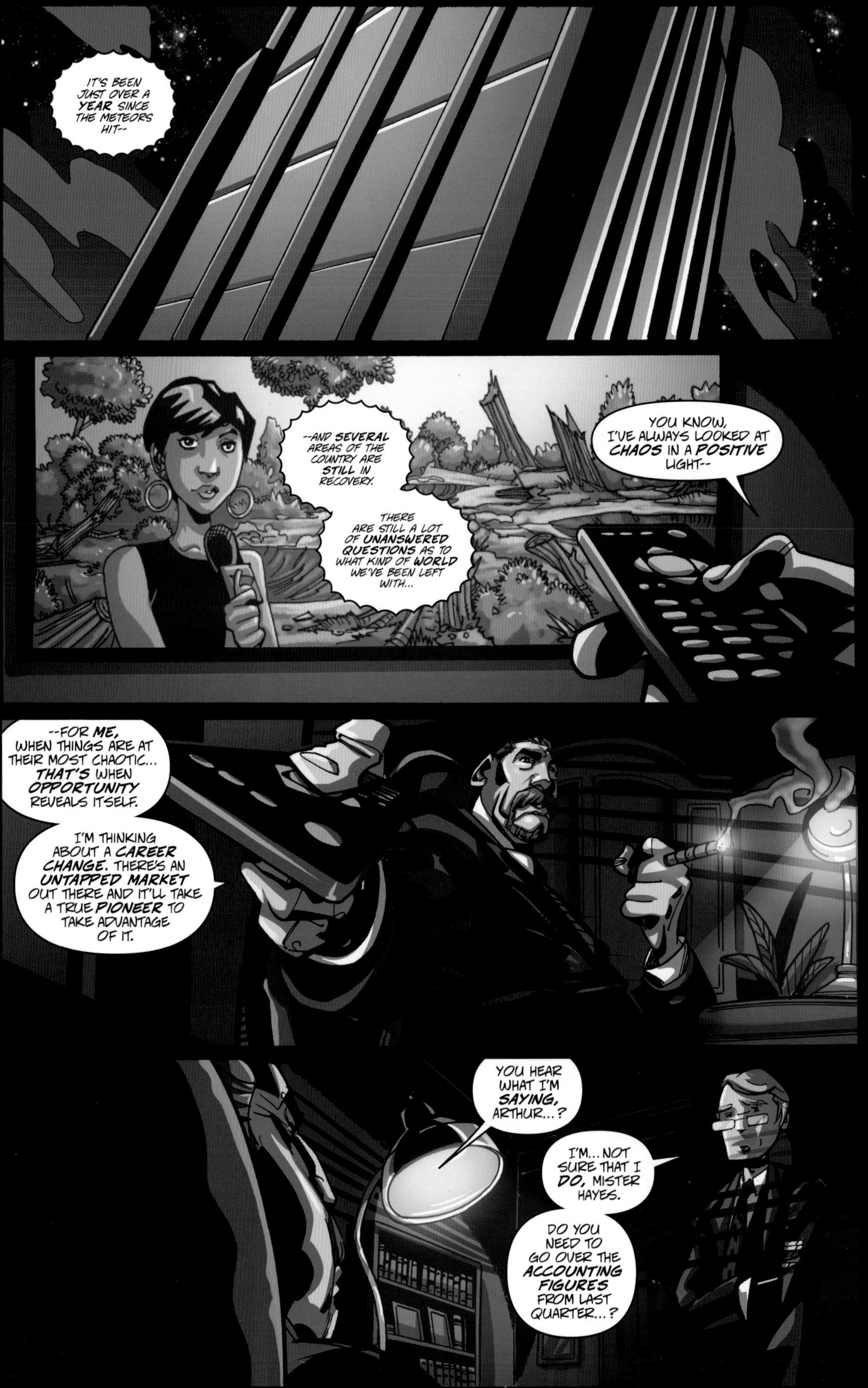
IT'S BEEN JUST OVER A YEAR SINCE THE METEORS HIT--
--AND SEVERAL AREAS OF THE COUNTRY ARE STILL IN RECOVERY.
THERE ARE STILL A LOT OF UNANSWERED QUESTIONS AS TO WHAT KIND OF WORLD WE'VE BEEN LEFT WITH...
YOU KNOW, I'VE ALWAYS LOOKED AT CHAOS IN A POSITIVE LIGHT--
--FOR ME, WHEN THINGS ARE AT THEIR MOST CHAOTIC... THAT'S WHEN OPPORTUNITY REVEALS ITSELF.
I'M THINKING ABOUT A CAREER CHANGE. THERE'S AN UNTAPPED MARKET OUT THERE AND IT'LL TAKE A TRUE PIONEER TO TAKE ADVANTAGE OF IT.
YOU HEAR WHAT I'M SAYING, ARTHUR...?
I'M... NOT SURE THAT I DO, MISTER HAYES.
DO YOU NEED TO GO OVER THE ACCOUNTING FIGURES FROM LAST QUARTER...?

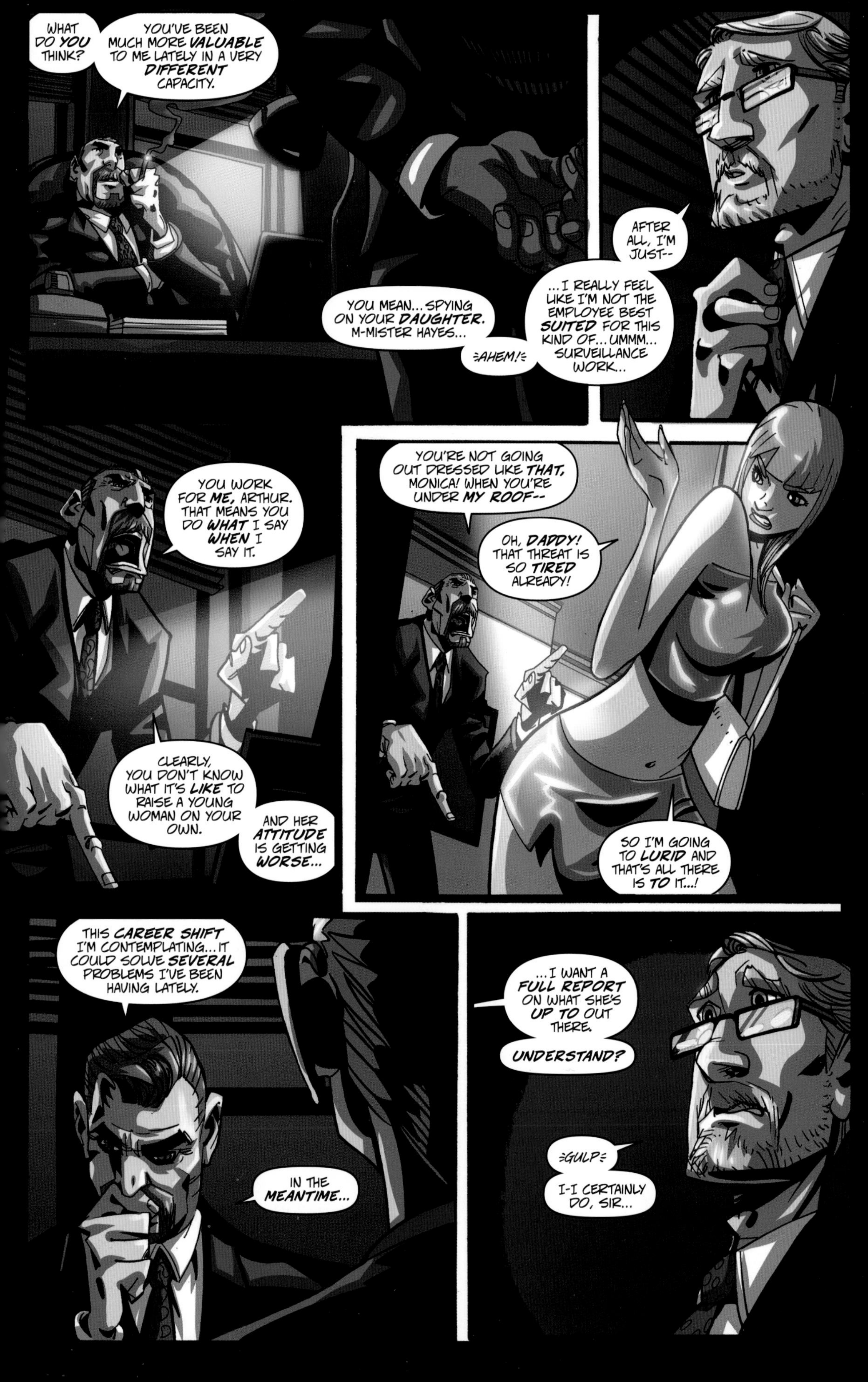
WHAT DO YOU THINK?
YOU'VE BEEN MUCH MORE VALUABLE TO ME LATELY IN A VERY DIFFERENT CAPACITY.
AFTER ALL, I'M JUST--
YOU MEAN... SPYING ON YOUR DAUGHTER. M-MISTER HAYES...
=AHEM!=
...I REALLY FEEL LIKE I'M NOT THE EMPLOYEE BEST SUITED FOR THIS KIND OF... UMMM... SURVEILLANCE WORK...
YOU WORK FOR ME, ARTHUR. THAT MEANS YOU DO WHAT I SAY WHEN I SAY IT.
CLEARLY, YOU DON'T KNOW WHAT IT'S LIKE TO RAISE A YOUNG WOMAN ON YOUR OWN.
AND HER ATTITUDE IS GETTING WORSE...
YOU'RE NOT GOING OUT DRESSED LIKE THAT, MONICA! WHEN YOU'RE UNDER MY ROOF--
OH, DADDY! THAT THREAT IS SO TIRED ALREADY!
SO I'M GOING TO LURID AND THAT'S ALL THERE IS TO IT...!
THIS CAREER SHIFT I'M CONTEMPLATING... IT COULD SOLVE SEVERAL PROBLEMS I'VE BEEN HAVING LATELY.
IN THE MEANTIME...
...I WANT A FULL REPORT ON WHAT SHE'S UP TO OUT THERE.
UNDERSTAND?
=GULP=
I-I CERTAINLY DO, SIR...

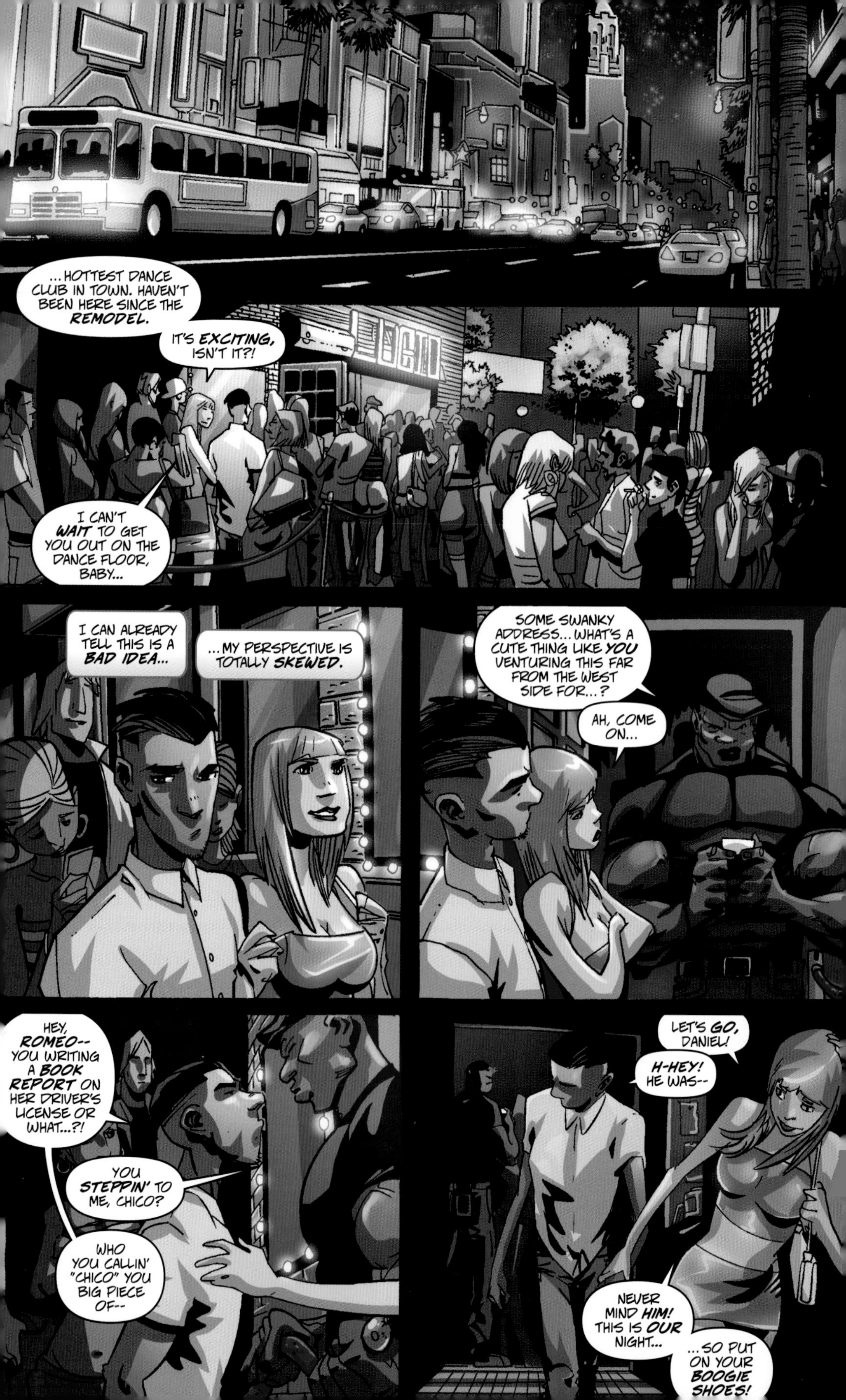

...HOTTEST DANCE CLUB IN TOWN. HAVEN'T BEEN HERE SINCE THE REMODEL.
IT'S EXCITING, ISN'T IT?!
I CAN'T WAIT TO GET YOU OUT ON THE DANCE FLOOR, BABY...
I CAN ALREADY TELL THIS IS A BAD IDEA...
...MY PERSPECTIVE IS TOTALLY SKEWED.
SOME SWANKY ADDRESS... WHAT'S A CUTE THING LIKE YOU VENTURING THIS FAR FROM THE WEST SIDE FOR...?
AH, COME ON...
HEY, ROMEO-- YOU WRITING A BOOK REPORT ON HER DRIVER'S LICENSE OR WHAT...?!
YOU STEPPIN' TO ME, CHICO?
WHO YOU CALLIN' "CHICO" YOU BIG PIECE OF--
LET'S GO, DANIEL!
H-HEY! HE WAS--
NEVER MIND HIM! THIS IS OUR NIGHT...
...SO PUT ON YOUR BOOGIE SHOES!

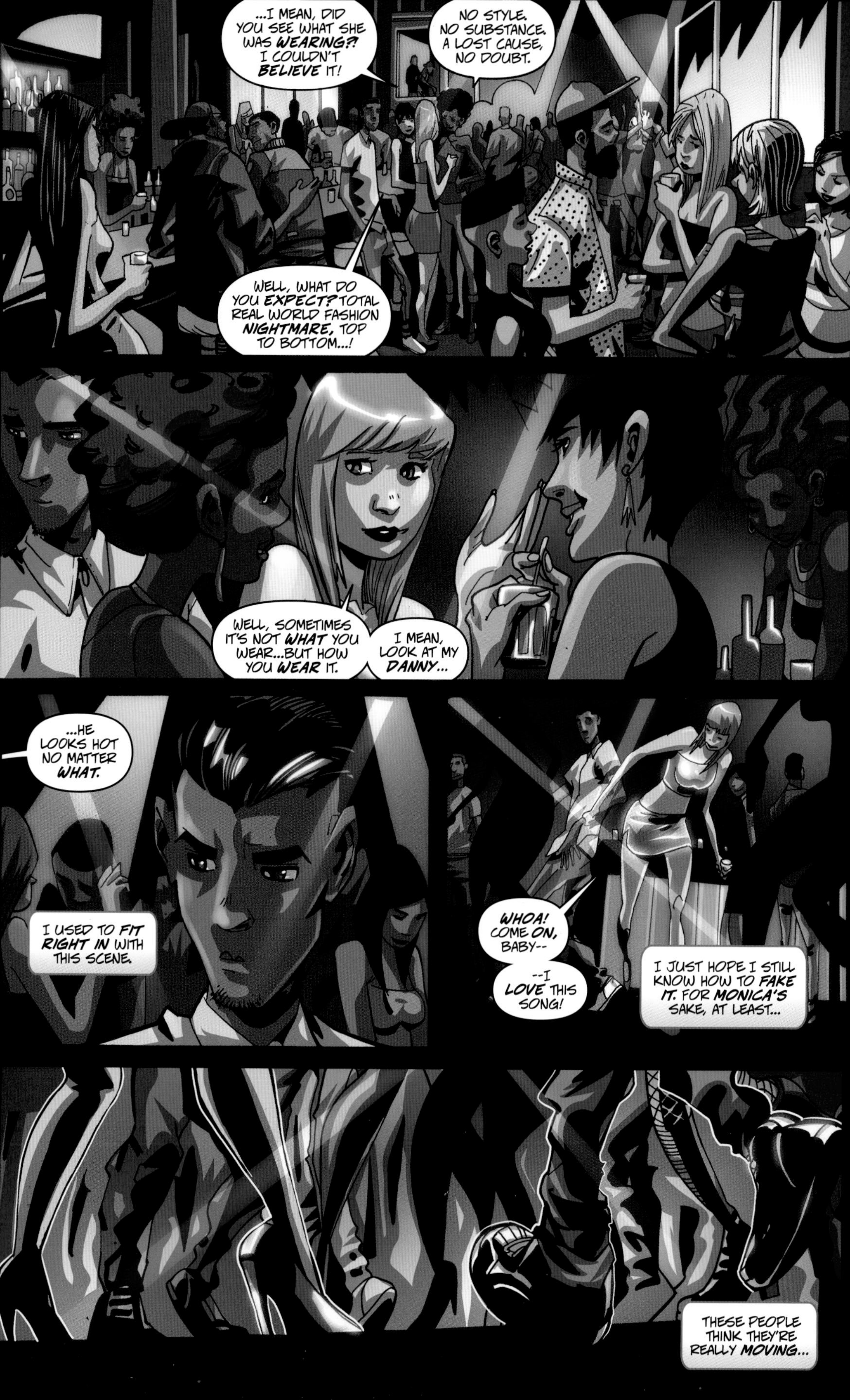
...I MEAN, DID YOU SEE WHAT SHE WAS WEARING?! I COULDN'T BELIEVE IT!
NO STYLE. NO SUBSTANCE. A LOST CAUSE, NO DOUBT.
WELL, WHAT DO YOU EXPECT? TOTAL REAL WORLD FASHION NIGHTMARE, TOP TO BOTTOM...!
WELL, SOMETIMES IT'S NOT WHAT YOU WEAR...BUT HOW YOU WEAR IT.
I MEAN, LOOK AT MY DANNY...
...HE LOOKS HOT NO MATTER WHAT.
I USED TO FIT RIGHT IN WITH THIS SCENE.
WHOA! COME ON, BABY--
--I LOVE THIS SONG!
I JUST HOPE I STILL KNOW HOW TO FAKE IT. FOR MONICA'S SAKE, AT LEAST...
THESE PEOPLE THINK THEY'RE REALLY MOVING...

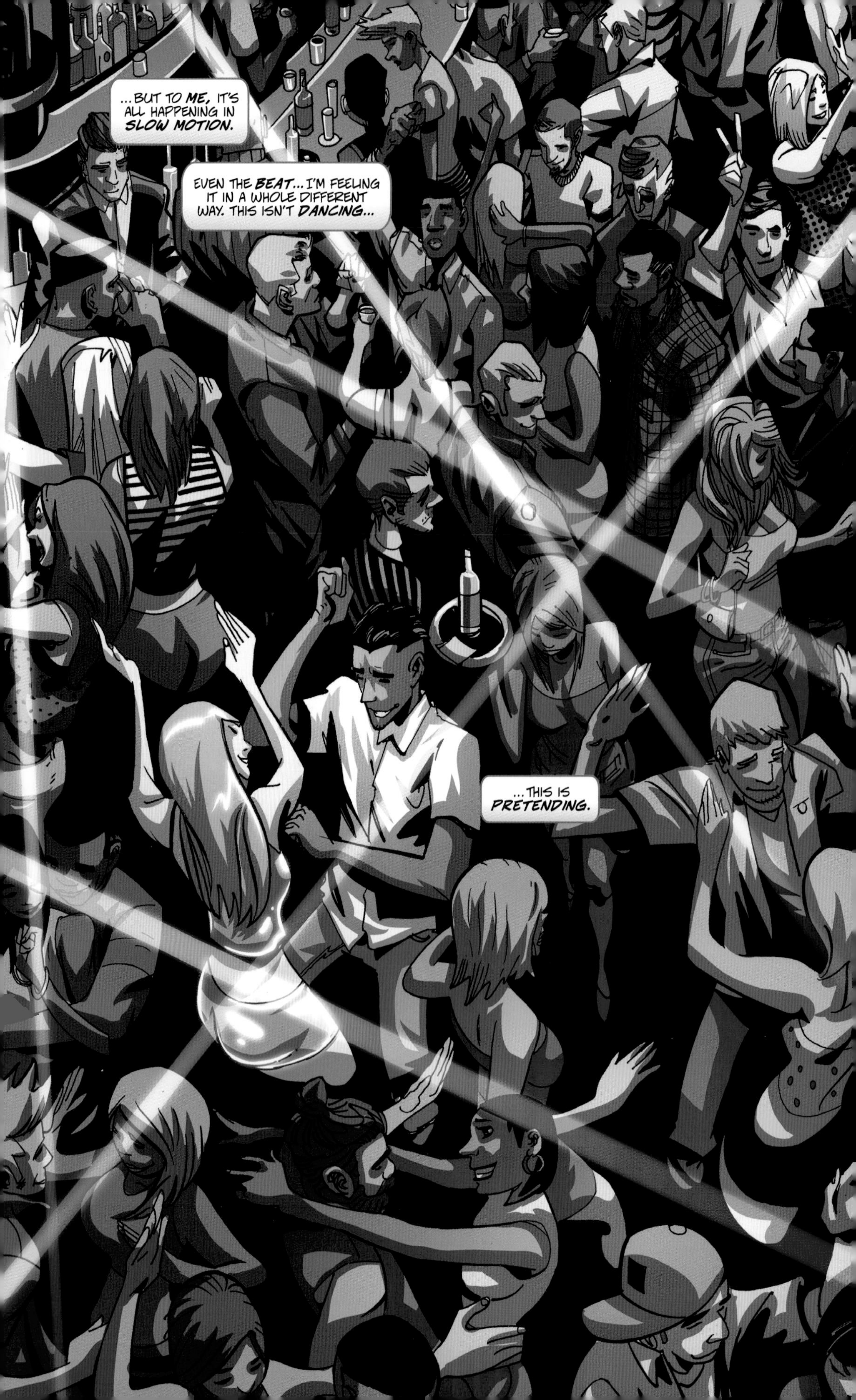
...BUT TO ME, IT'S ALL HAPPENING IN SLOW MOTION.
EVEN THE BEAT... I'M FEELING IT IN A WHOLE DIFFERENT WAY. THIS ISN'T DANCING...
...THIS IS PRETENDING.

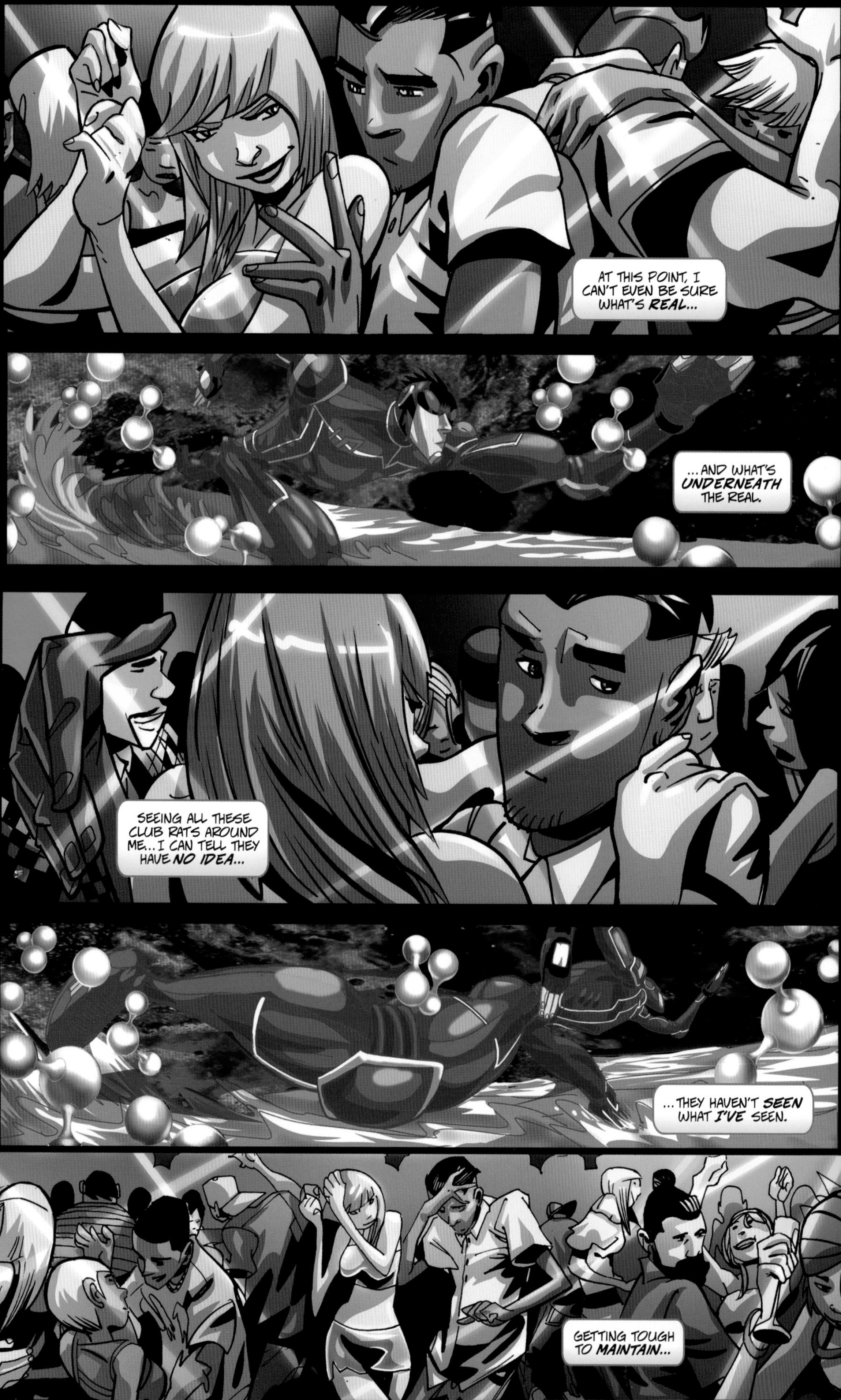
AT THIS POINT, I CAN'T EVEN BE SURE WHAT'S REAL...
...AND WHAT'S UNDERNEATH THE REAL.
SEEING ALL THESE CLUB RATS AROUND ME...I CAN TELL THEY HAVE NO IDEA...
...THEY HAVEN'T SEEN WHAT I'VE SEEN.
GETTING TOUGH TO MAINTAIN...

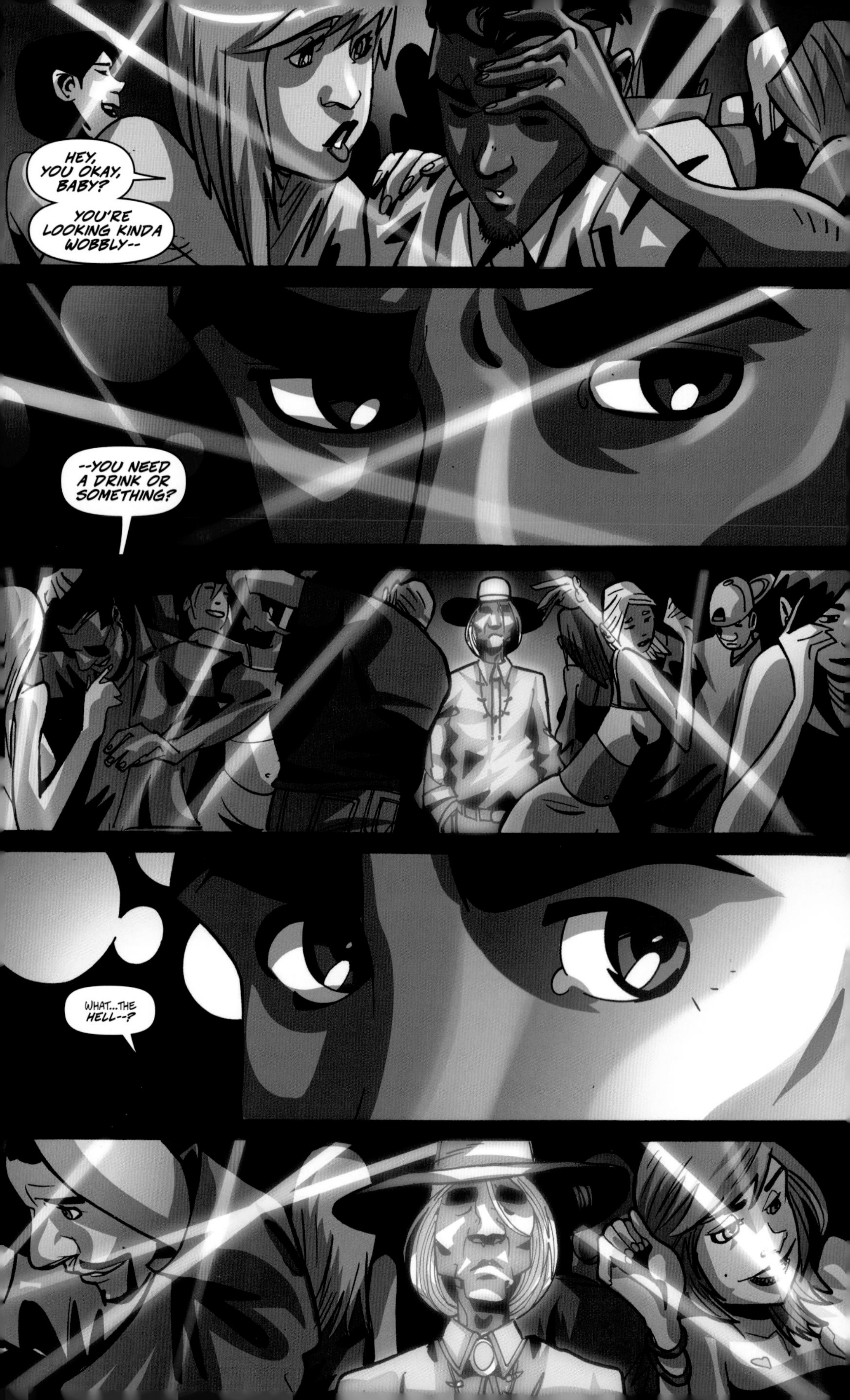
HEY, YOU OKAY, BABY?
YOU'RE LOOKING KINDA WOBBLY--
--YOU NEED A DRINK OR SOMETHING?
WHAT...THE HELL--?

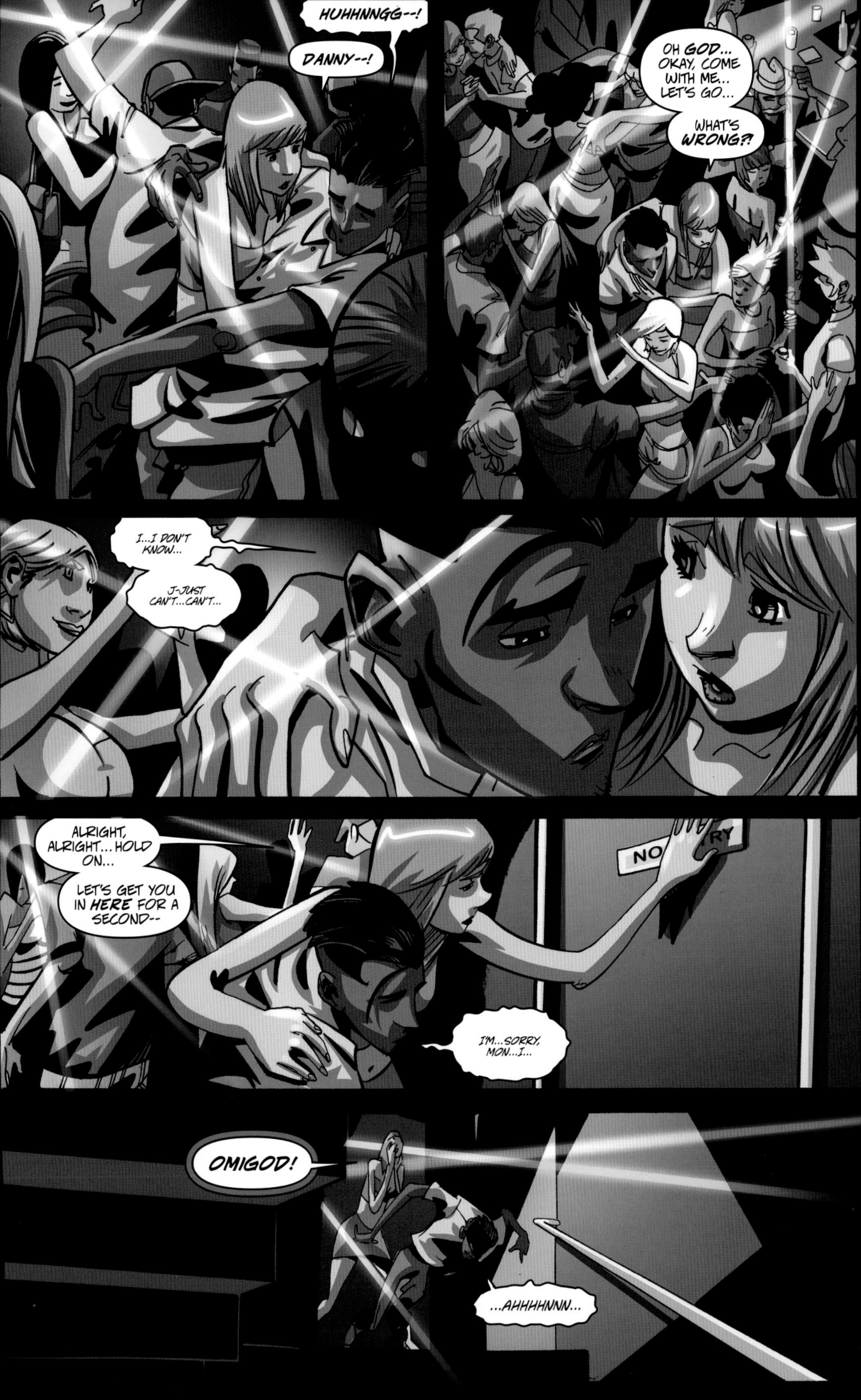
HUHHNNGG--!
DANNY--!
OH GOD... OKAY, COME WITH ME... LET'S GO...
WHAT'S WRONG?!
I...I DON'T KNOW...
J-JUST CAN'T...CAN'T...
ALRIGHT, ALRIGHT... HOLD ON...
LET'S GET YOU IN HERE FOR A SECOND--
I'M...SORRY, MON...I...
OMIGOD!
...AHHHHNNN...

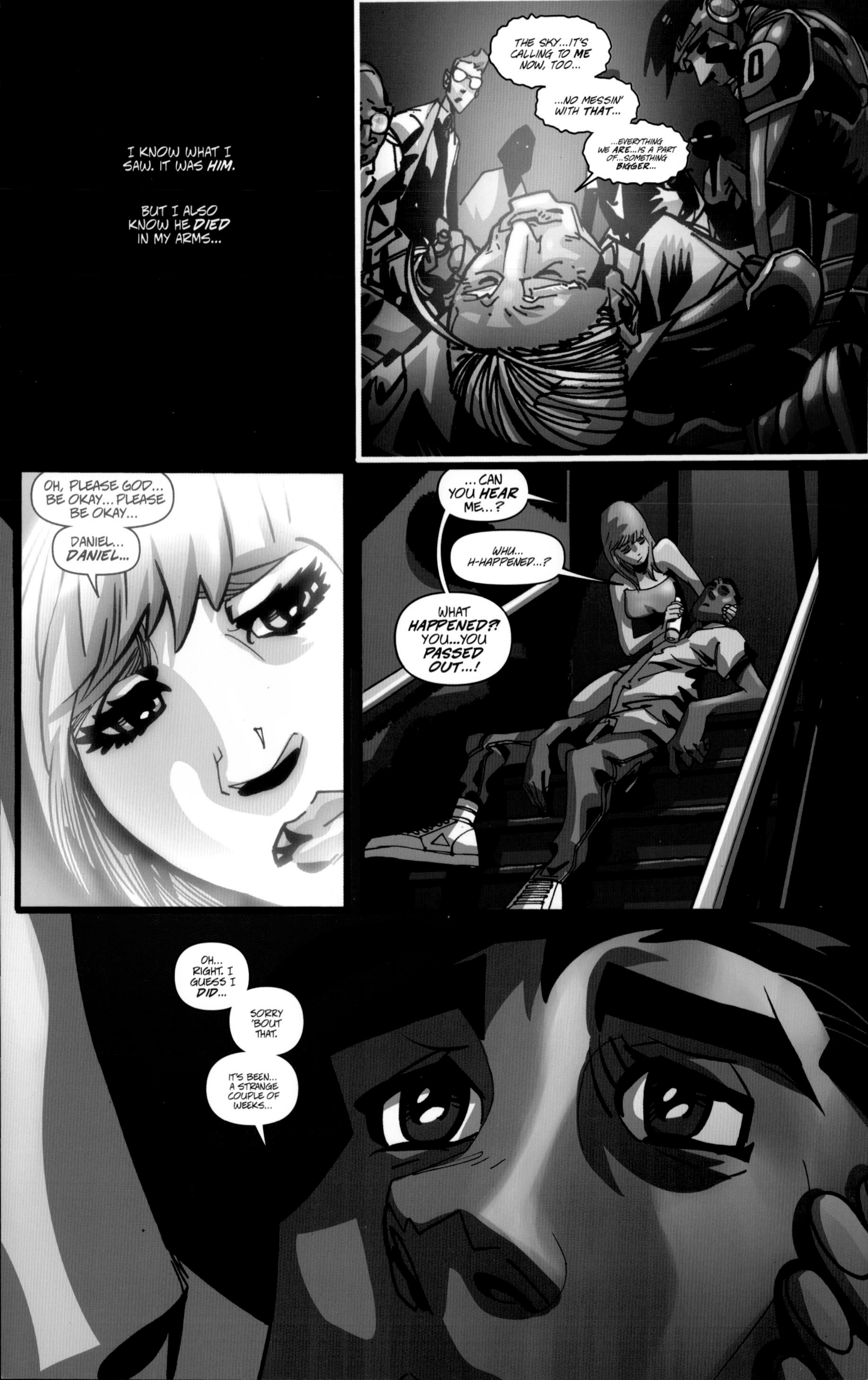
I KNOW WHAT I SAW. IT WAS HIM.
BUT I ALSO KNOW HE DIED IN MY ARMS...
THE SKY...IT'S CALLING TO ME NOW, TOO...
...NO MESSIN' WITH THAT...
...EVERYTHING WE ARE...IS A PART OF...SOMETHING BIGGER...
OH, PLEASE GOD... BE OKAY... PLEASE BE OKAY...
DANIEL... DANIEL...
...CAN YOU HEAR ME...?
WHU... H-HAPPENED...?
WHAT HAPPENED?! YOU...YOU PASSED OUT...!
OH... RIGHT. I GUESS I DID...
SORRY 'BOUT THAT.
IT'S BEEN... A STRANGE COUPLE OF WEEKS...

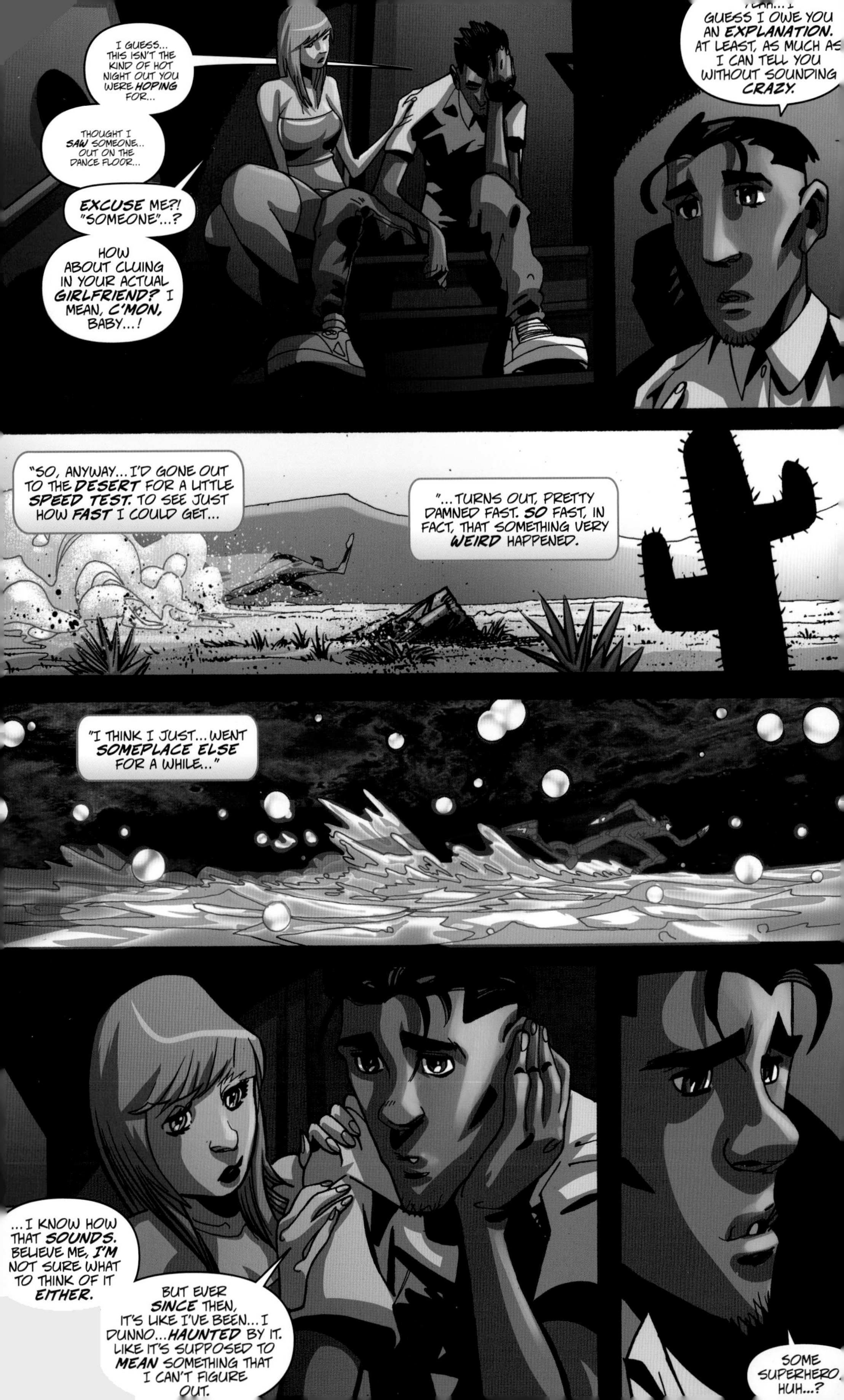
I GUESS... THIS ISN'T THE KIND OF HOT NIGHT OUT YOU WERE HOPING FOR...
THOUGHT I SAW SOMEONE... OUT ON THE DANCE FLOOR...
EXCUSE ME?! "SOMEONE"...?
HOW ABOUT CLUING IN YOUR ACTUAL GIRLFRIEND? I MEAN, C'MON, BABY...!
GUESS I OWE YOU AN EXPLANATION. AT LEAST, AS MUCH AS I CAN TELL YOU WITHOUT SOUNDING CRAZY.
"SO, ANYWAY... I'D GONE OUT TO THE DESERT FOR A LITTLE SPEED TEST. TO SEE JUST HOW FAST I COULD GET...
"...TURNS OUT, PRETTY DAMNED FAST. SO FAST, IN FACT, THAT SOMETHING VERY WEIRD HAPPENED.
"I THINK I JUST... WENT SOMEPLACE ELSE FOR A WHILE..."
...I KNOW HOW THAT SOUNDS. BELIEVE ME, I'M NOT SURE WHAT TO THINK OF IT EITHER.
BUT EVER SINCE THEN, IT'S LIKE I'VE BEEN... I DUNNO... HAUNTED BY IT. LIKE IT'S SUPPOSED TO MEAN SOMETHING THAT I CAN'T FIGURE OUT.
SOME SUPERHERO, HUH...?

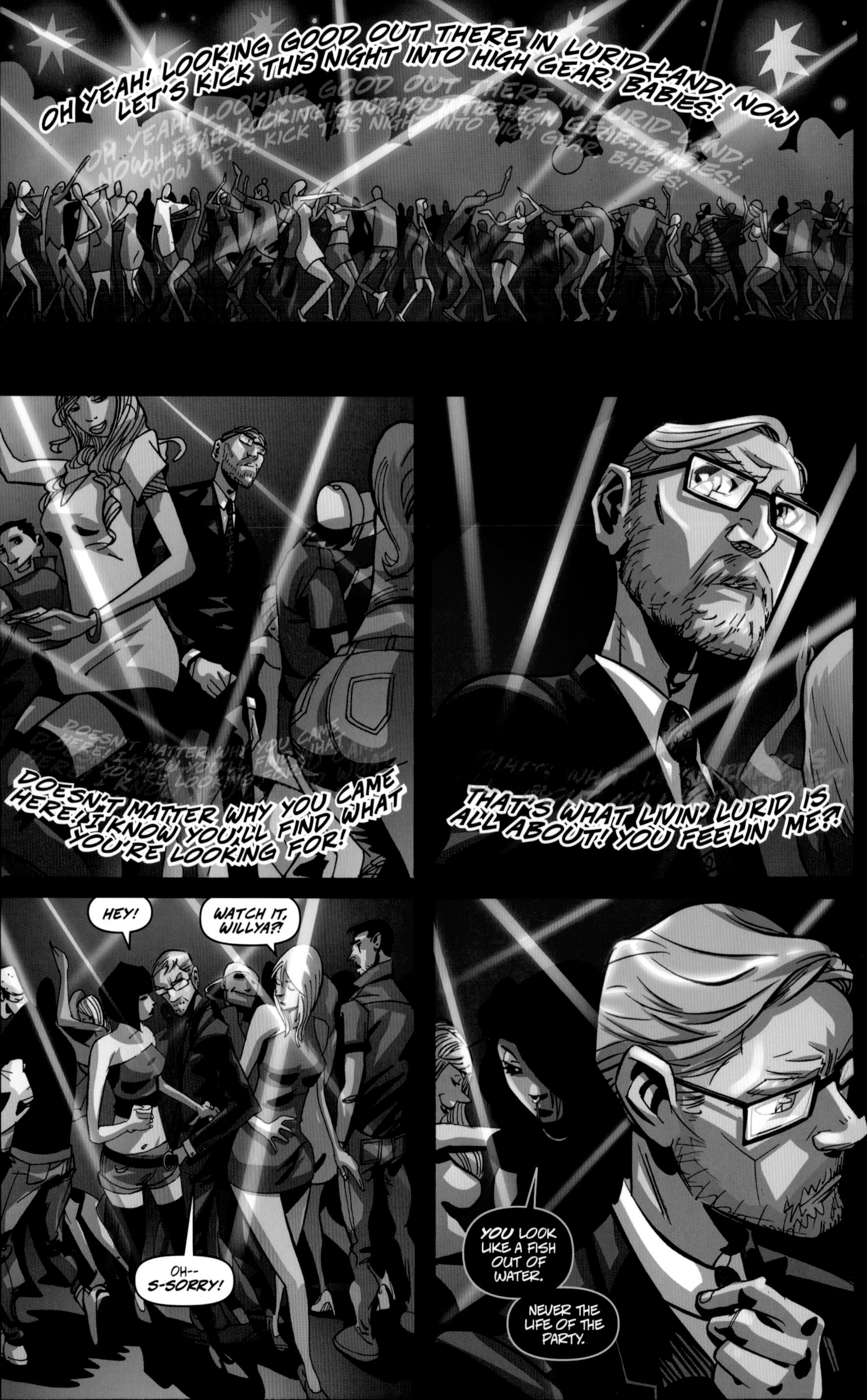
OH YEAH! LOOKING GOOD OUT THERE IN LURID-LAND! NOW LET'S KICK THIS NIGHT INTO HIGH GEAR, BABIES!
DOESN'T MATTER WHY YOU CAME HERE! I KNOW YOU'LL FIND WHAT YOU'RE LOOKING FOR!
THAT'S WHAT LIVIN' LURID IS ALL ABOUT! YOU FEELIN' ME?!
HEY!
WATCH IT, WILLYA?!
OH-- S-SORRY!
YOU LOOK LIKE A FISH OUT OF WATER.
NEVER THE LIFE OF THE PARTY.

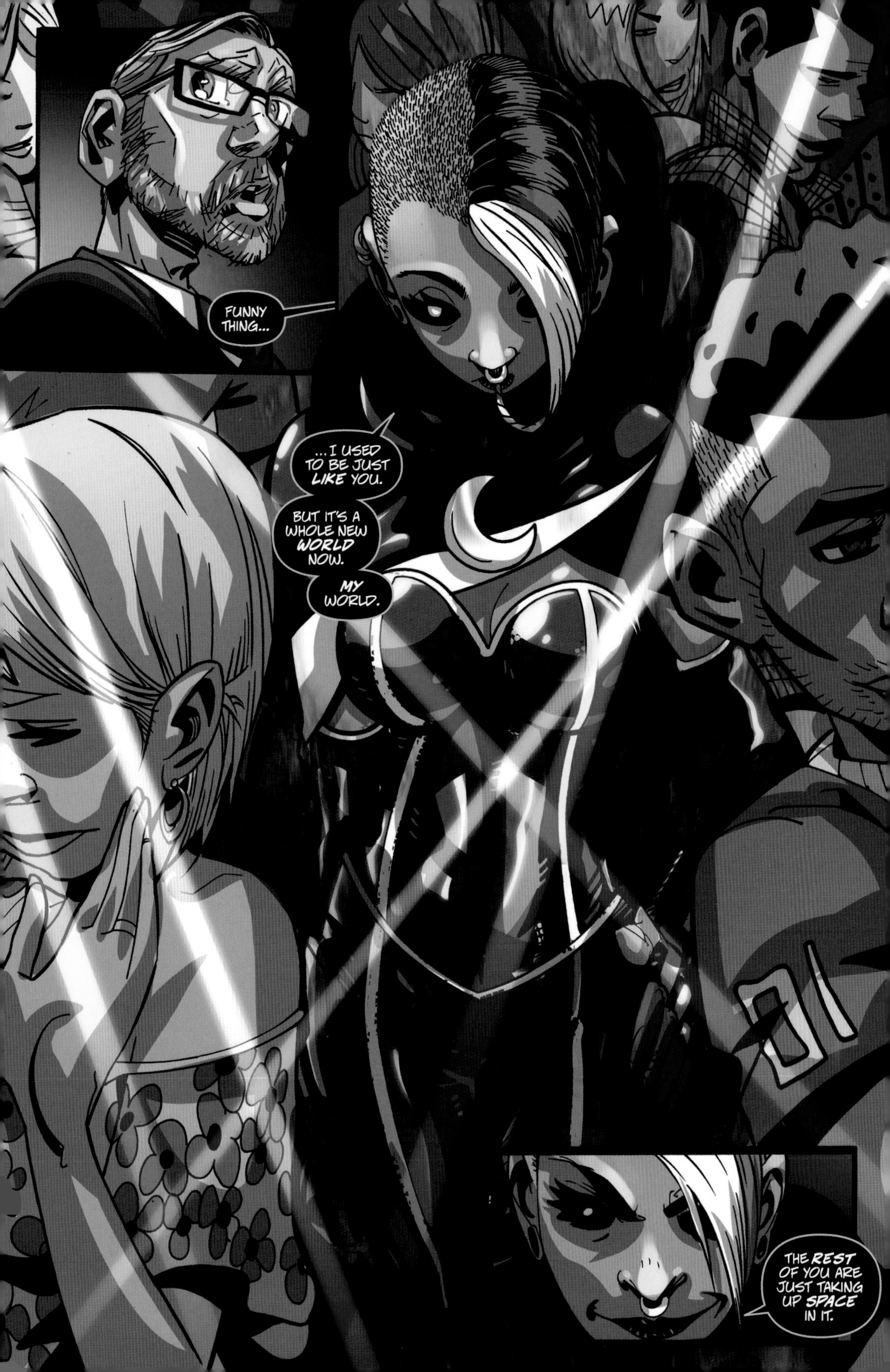
FUNNY THING...
...I USED TO BE JUST LIKE YOU.
BUT IT'S A WHOLE NEW WORLD NOW.
MY WORLD.
THE REST OF YOU ARE JUST TAKING UP SPACE IN IT.

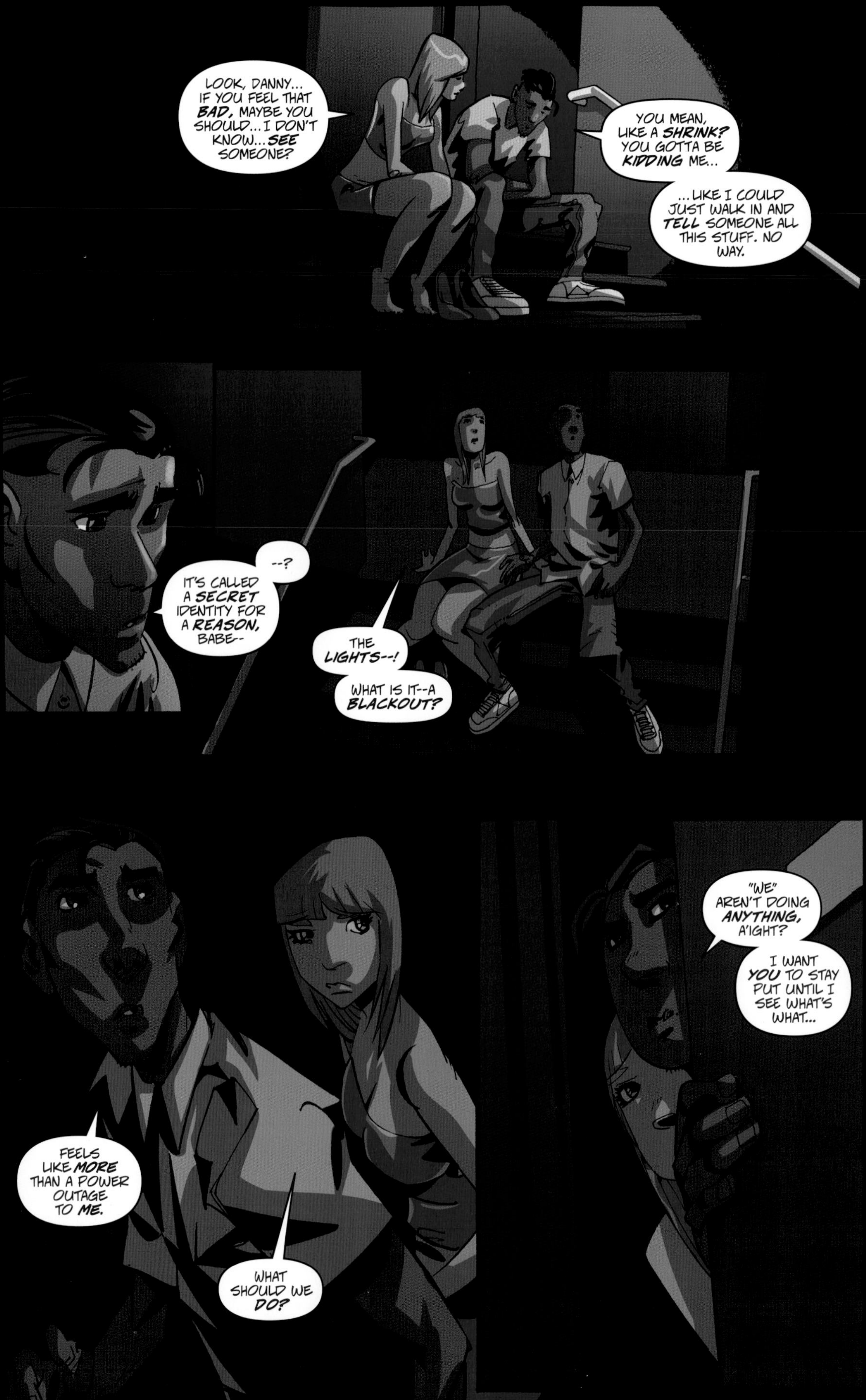
LOOK, DANNY... IF YOU FEEL THAT BAD, MAYBE YOU SHOULD... I DON'T KNOW... SEE SOMEONE?
YOU MEAN, LIKE A SHRINK? YOU GOTTA BE KIDDING ME...
...LIKE I COULD JUST WALK IN AND TELL SOMEONE ALL THIS STUFF. NO WAY.
IT'S CALLED A SECRET IDENTITY FOR A REASON, BABE--
--?
THE LIGHTS--!
WHAT IS IT--A BLACKOUT?
FEELS LIKE MORE THAN A POWER OUTAGE TO ME.
WHAT SHOULD WE DO?
"WE" AREN'T DOING ANYTHING, A'IGHT?
I WANT YOU TO STAY PUT UNTIL I SEE WHAT'S WHAT...

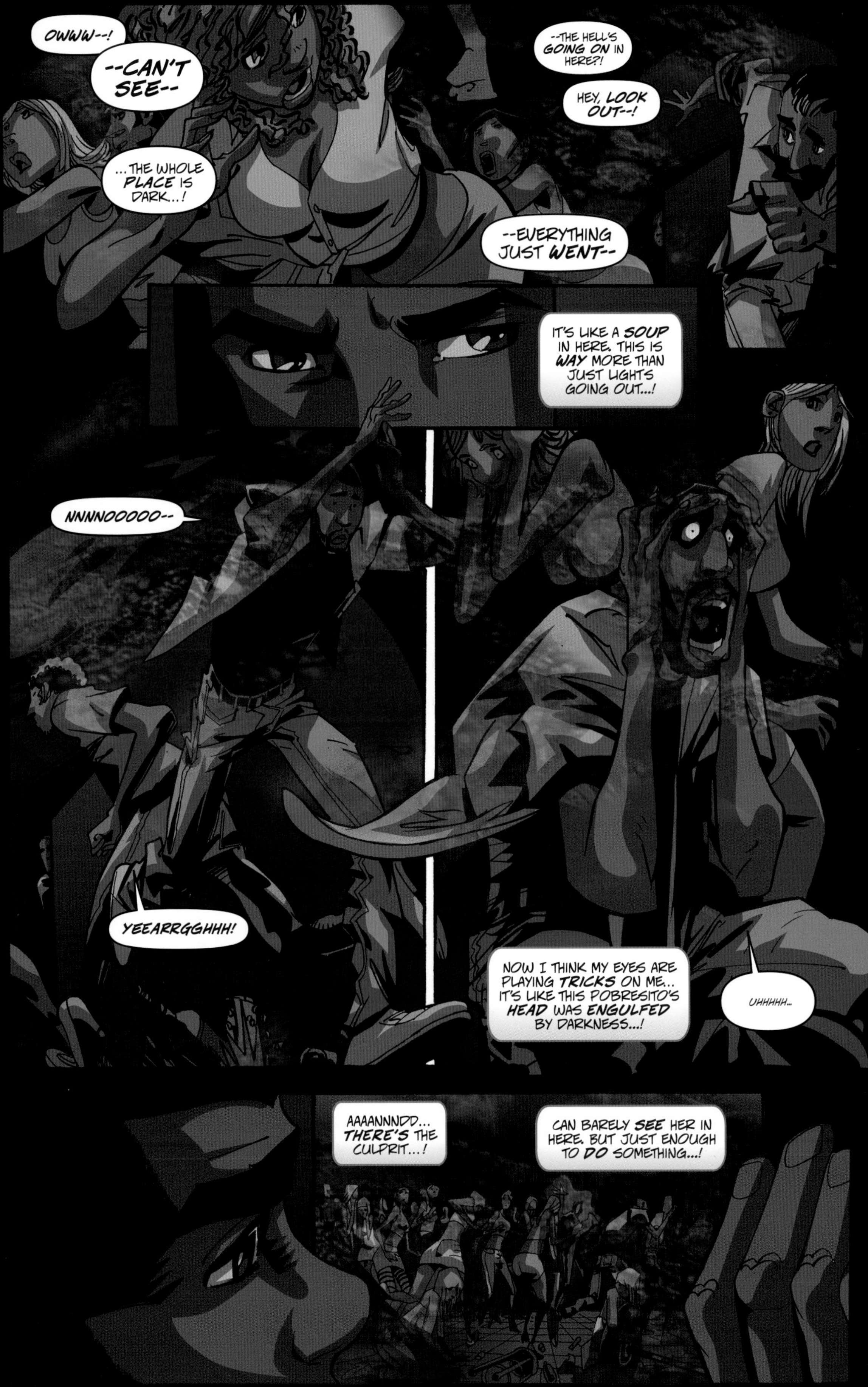
OWWW--!
--CAN'T SEE--
...THE WHOLE PLACE IS DARK...!
--THE HELL'S GOING ON IN HERE?!
HEY, LOOK OUT--!
--EVERYTHING JUST WENT--
IT'S LIKE A SOUP IN HERE. THIS IS WAY MORE THAN JUST LIGHTS GOING OUT...!
NNNNOOOOO--
YEEARRGGHHH!
NOW I THINK MY EYES ARE PLAYING TRICKS ON ME... IT'S LIKE THIS POBRESITO'S HEAD WAS ENGULFED BY DARKNESS...!
UHHHHH...
AAAANNNDD... THERE'S THE CULPRIT...!
CAN BARELY SEE HER IN HERE. BUT JUST ENOUGH TO DO SOMETHING...!

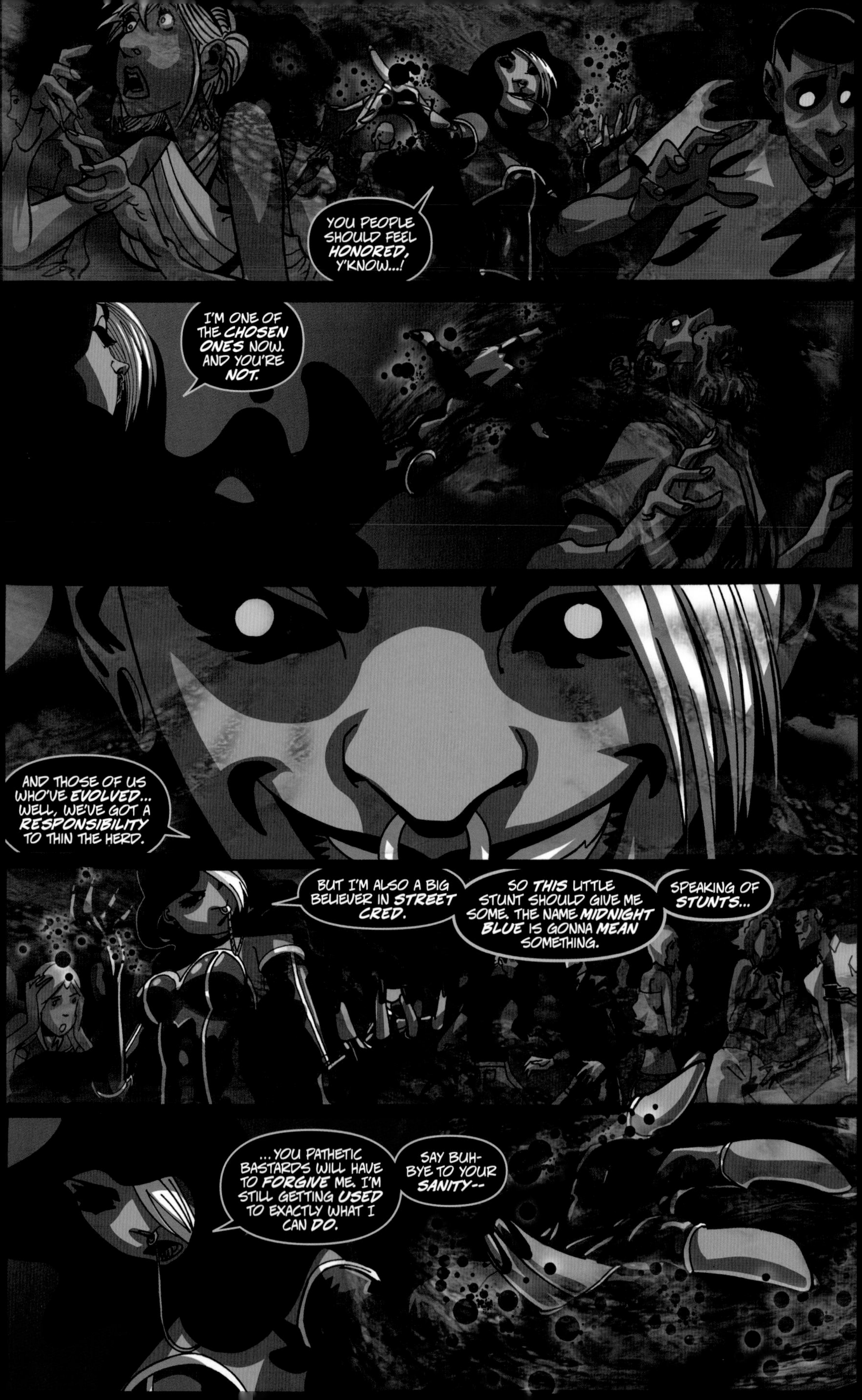
YOU PEOPLE SHOULD FEEL HONORED, Y'KNOW...!
I'M ONE OF THE CHOSEN ONES NOW. AND YOU'RE NOT.
AND THOSE OF US WHO'VE EVOLVED... WELL, WE'VE GOT A RESPONSIBILITY TO THIN THE HERD.
BUT I'M ALSO A BIG BELIEVER IN STREET CRED.
SO THIS LITTLE STUNT SHOULD GIVE ME SOME. THE NAME MIDNIGHT BLUE IS GONNA MEAN SOMETHING.
SPEAKING OF STUNTS...
...YOU PATHETIC BASTARDS WILL HAVE TO FORGIVE ME. I'M STILL GETTING USED TO EXACTLY WHAT I CAN DO.
SAY BUH-BYE TO YOUR SANITY--

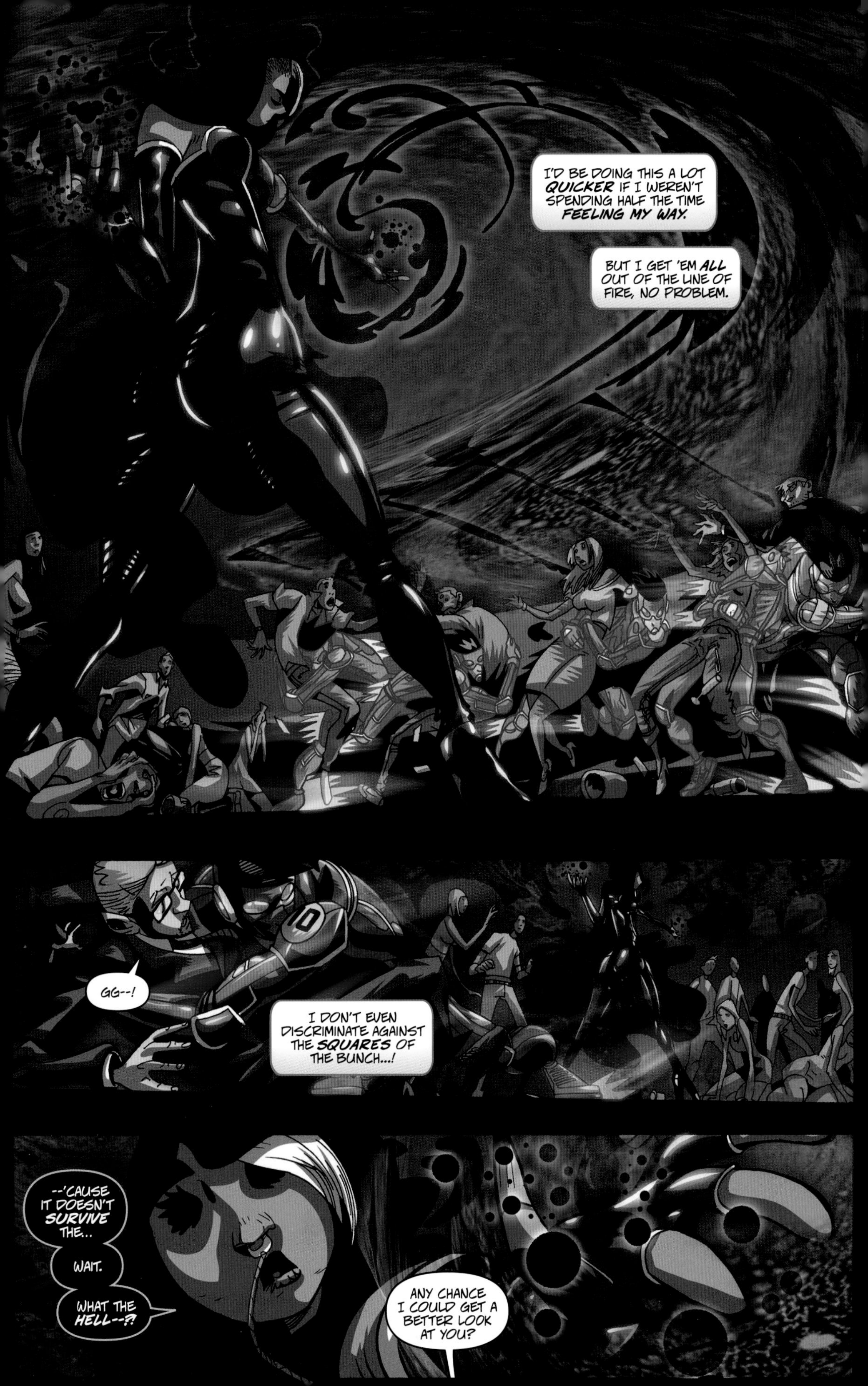
I'D BE DOING THIS A LOT QUICKER IF I WEREN'T SPENDING HALF THE TIME FEELING MY WAY.
BUT I GET 'EM ALL OUT OF THE LINE OF FIRE, NO PROBLEM.
GG--!
I DON'T EVEN DISCRIMINATE AGAINST THE SQUARES OF THE BUNCH...!
--'CAUSE IT DOESN'T SURVIVE THE...
WAIT.
WHAT THE HELL--?!
ANY CHANCE I COULD GET A BETTER LOOK AT YOU?

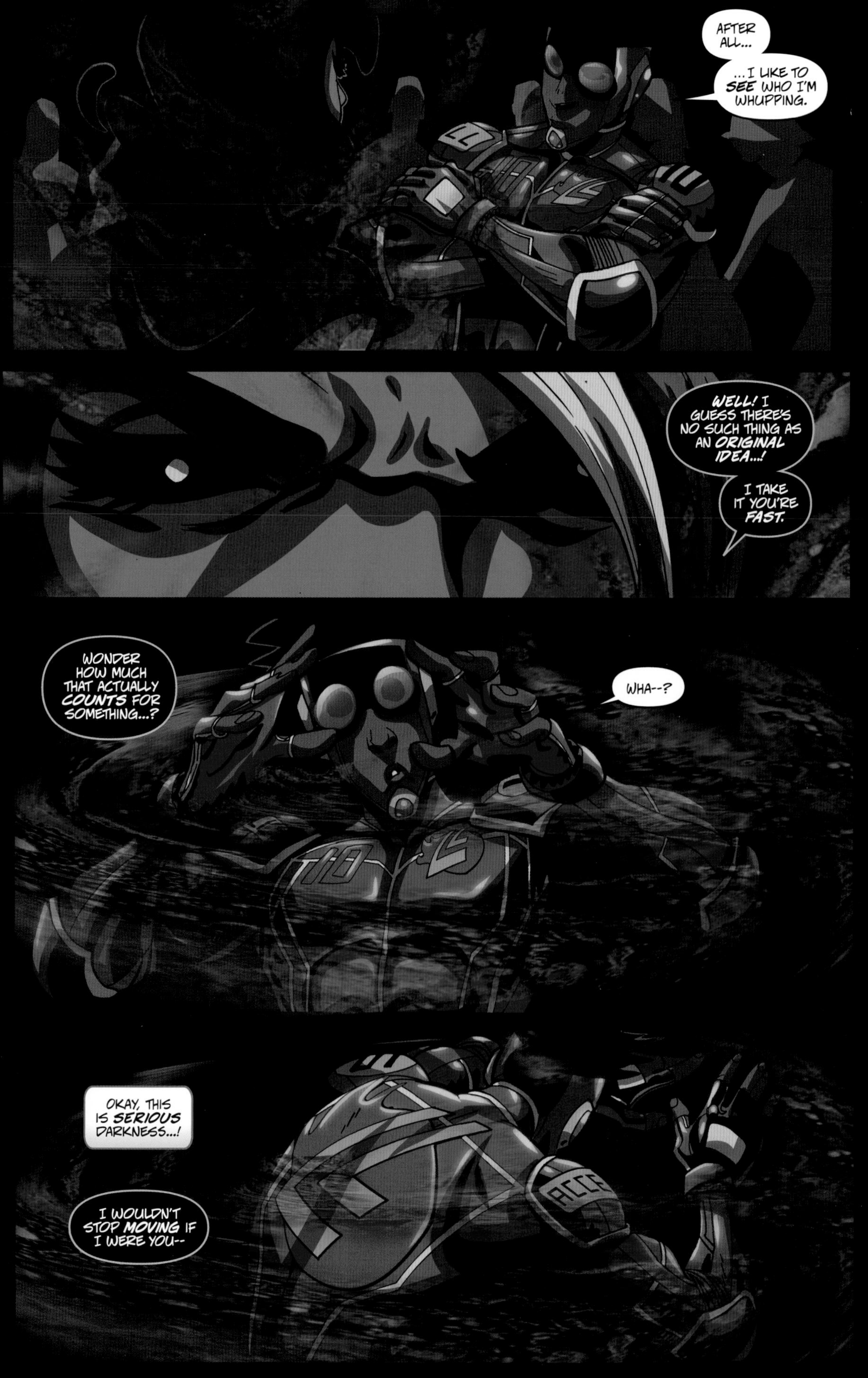

AFTER ALL...
...I LIKE TO SEE WHO I'M WHUPPING.
WELL! I GUESS THERE'S NO SUCH THING AS AN ORIGINAL IDEA...!
I TAKE IT YOU'RE FAST.
WONDER HOW MUCH THAT ACTUALLY COUNTS FOR SOMETHING...?
WHA--?
OKAY, THIS IS SERIOUS DARKNESS...!
I WOULDN'T STOP MOVING IF I WERE YOU--

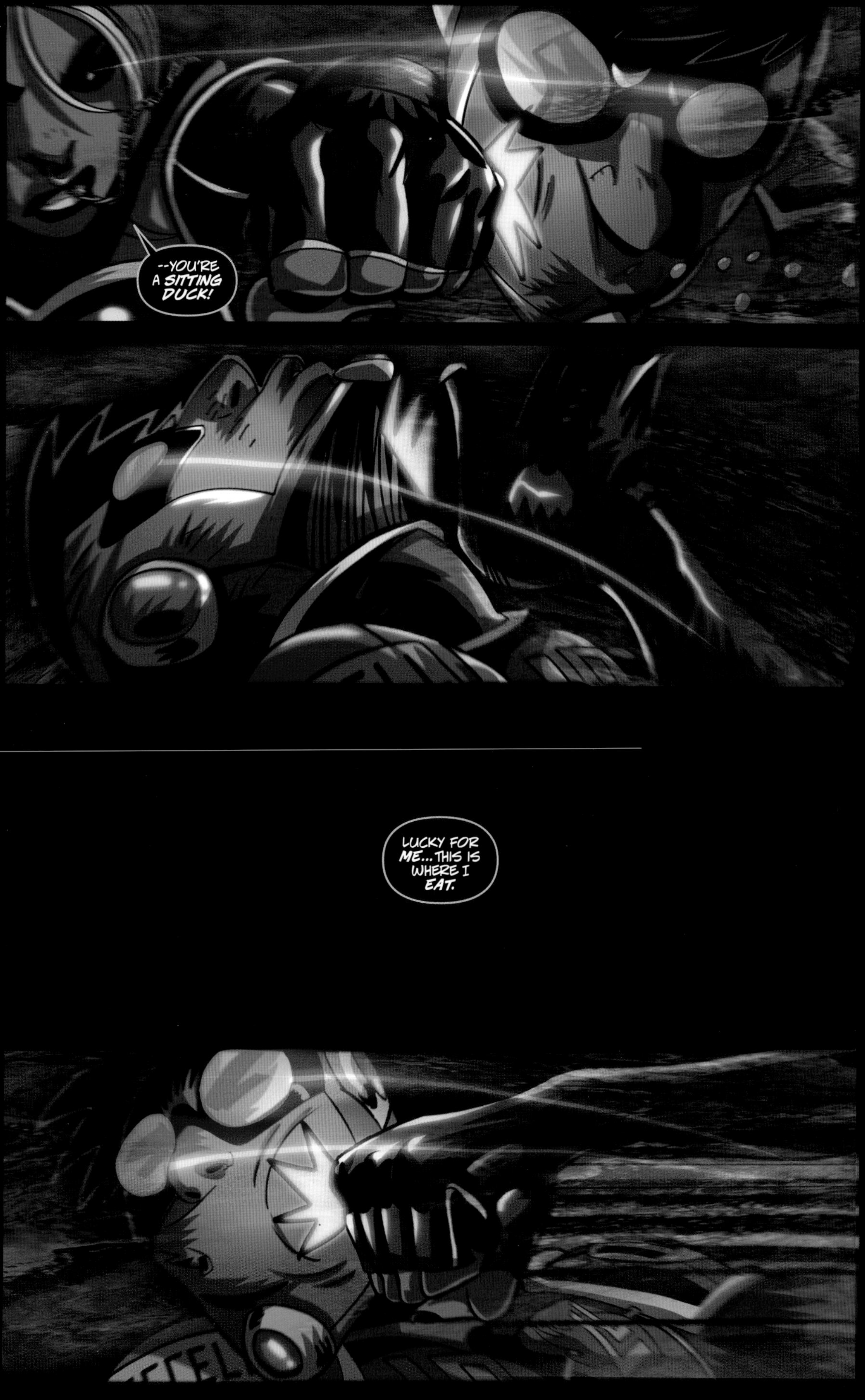
--YOU'RE A SITTING DUCK!
LUCKY FOR ME... THIS IS WHERE I EAT.

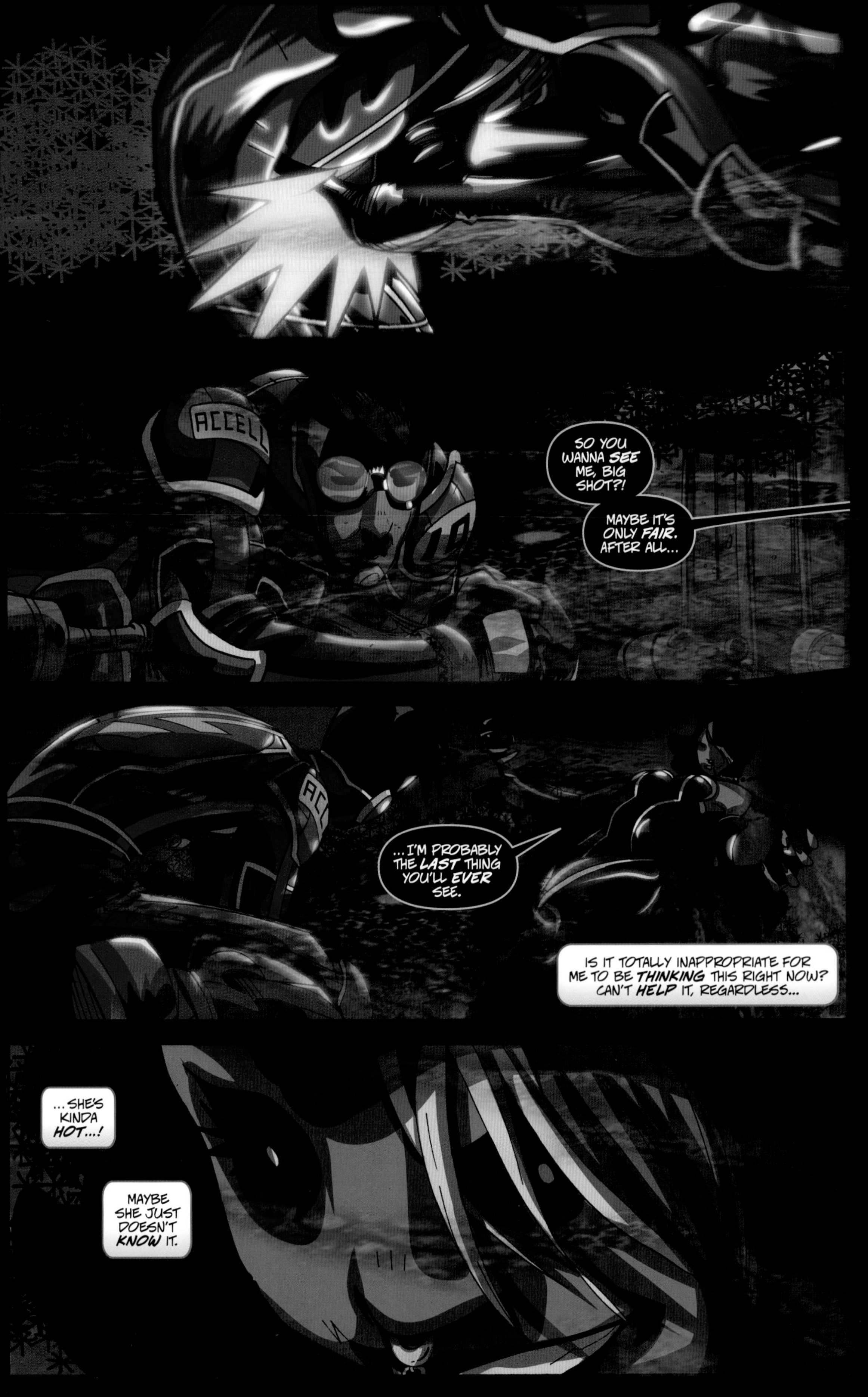

SO YOU WANNA SEE ME, BIG SHOT?!
MAYBE IT'S ONLY FAIR. AFTER ALL...
...I'M PROBABLY THE LAST THING YOU'LL EVER SEE.
IS IT TOTALLY INAPPROPRIATE FOR ME TO BE THINKING THIS RIGHT NOW? CAN'T HELP IT, REGARDLESS...
...SHE'S KINDA HOT...!
MAYBE SHE JUST DOESN'T KNOW IT.

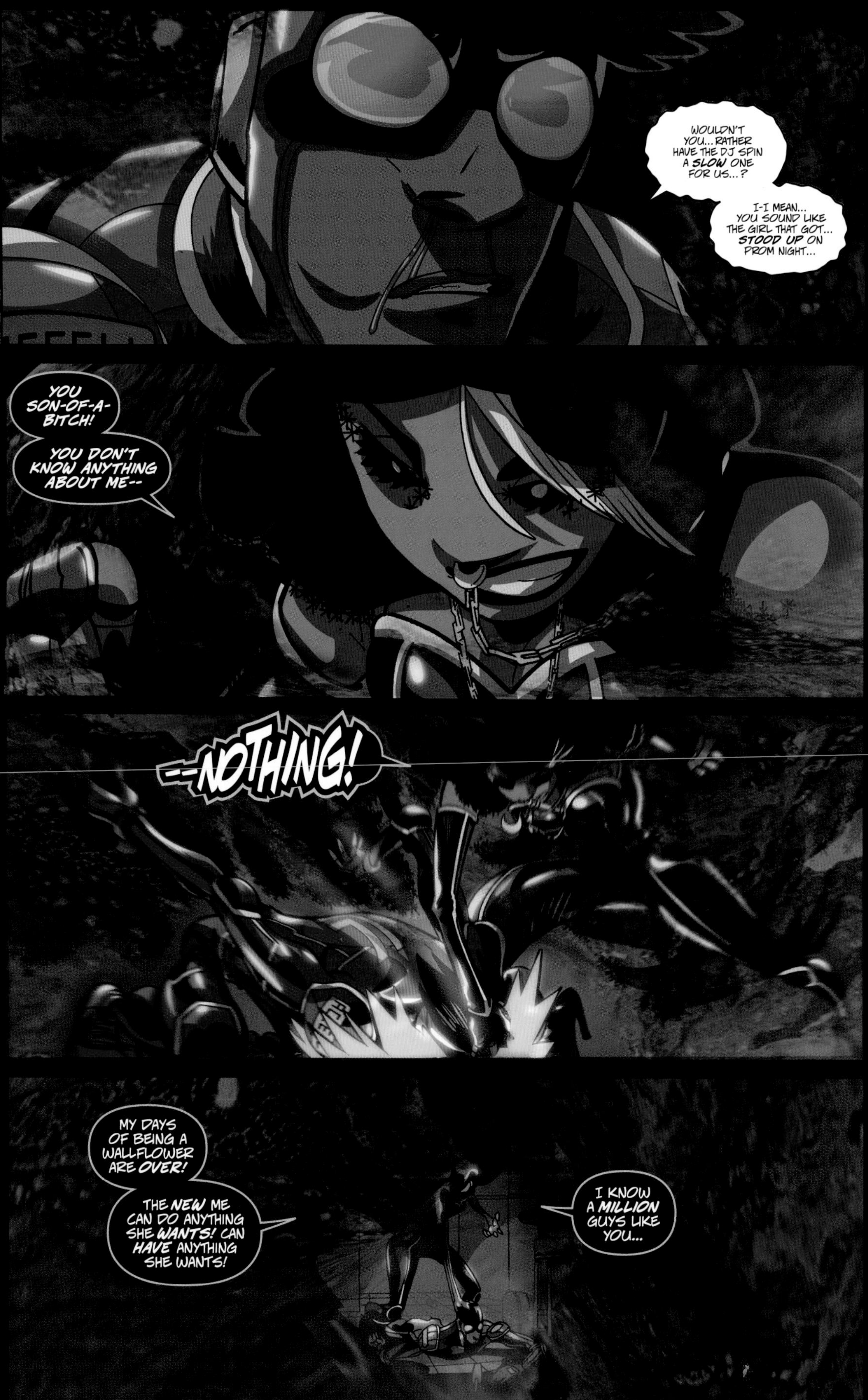
WOULDN'T YOU...RATHER HAVE THE DJ SPIN A SLOW ONE FOR US...?
I-I MEAN... YOU SOUND LIKE THE GIRL THAT GOT... STOOD UP ON PROM NIGHT...
YOU SON-OF-A-BITCH!
YOU DON'T KNOW ANYTHING ABOUT ME--
--NOTHING!
MY DAYS OF BEING A WALLFLOWER ARE OVER!
THE NEW ME CAN DO ANYTHING SHE WANTS! CAN HAVE ANYTHING SHE WANTS!
I KNOW A MILLION GUYS LIKE YOU...

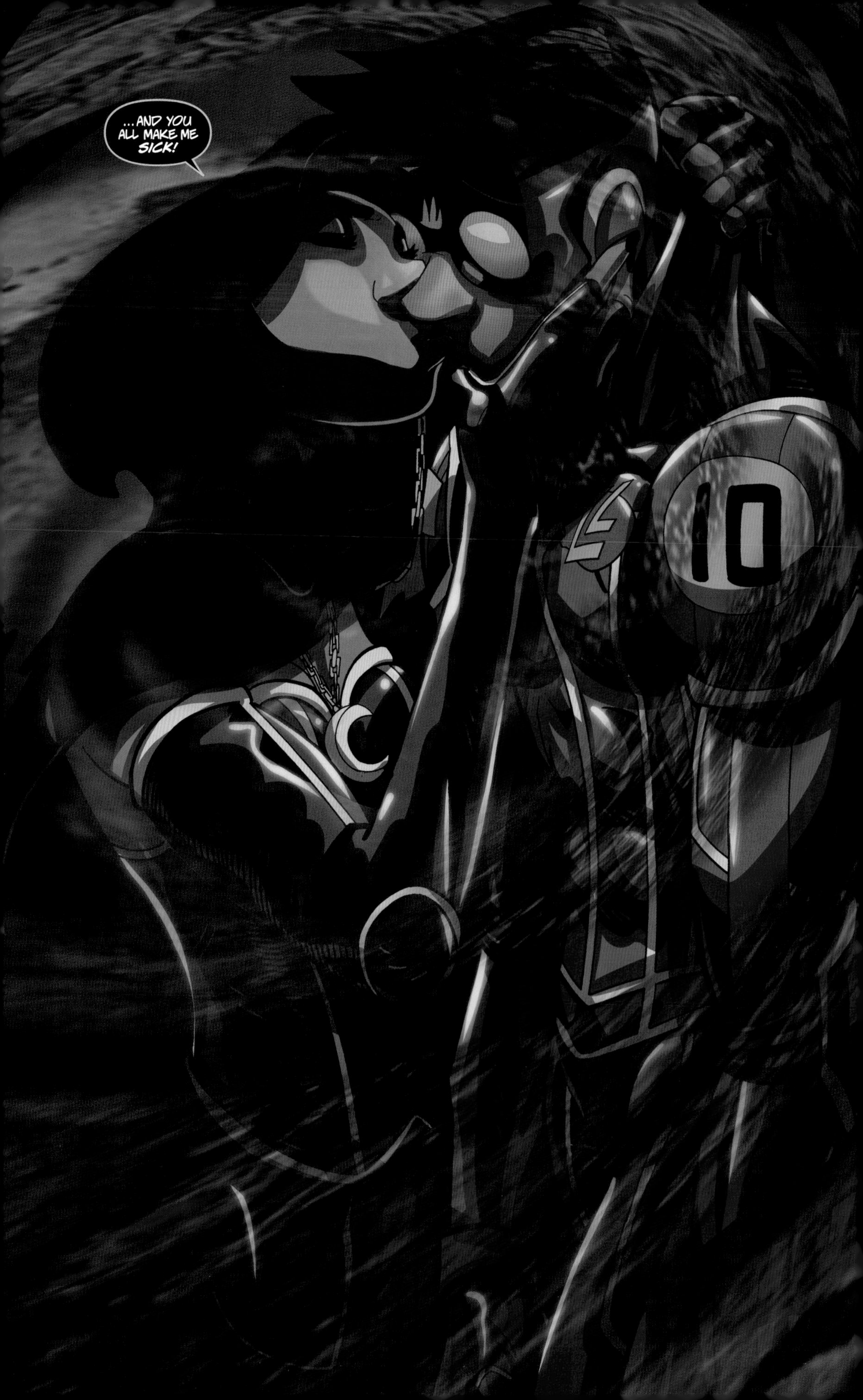
...AND YOU ALL MAKE ME SICK!

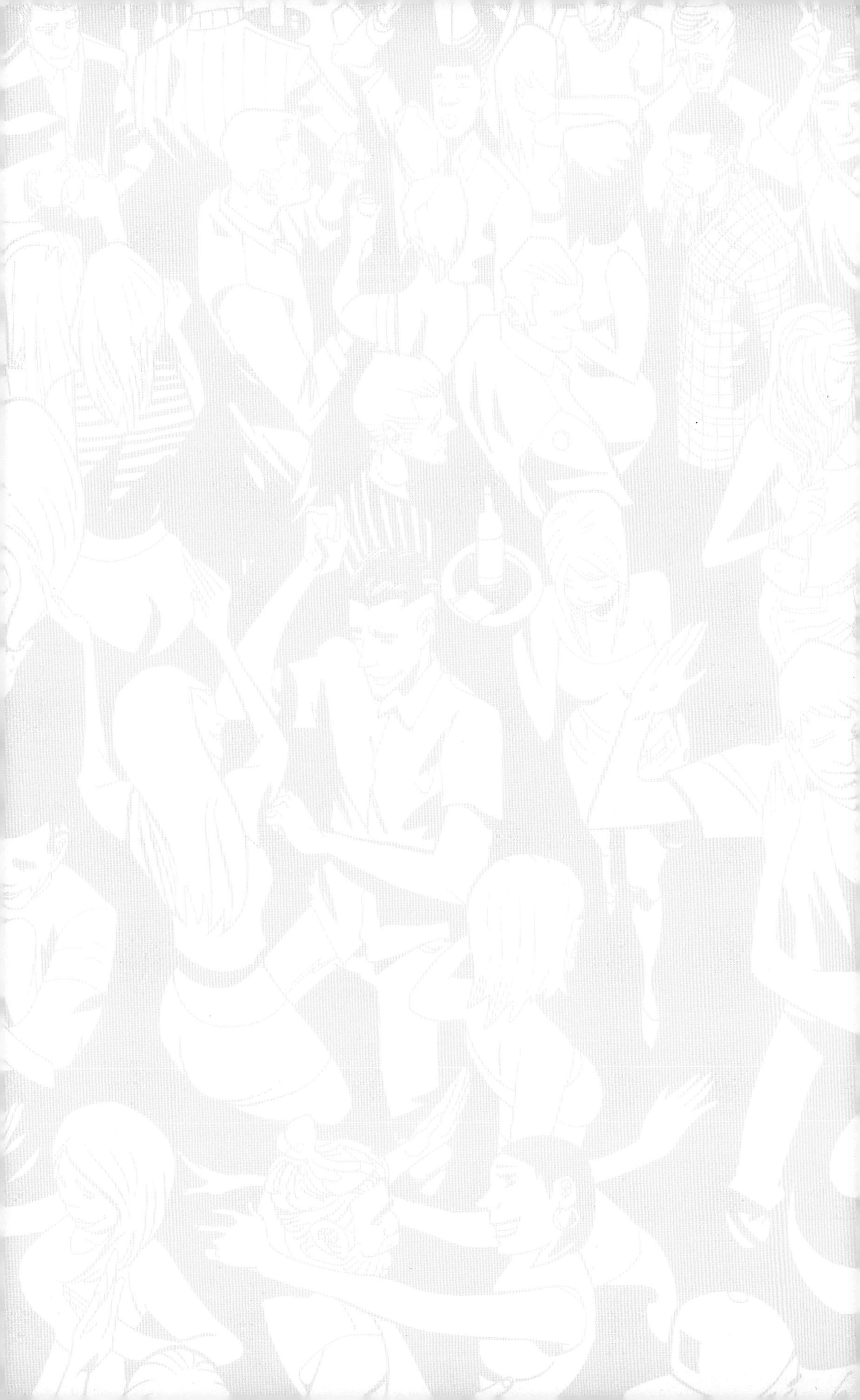

CHAPTER TWO

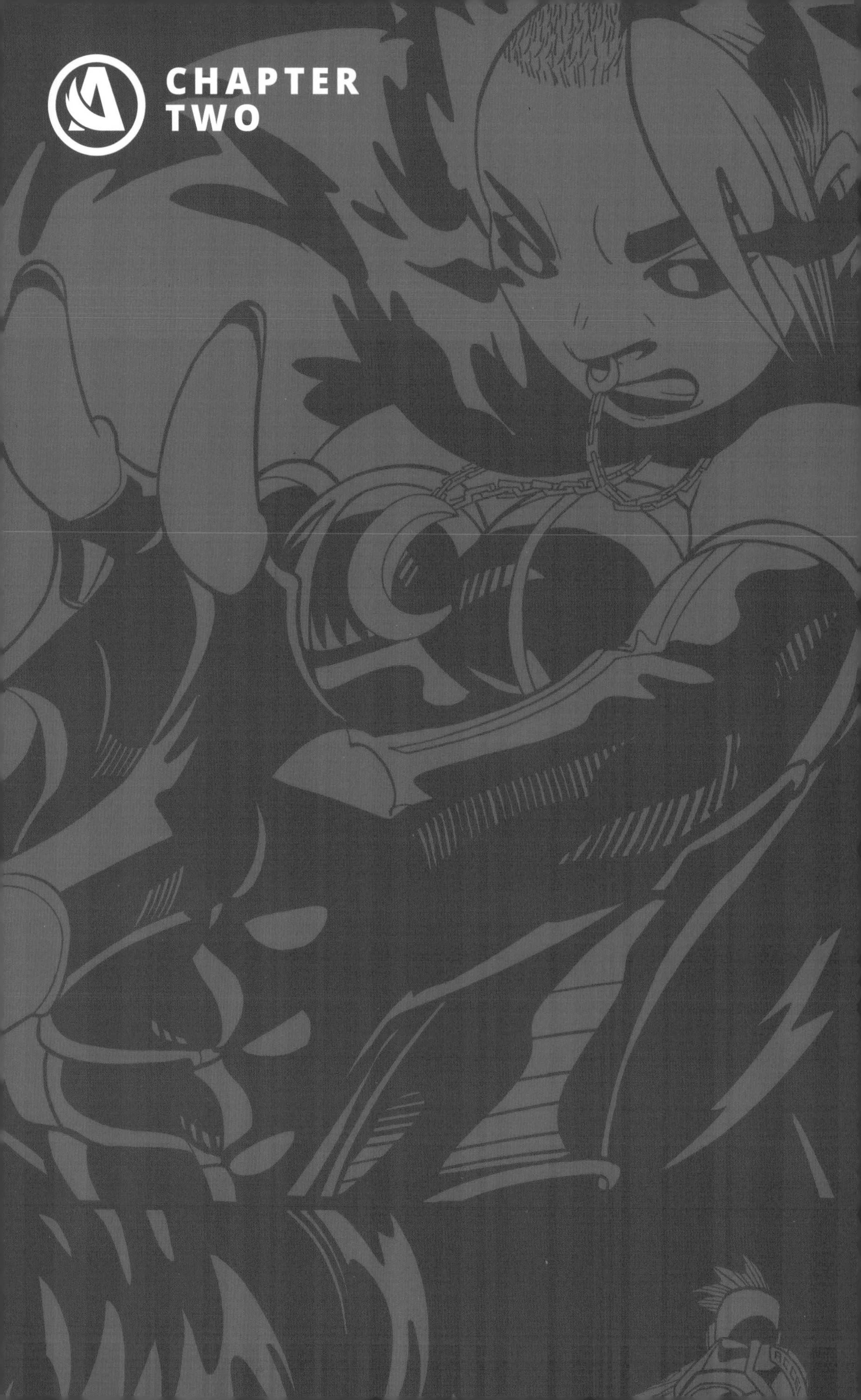

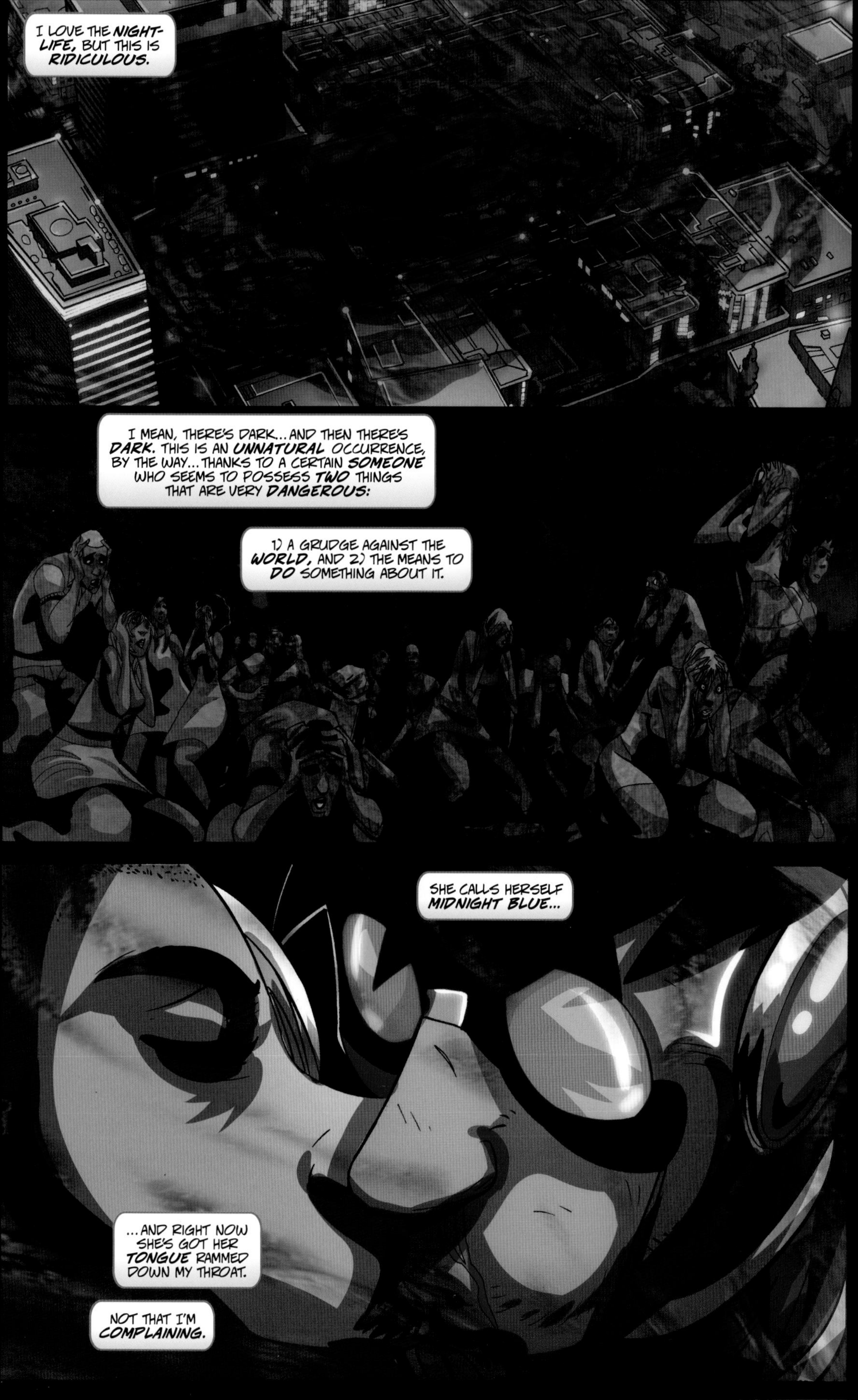
I LOVE THE NIGHT-LIFE, BUT THIS IS RIDICULOUS.
I MEAN, THERE'S DARK... AND THEN THERE'S DARK. THIS IS AN UNNATURAL OCCURRENCE, BY THE WAY... THANKS TO A CERTAIN SOMEONE WHO SEEMS TO POSSESS TWO THINGS THAT ARE VERY DANGEROUS:
1) A GRUDGE AGAINST THE WORLD, AND 2) THE MEANS TO DO SOMETHING ABOUT IT.
SHE CALLS HERSELF MIDNIGHT BLUE...
...AND RIGHT NOW SHE'S GOT HER TONGUE RAMMED DOWN MY THROAT.
NOT THAT I'M COMPLAINING.

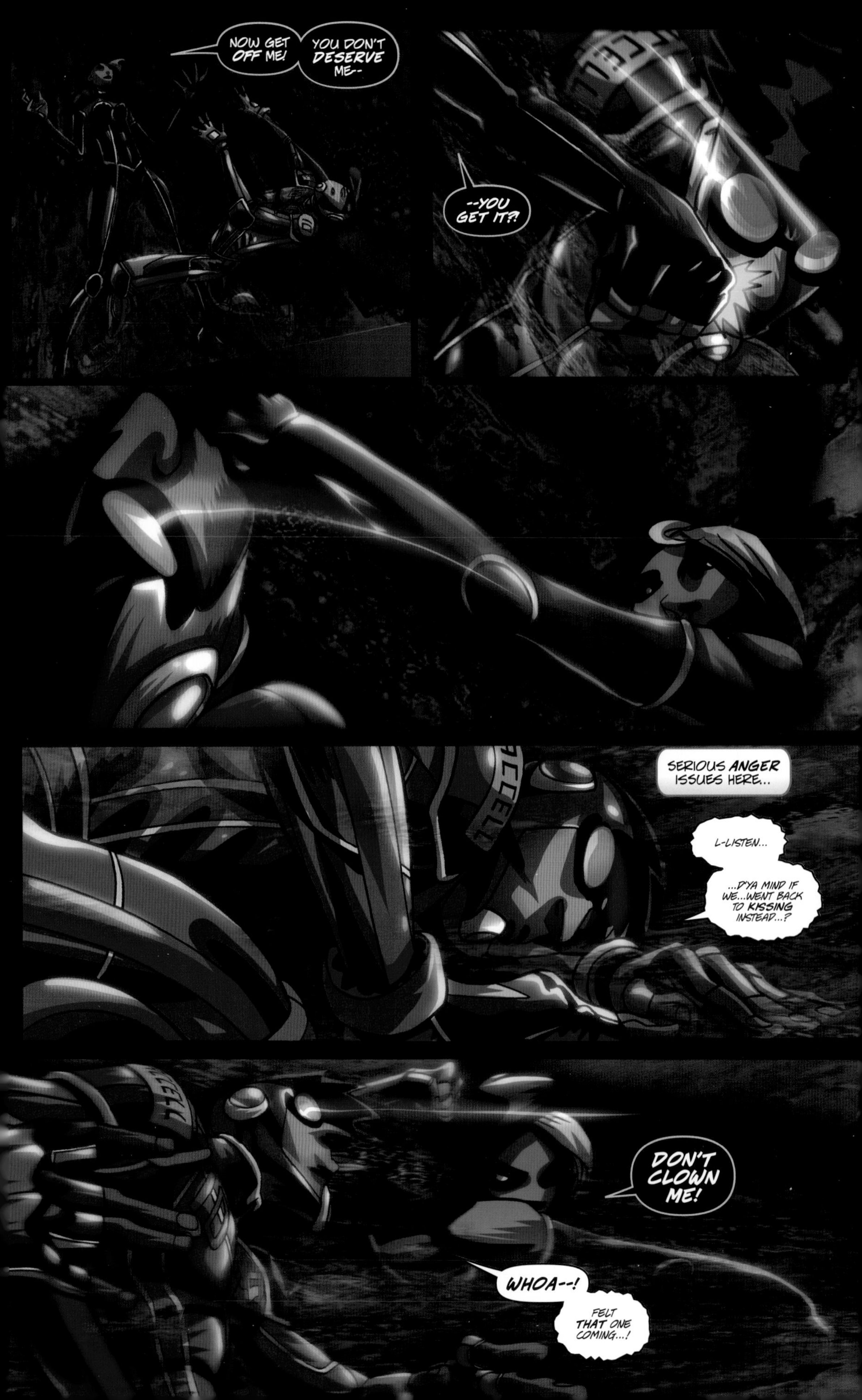
NOW GET OFF ME!
YOU DON'T DESERVE ME--
--YOU GET IT?!
SERIOUS ANGER ISSUES HERE...
L-LISTEN...
...D'YA MIND IF WE...WENT BACK TO KISSING INSTEAD...?
DON'T CLOWN ME!
WHOA--!
FELT THAT ONE COMING...!

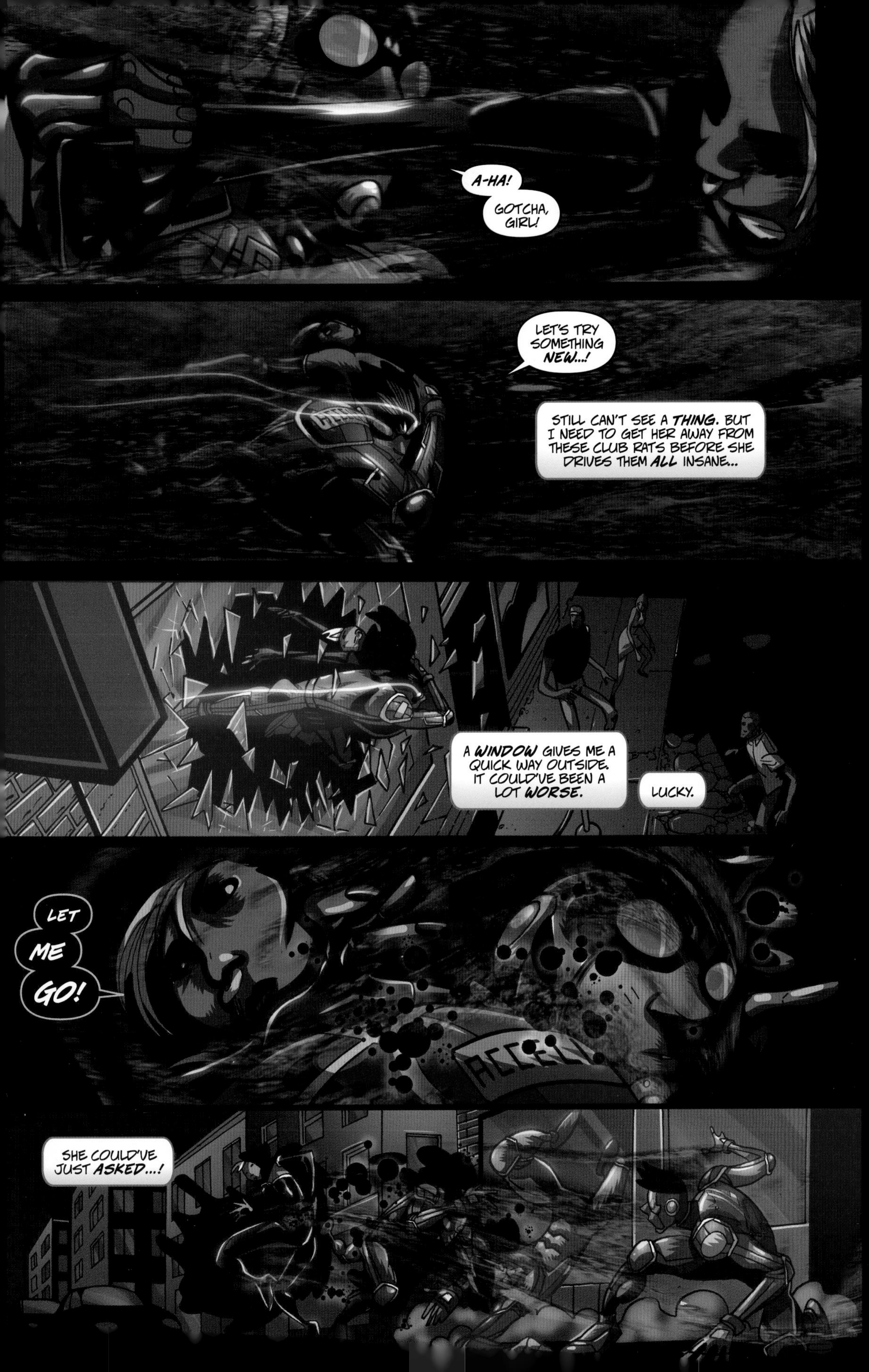
A-HA!
GOTCHA, GIRL!
LET'S TRY SOMETHING NEW...!
STILL CAN'T SEE A THING. BUT I NEED TO GET HER AWAY FROM THESE CLUB RATS BEFORE SHE DRIVES THEM ALL INSANE...
A WINDOW GIVES ME A QUICK WAY OUTSIDE. IT COULD'VE BEEN A LOT WORSE.
LUCKY.
LET ME GO!
SHE COULD'VE JUST ASKED...!

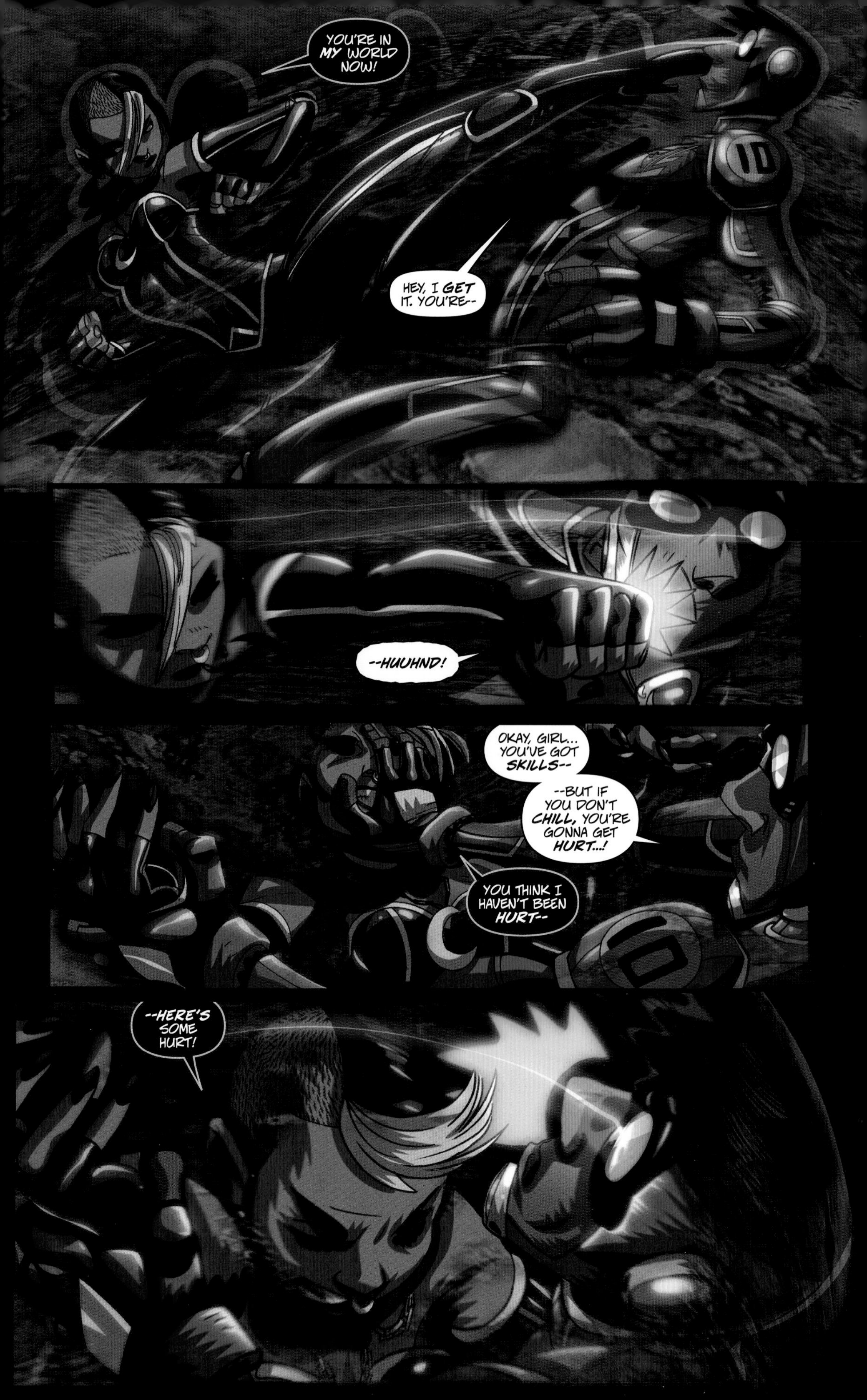
YOU'RE IN MY WORLD NOW!
HEY, I GET IT. YOU'RE--
--HUUHND!
OKAY, GIRL... YOU'VE GOT SKILLS--
--BUT IF YOU DON'T CHILL, YOU'RE GONNA GET HURT...!
YOU THINK I HAVEN'T BEEN HURT--
--HERE'S SOME HURT!

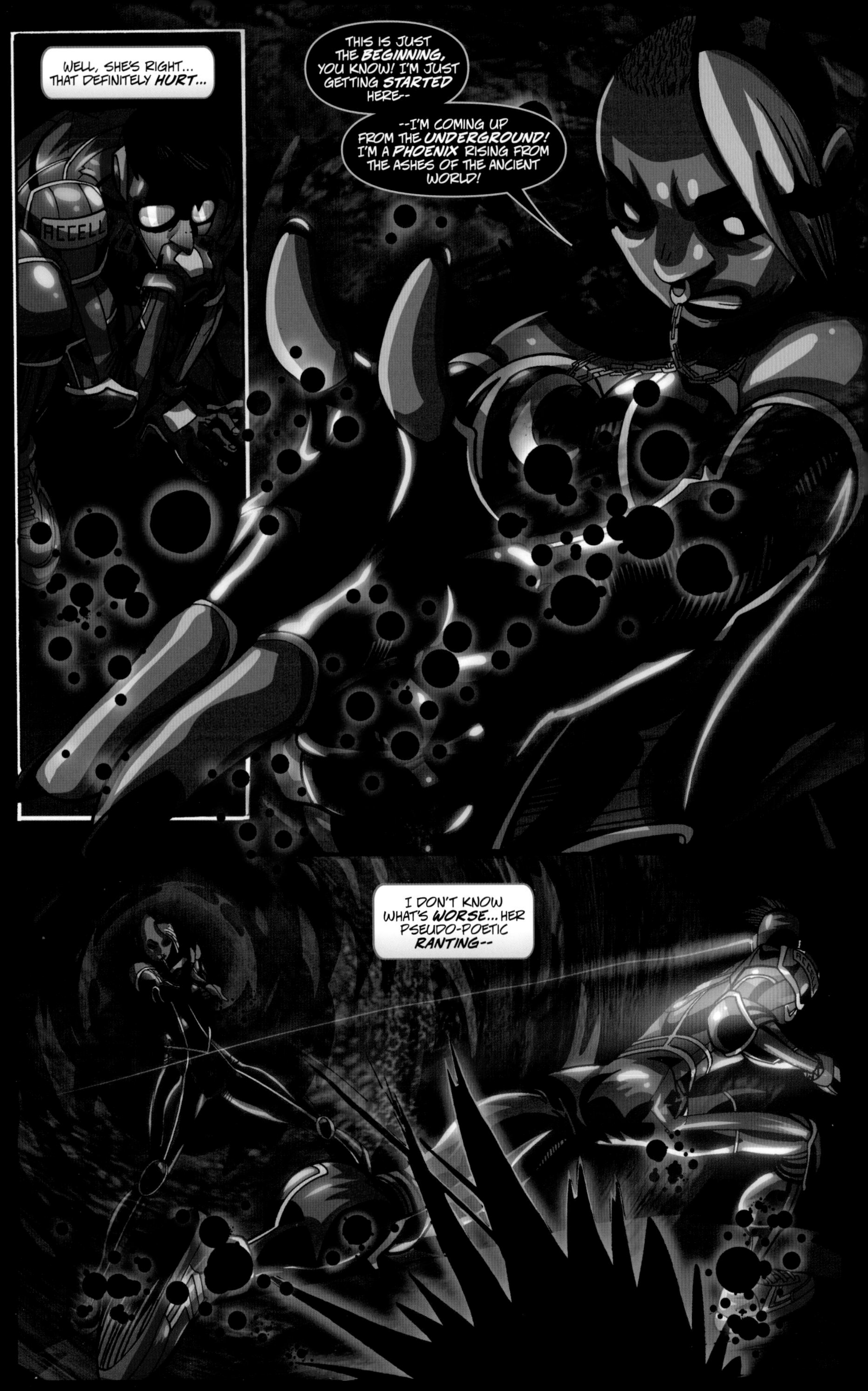

WELL, SHE'S RIGHT... THAT DEFINITELY HURT...
THIS IS JUST THE BEGINNING, YOU KNOW! I'M JUST GETTING STARTED HERE--
--I'M COMING UP FROM THE UNDERGROUND! I'M A PHOENIX RISING FROM THE ASHES OF THE ANCIENT WORLD!
I DON'T KNOW WHAT'S WORSE... HER PSEUDO-POETIC RANTING--

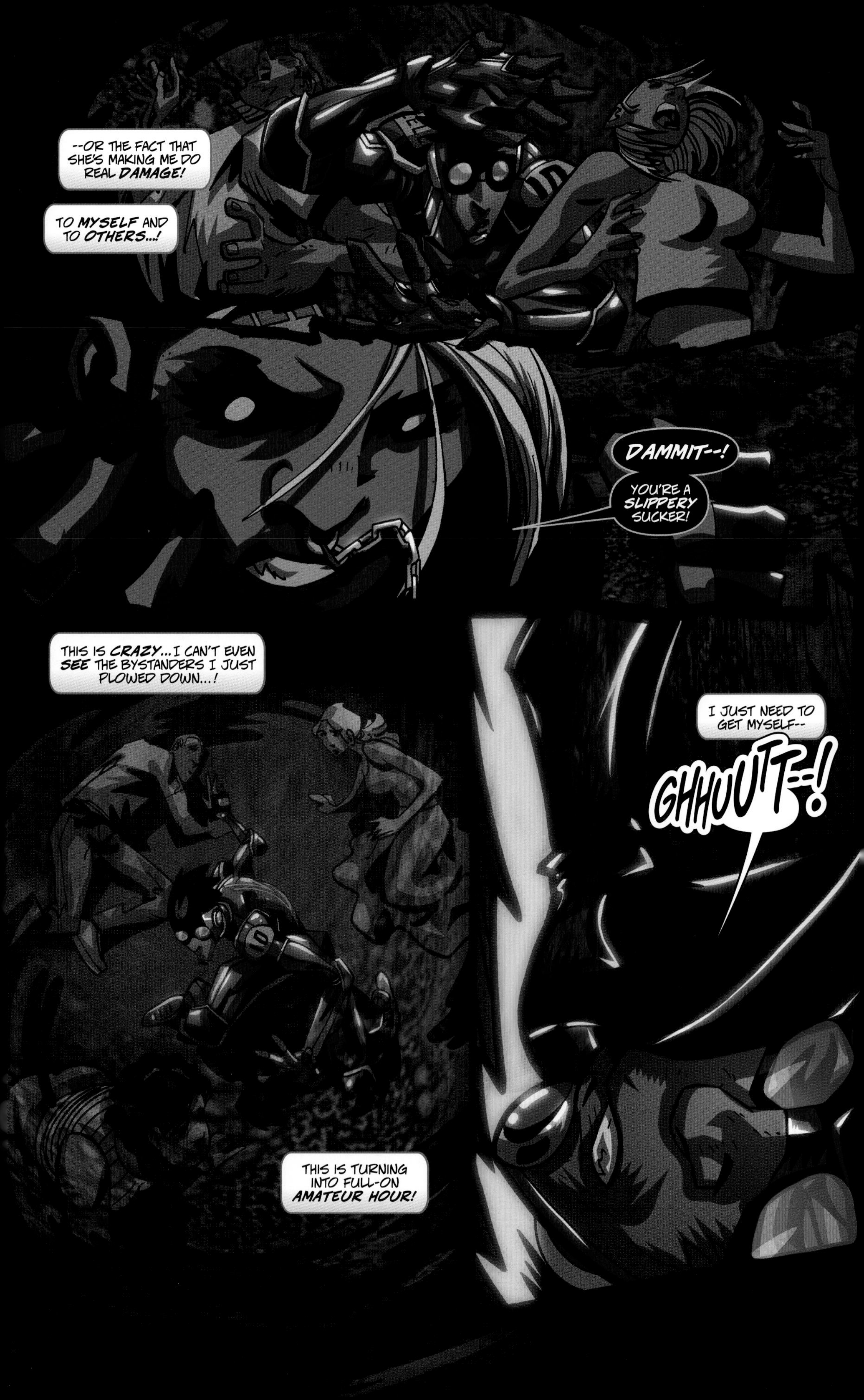
--OR THE FACT THAT SHE'S MAKING ME DO REAL DAMAGE!
TO MYSELF AND TO OTHERS...!
DAMMIT--!
YOU'RE A SLIPPERY SUCKER!
THIS IS CRAZY...I CAN'T EVEN SEE THE BYSTANDERS I JUST PLOWED DOWN...!
THIS IS TURNING INTO FULL-ON AMATEUR HOUR!
I JUST NEED TO GET MYSELF--
GHHUUTT--!

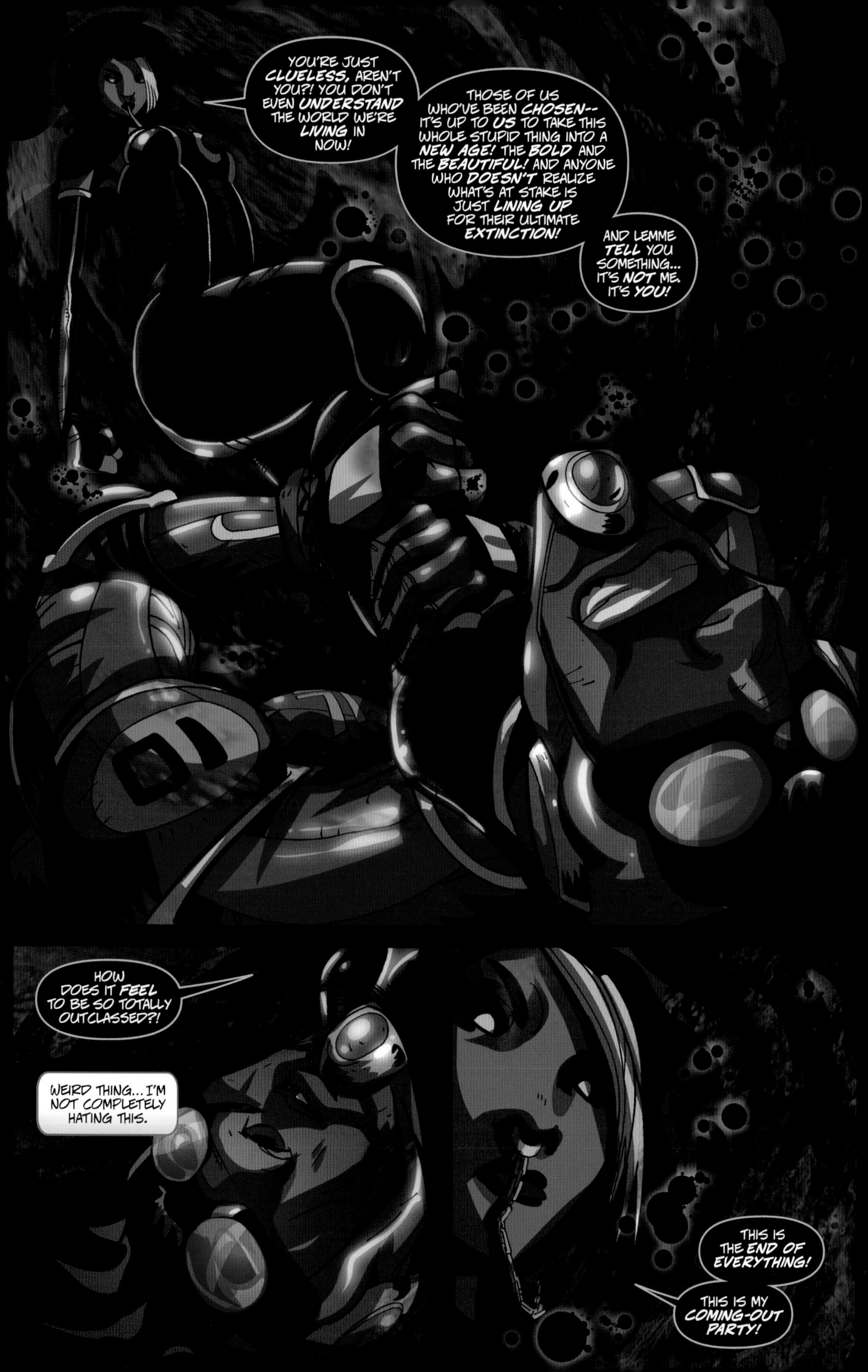
YOU'RE JUST CLUELESS, AREN'T YOU?! YOU DON'T EVEN UNDERSTAND THE WORLD WE'RE LIVING IN NOW!
THOSE OF US WHO'VE BEEN CHOSEN-- IT'S UP TO US TO TAKE THIS WHOLE STUPID THING INTO A NEW AGE! THE BOLD AND THE BEAUTIFUL! AND ANYONE WHO DOESN'T REALIZE WHAT'S AT STAKE IS JUST LINING UP FOR THEIR ULTIMATE EXTINCTION!
AND LEMME TELL YOU SOMETHING... IT'S NOT ME. IT'S YOU!
HOW DOES IT FEEL TO BE SO TOTALLY OUTCLASSED?!
WEIRD THING... I'M NOT COMPLETELY HATING THIS.
THIS IS THE END OF EVERYTHING!
THIS IS MY COMING-OUT PARTY!

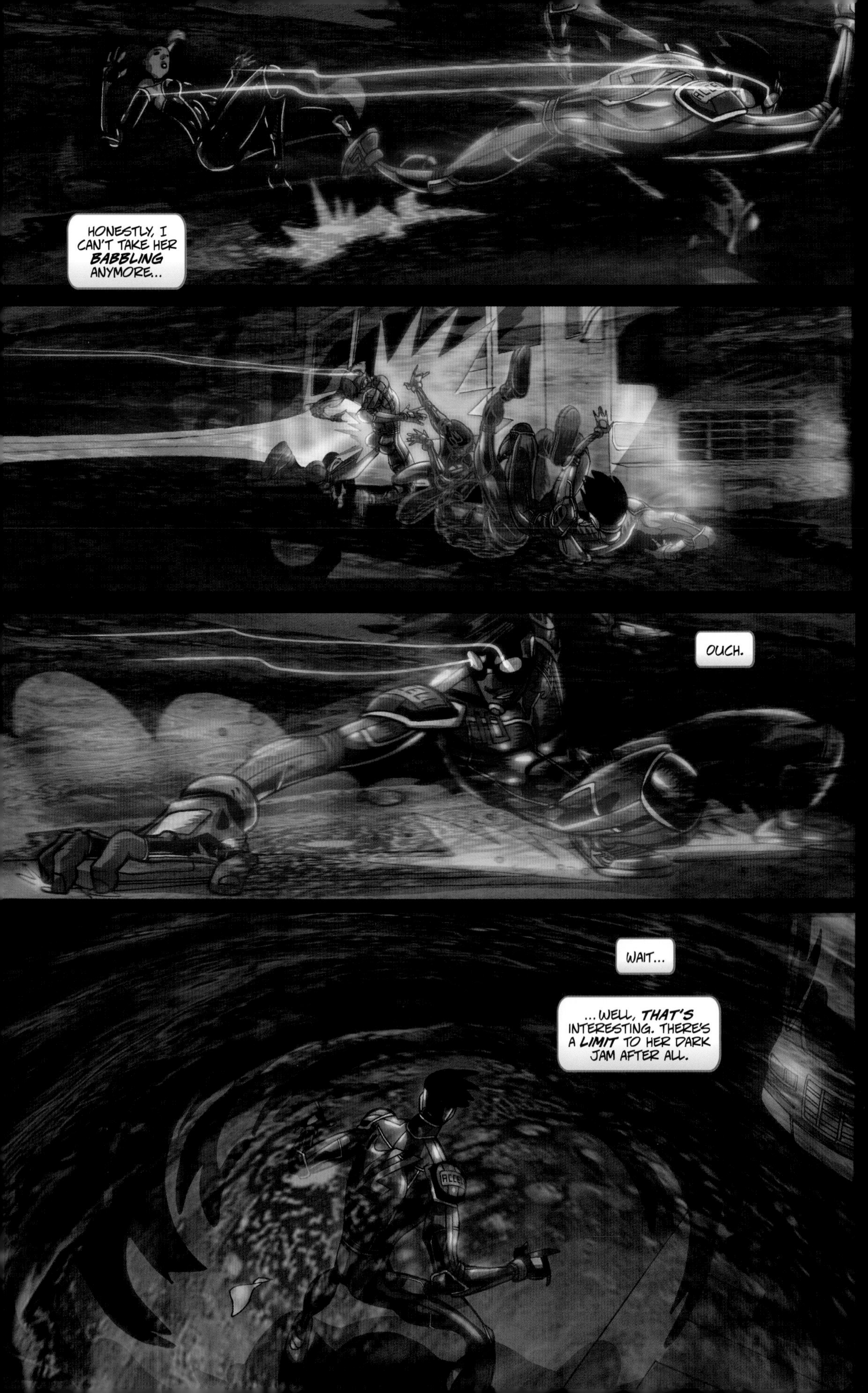
HONESTLY, I CAN'T TAKE HER BABBLING ANYMORE...
OUCH.
WAIT...
...WELL, THAT'S INTERESTING. THERE'S A LIMIT TO HER DARK JAM AFTER ALL.

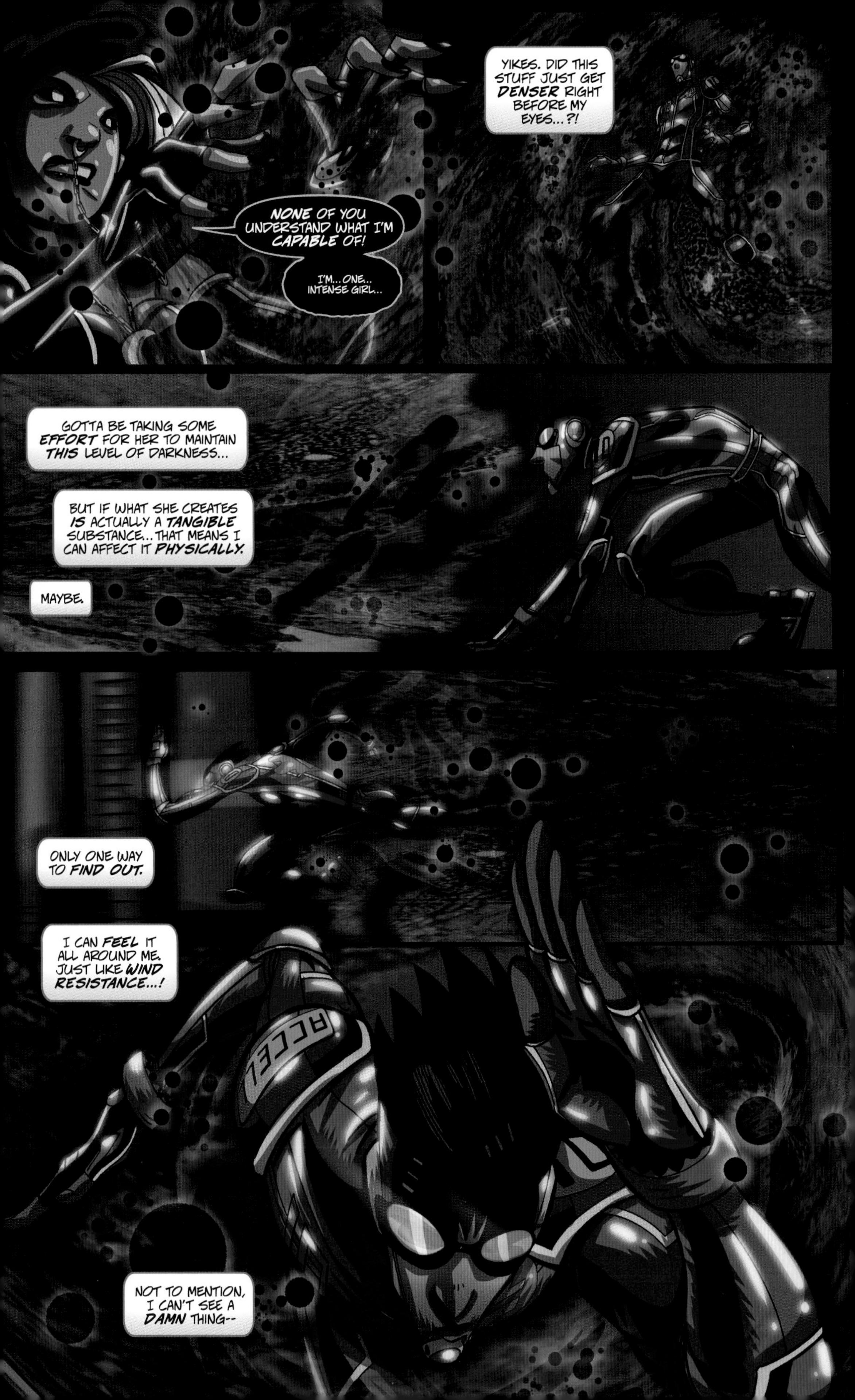
NONE OF YOU UNDERSTAND WHAT I'M CAPABLE OF!
I'M... ONE... INTENSE GIRL...
YIKES. DID THIS STUFF JUST GET DENSER RIGHT BEFORE MY EYES...?!
GOTTA BE TAKING SOME EFFORT FOR HER TO MAINTAIN THIS LEVEL OF DARKNESS...
BUT IF WHAT SHE CREATES IS ACTUALLY A TANGIBLE SUBSTANCE... THAT MEANS I CAN AFFECT IT PHYSICALLY.
MAYBE.
ONLY ONE WAY TO FIND OUT.
I CAN FEEL IT ALL AROUND ME. JUST LIKE WIND RESISTANCE...!
ACCEL
NOT TO MENTION, I CAN'T SEE A DAMN THING--

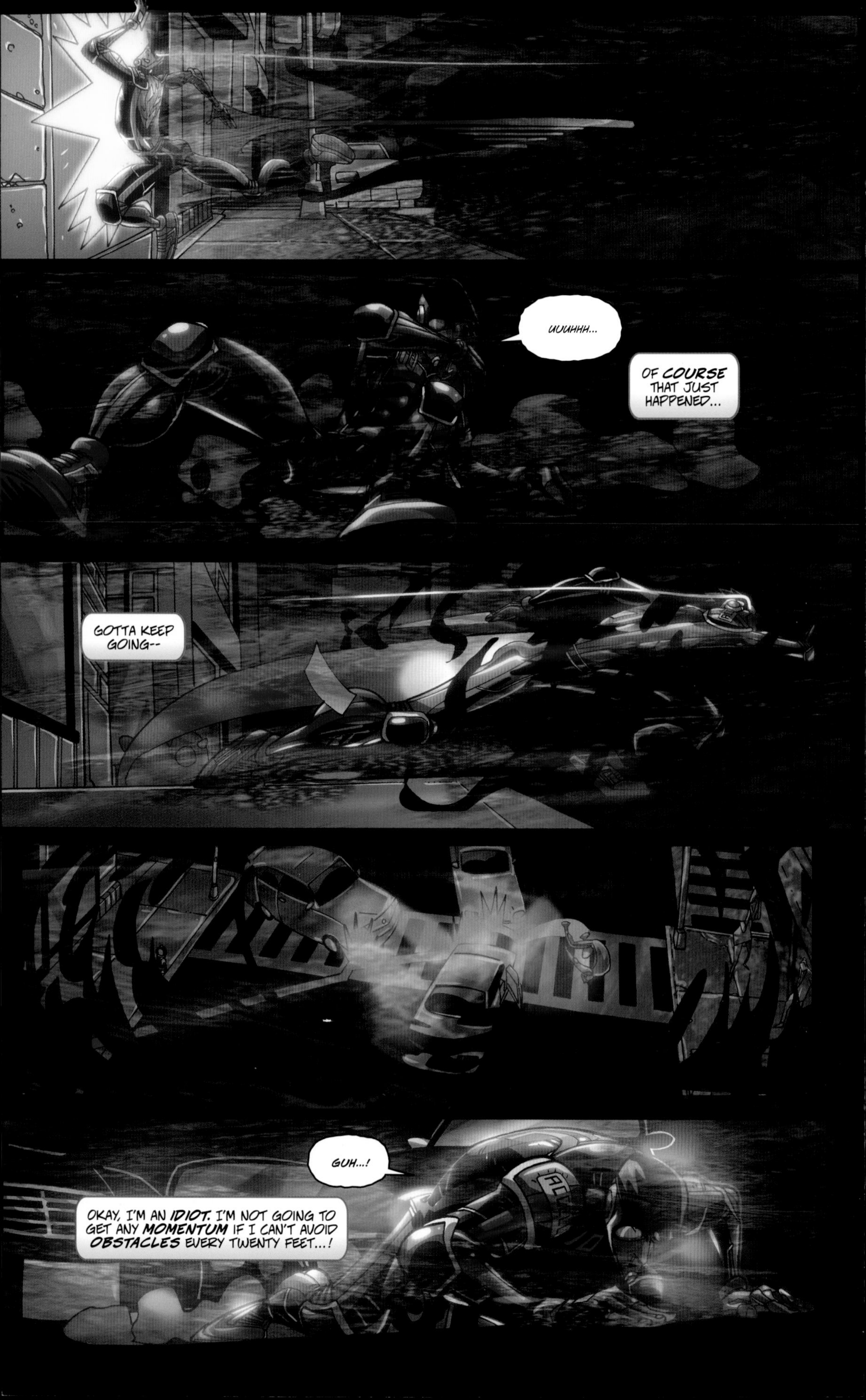
UUUHHH...
OF COURSE THAT JUST HAPPENED...
GOTTA KEEP GOING--
GUH...!
OKAY, I'M AN IDIOT. I'M NOT GOING TO GET ANY MOMENTUM IF I CAN'T AVOID OBSTACLES EVERY TWENTY FEET...!

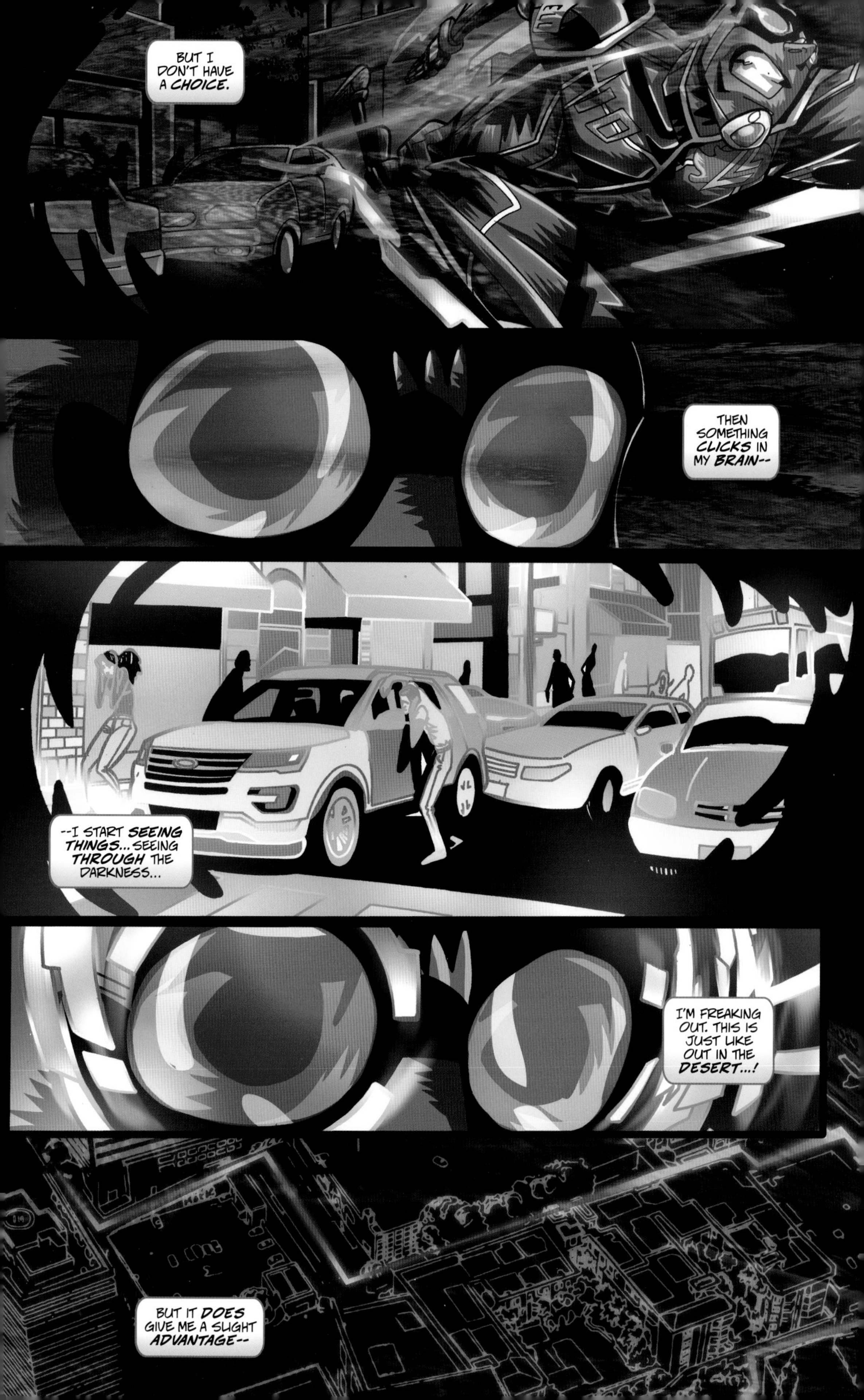
BUT I DON'T HAVE A CHOICE.
THEN SOMETHING CLICKS IN MY BRAIN--
--I START SEEING THINGS... SEEING THROUGH THE DARKNESS...
I'M FREAKING OUT. THIS IS JUST LIKE OUT IN THE DESERT...!
BUT IT DOES GIVE ME A SLIGHT ADVANTAGE--

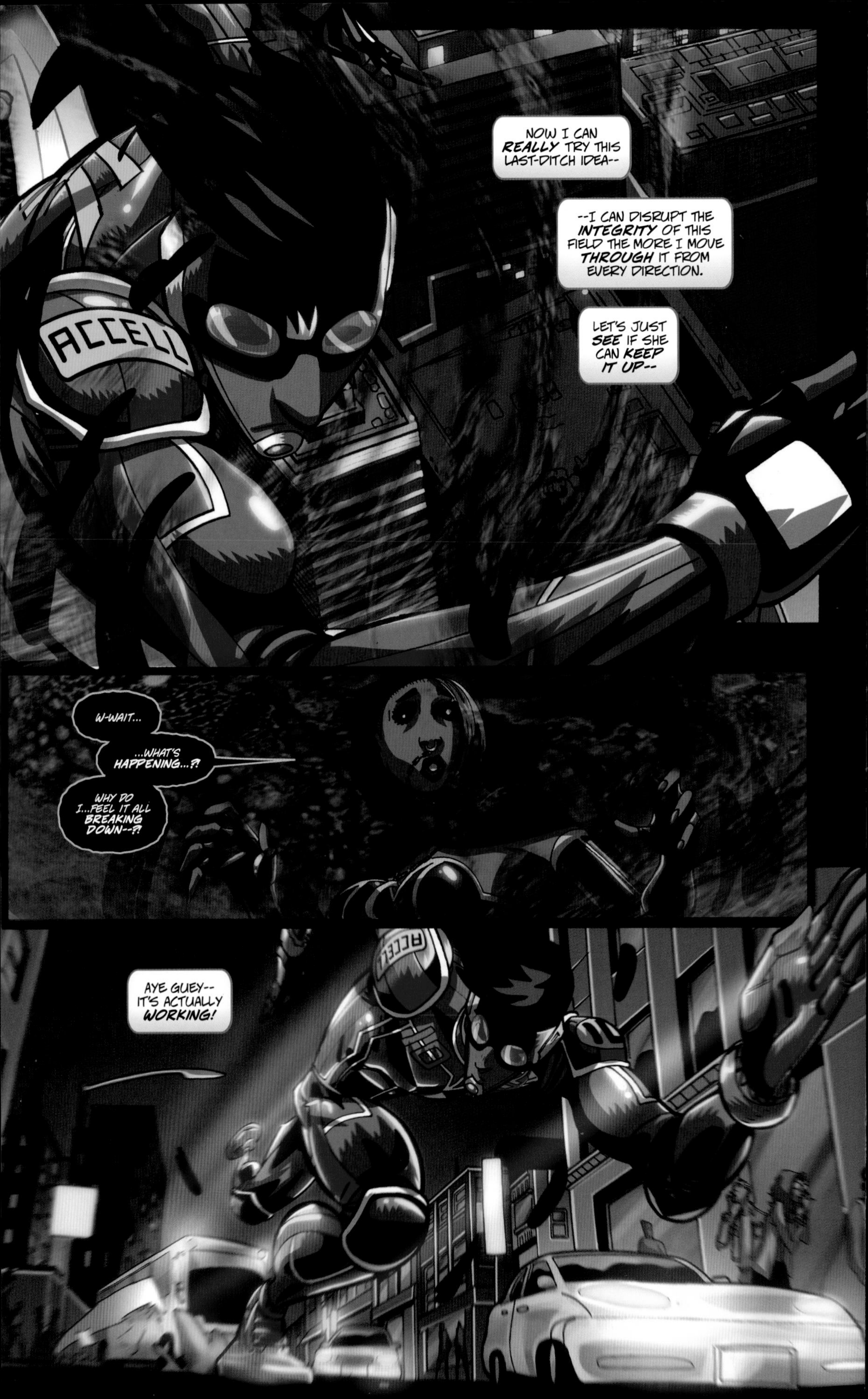

NOW I CAN REALLY TRY THIS LAST-DITCH IDEA--
--I CAN DISRUPT THE INTEGRITY OF THIS FIELD THE MORE I MOVE THROUGH IT FROM EVERY DIRECTION.
LET'S JUST SEE IF SHE CAN KEEP IT UP--
W-WAIT...
...WHAT'S HAPPENING...?!
WHY DO I...FEEL IT ALL BREAKING DOWN--?!
ACCELL
AYE GUEY-- IT'S ACTUALLY WORKING!

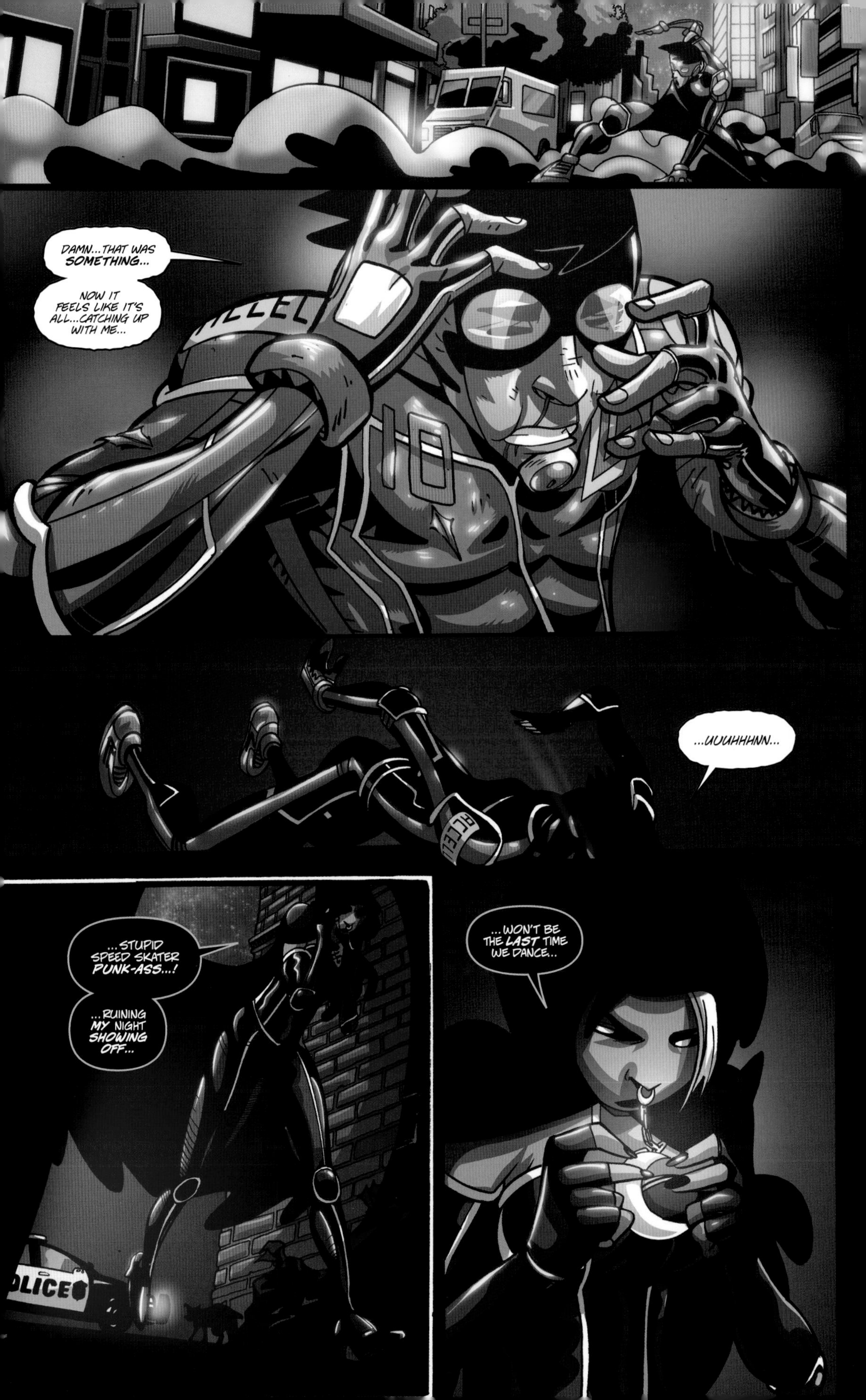
DAMN...THAT WAS SOMETHING...
NOW IT FEELS LIKE IT'S ALL...CATCHING UP WITH ME...
...UUUHHHNN...
...STUPID SPEED SKATER PUNK-ASS...!
...RUINING MY NIGHT SHOWING OFF...
...WON'T BE THE LAST TIME WE DANCE...
POLICE

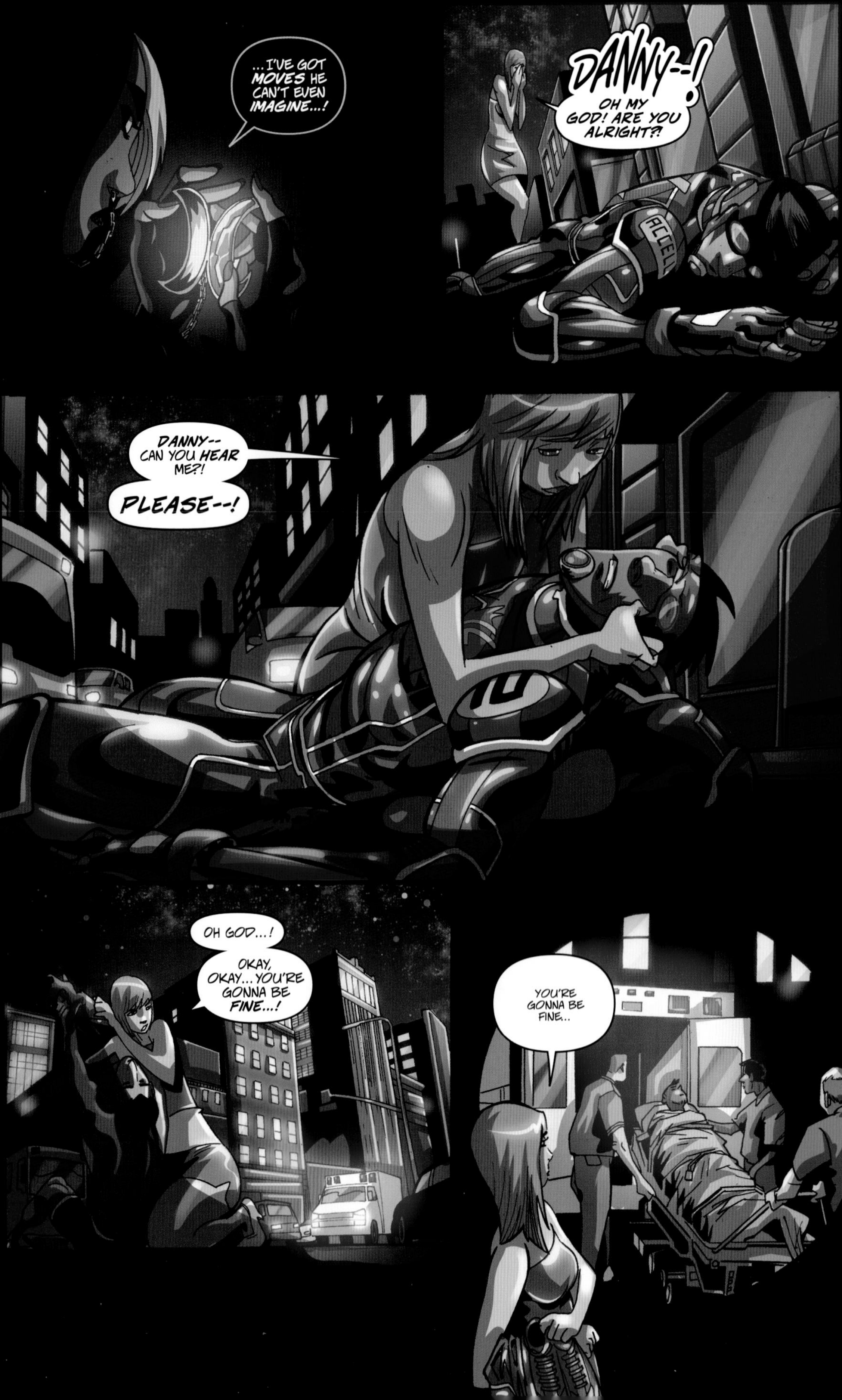
...I'VE GOT MOVES HE CAN'T EVEN IMAGINE...!
DANNY--!
OH MY GOD! ARE YOU ALRIGHT?!
DANNY-- CAN YOU HEAR ME?!
PLEASE--!
OH GOD...!
OKAY, OKAY...YOU'RE GONNA BE FINE...!
YOU'RE GONNA BE FINE...

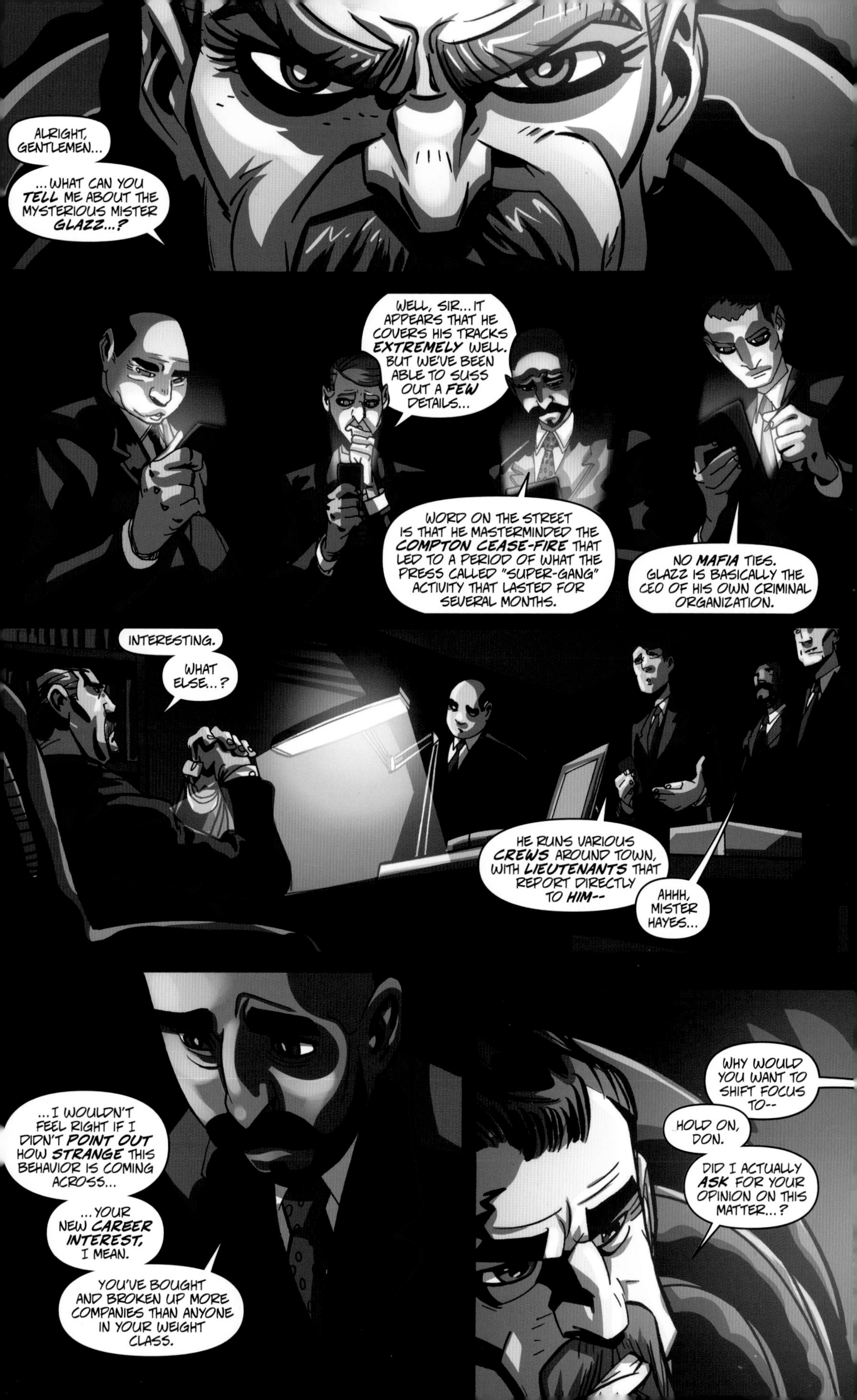

ALRIGHT, GENTLEMEN...
...WHAT CAN YOU TELL ME ABOUT THE MYSTERIOUS MISTER GLAZZ...?
WELL, SIR... IT APPEARS THAT HE COVERS HIS TRACKS EXTREMELY WELL. BUT WE'VE BEEN ABLE TO SUSS OUT A FEW DETAILS...
WORD ON THE STREET IS THAT HE MASTERMINDED THE COMPTON CEASE-FIRE THAT LED TO A PERIOD OF WHAT THE PRESS CALLED "SUPER-GANG" ACTIVITY THAT LASTED FOR SEVERAL MONTHS.
NO MAFIA TIES. GLAZZ IS BASICALLY THE CEO OF HIS OWN CRIMINAL ORGANIZATION.
INTERESTING.
WHAT ELSE...?
HE RUNS VARIOUS CREWS AROUND TOWN, WITH LIEUTENANTS THAT REPORT DIRECTLY TO HIM--
AHHH, MISTER HAYES...
...I WOULDN'T FEEL RIGHT IF I DIDN'T POINT OUT HOW STRANGE THIS BEHAVIOR IS COMING ACROSS...
...YOUR NEW CAREER INTEREST, I MEAN.
YOU'VE BOUGHT AND BROKEN UP MORE COMPANIES THAN ANYONE IN YOUR WEIGHT CLASS.
WHY WOULD YOU WANT TO SHIFT FOCUS TO--
HOLD ON, DON.
DID I ACTUALLY ASK FOR YOUR OPINION ON THIS MATTER...?

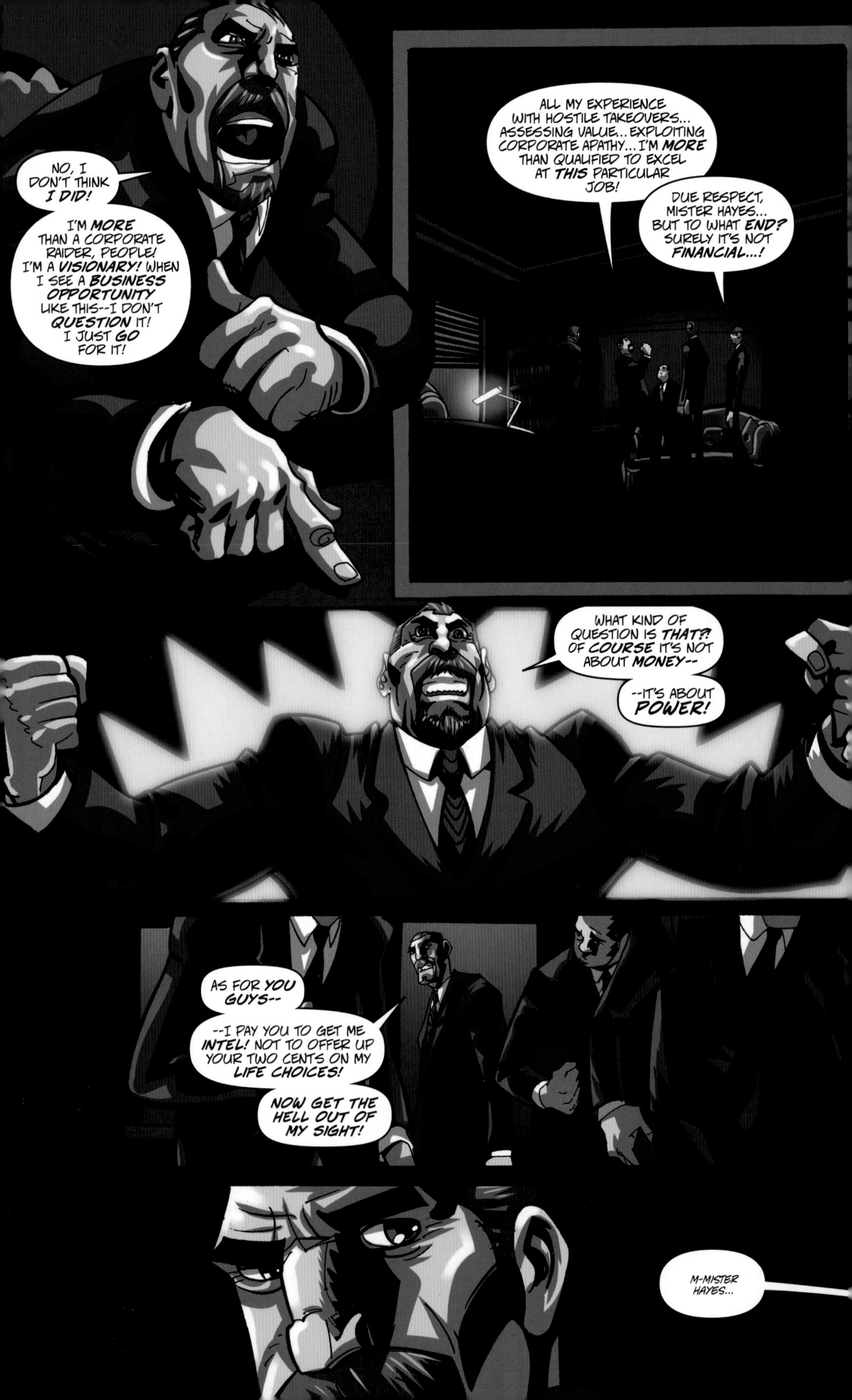
NO, I DON'T THINK I DID!
I'M MORE THAN A CORPORATE RAIDER, PEOPLE! I'M A VISIONARY! WHEN I SEE A BUSINESS OPPORTUNITY LIKE THIS--I DON'T QUESTION IT! I JUST GO FOR IT!
ALL MY EXPERIENCE WITH HOSTILE TAKEOVERS... ASSESSING VALUE... EXPLOITING CORPORATE APATHY... I'M MORE THAN QUALIFIED TO EXCEL AT THIS PARTICULAR JOB!
DUE RESPECT, MISTER HAYES... BUT TO WHAT END? SURELY IT'S NOT FINANCIAL...!
WHAT KIND OF QUESTION IS THAT?! OF COURSE IT'S NOT ABOUT MONEY--
--IT'S ABOUT POWER!
AS FOR YOU GUYS--
--I PAY YOU TO GET ME INTEL! NOT TO OFFER UP YOUR TWO CENTS ON MY LIFE CHOICES!
NOW GET THE HELL OUT OF MY SIGHT!
M-MISTER HAYES...

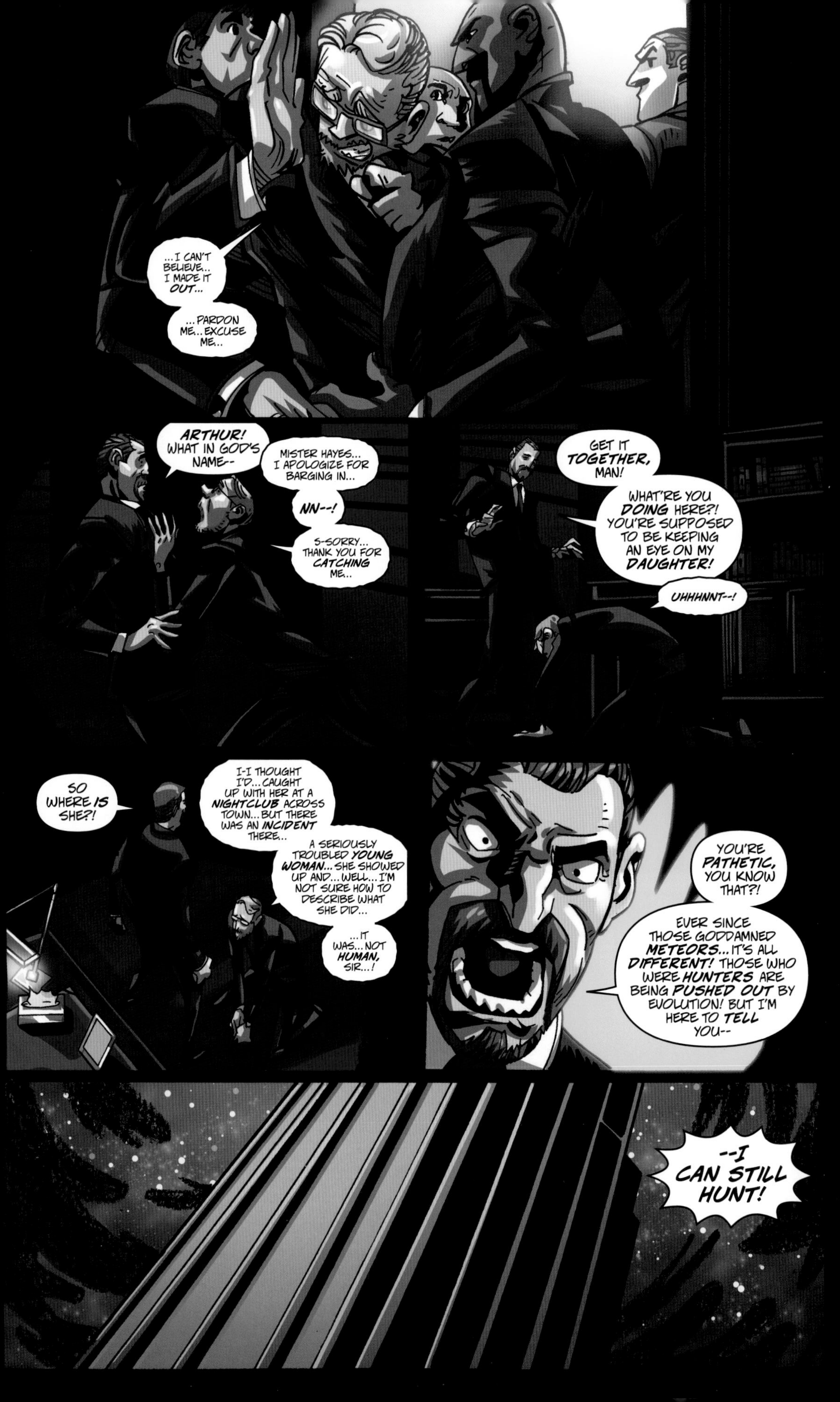
...I CAN'T BELIEVE... I MADE IT OUT...
...PARDON ME...EXCUSE ME...
ARTHUR! WHAT IN GOD'S NAME--
MISTER HAYES... I APOLOGIZE FOR BARGING IN...
NN--!
S-SORRY... THANK YOU FOR CATCHING ME...
GET IT TOGETHER, MAN!
WHAT'RE YOU DOING HERE?! YOU'RE SUPPOSED TO BE KEEPING AN EYE ON MY DAUGHTER!
UHHHNNT--!
SO WHERE IS SHE?!
I-I THOUGHT I'D...CAUGHT UP WITH HER AT A NIGHTCLUB ACROSS TOWN...BUT THERE WAS AN INCIDENT THERE...
A SERIOUSLY TROUBLED YOUNG WOMAN...SHE SHOWED UP AND...WELL...I'M NOT SURE HOW TO DESCRIBE WHAT SHE DID...
...IT WAS...NOT HUMAN, SIR...!
YOU'RE PATHETIC, YOU KNOW THAT?!
EVER SINCE THOSE GODDAMNED METEORS...IT'S ALL DIFFERENT! THOSE WHO WERE HUNTERS ARE BEING PUSHED OUT BY EVOLUTION! BUT I'M HERE TO TELL YOU--
--I CAN STILL HUNT!

NEW VERSE, SAME AS THE FIRST...

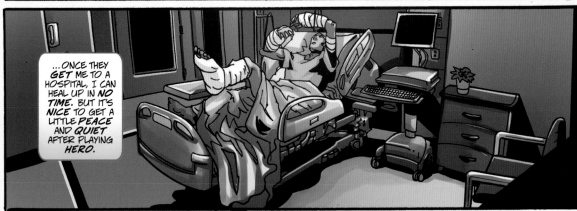

...ONCE THEY *GET* ME TO A HOSPITAL, I CAN HEAL UP IN *NO TIME.* BUT IT'S *NICE* TO GET A LITTLE *PEACE* AND *QUIET* AFTER PLAYING *HERO.*

STILL NOT SURE HOW MUCH I *TRUST* MYSELF...

...AND I HATE TO THINK MY MIND'S STILL PLAYING *TRICKS* ON ME...

WHAT DO YOU *MEAN* "CALM DOWN"?!

THAT BITCH COULD'VE *KILLED* YOU, DANNY--!

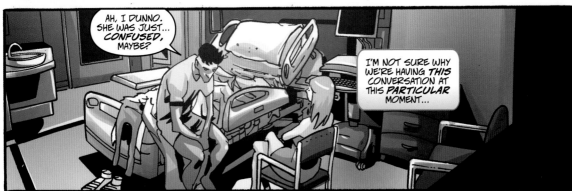

AH, I DUNNO. SHE WAS JUST... *CONFUSED,* MAYBE?

I'M NOT SURE WHY WE'RE HAVING *THIS* CONVERSATION AT THIS *PARTICULAR* MOMENT...

HEY, THANKS FOR BRINGING A CHANGE OF *CLOTHES,* BOMBONCITA.

AND THANKS FOR GRABBING MY *RUNNING THREADS* SO I DIDN'T HAVE TO DEAL WITH ANY ANNOYING *QUESTIONS...*

LEAST I COULD DO, I GUESS. AFTER ALL, *YOU'RE* THE HERO WITH THE SECRET IDENTITY, RIGHT...?

RIGHT AS RAIN. AT LEAST, AS LONG AS I CAN KEEP IT UP. SEEMS *CLEANER...*

SO... ABOUT THIS *GIRL* CAUSING ALL THE TROUBLE...

...SHE *GOT AWAY?*

AS FAR AS I KNOW. HONESTLY, I WAS MORE CONCERNED WITH *SAVING LIVES* THAN GOING TOE-TO-TOE WITH SOME NEW *CARAJO* ON THE SCENE.

MAYBE *NEXT* TIME.

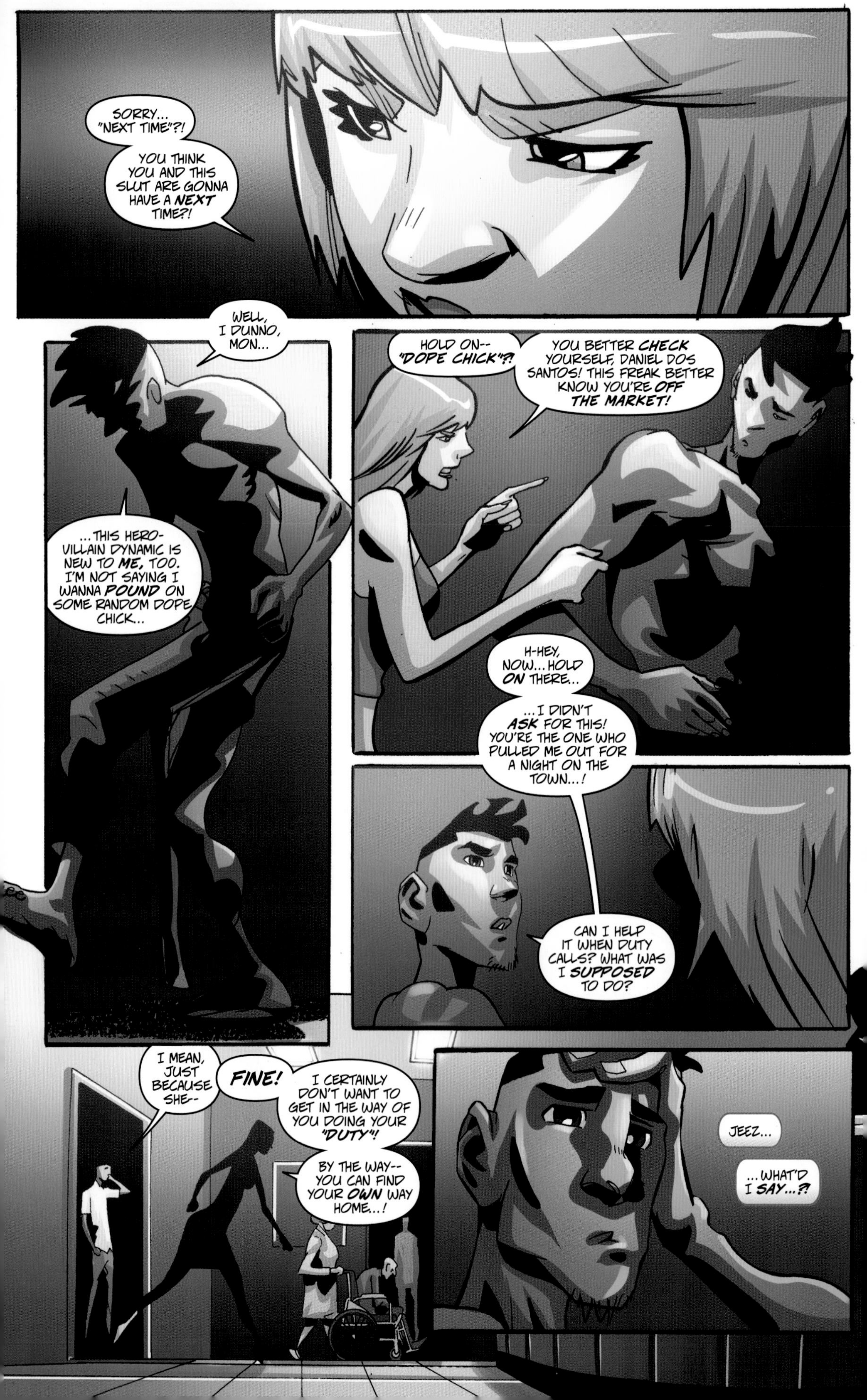
SORRY... "NEXT TIME"?!
YOU THINK YOU AND THIS SLUT ARE GONNA HAVE A **NEXT** TIME?!
WELL, I DUNNO, MON...
...THIS HERO-VILLAIN DYNAMIC IS NEW TO **ME,** TOO. I'M NOT SAYING I WANNA **POUND** ON SOME RANDOM DOPE CHICK...
HOLD ON-- **"DOPE CHICK"?!**
YOU BETTER **CHECK** YOURSELF, DANIEL DOS SANTOS! THIS FREAK BETTER KNOW YOU'RE **OFF THE MARKET!**
H-HEY, NOW... HOLD **ON** THERE...
...I DIDN'T **ASK** FOR THIS! YOU'RE THE ONE WHO PULLED ME OUT FOR A NIGHT ON THE TOWN...!
CAN I HELP IT WHEN DUTY CALLS? WHAT WAS I **SUPPOSED** TO DO?
I MEAN, JUST BECAUSE SHE--
FINE!
I CERTAINLY DON'T WANT TO GET IN THE WAY OF YOU DOING YOUR **"DUTY"!**
BY THE WAY-- YOU CAN FIND YOUR **OWN** WAY HOME...!
JEEZ...
...WHAT'D I **SAY...?!**

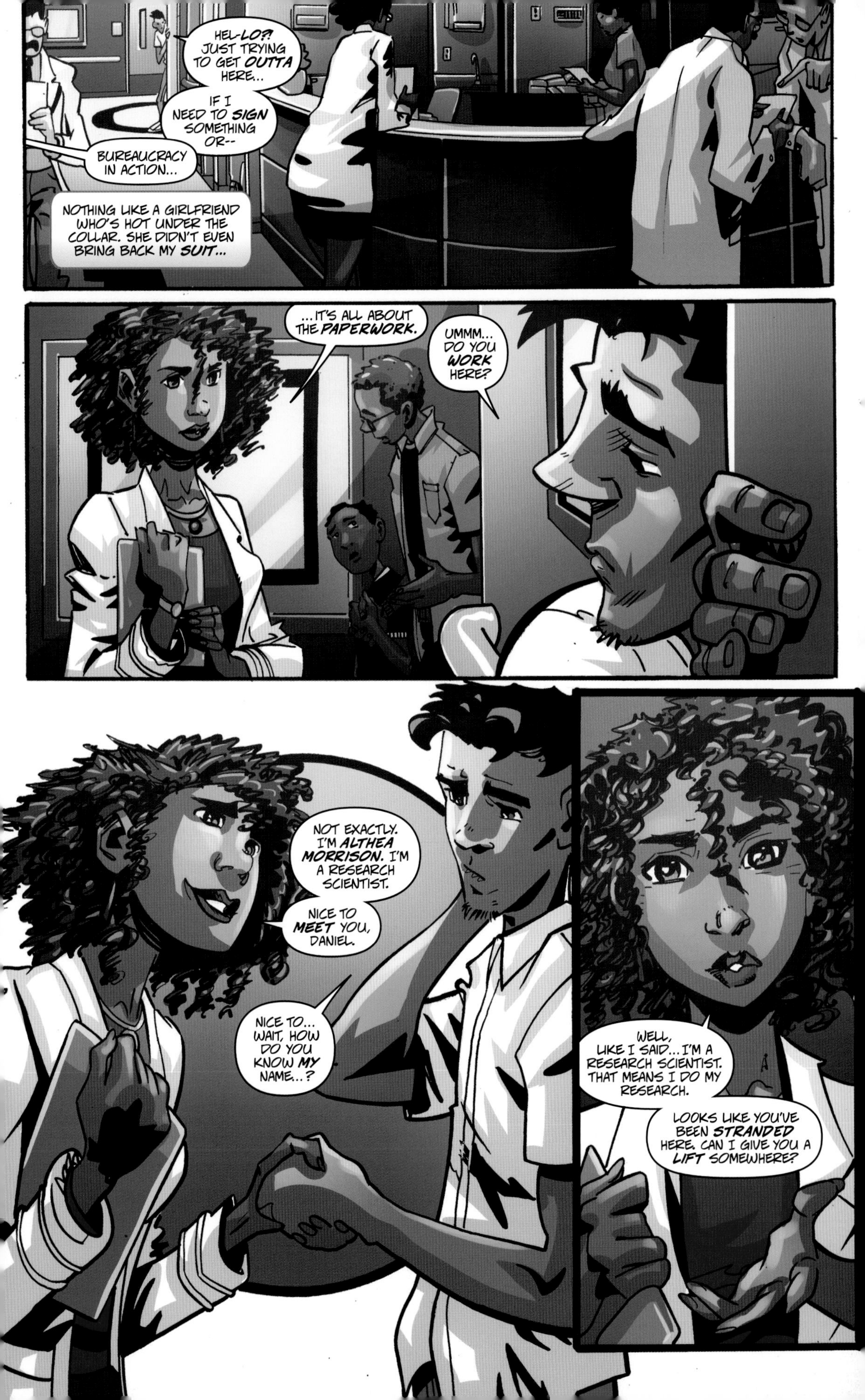
HEL-LO?! JUST TRYING TO GET OUTTA HERE...
IF I NEED TO SIGN SOMETHING OR--
BUREAUCRACY IN ACTION...
NOTHING LIKE A GIRLFRIEND WHO'S HOT UNDER THE COLLAR. SHE DIDN'T EVEN BRING BACK MY SUIT...
...IT'S ALL ABOUT THE PAPERWORK.
UMMM... DO YOU WORK HERE?
NOT EXACTLY. I'M ALTHEA MORRISON. I'M A RESEARCH SCIENTIST.
NICE TO MEET YOU, DANIEL.
NICE TO... WAIT, HOW DO YOU KNOW MY NAME...?
WELL, LIKE I SAID... I'M A RESEARCH SCIENTIST. THAT MEANS I DO MY RESEARCH.
LOOKS LIKE YOU'VE BEEN STRANDED HERE. CAN I GIVE YOU A LIFT SOMEWHERE?

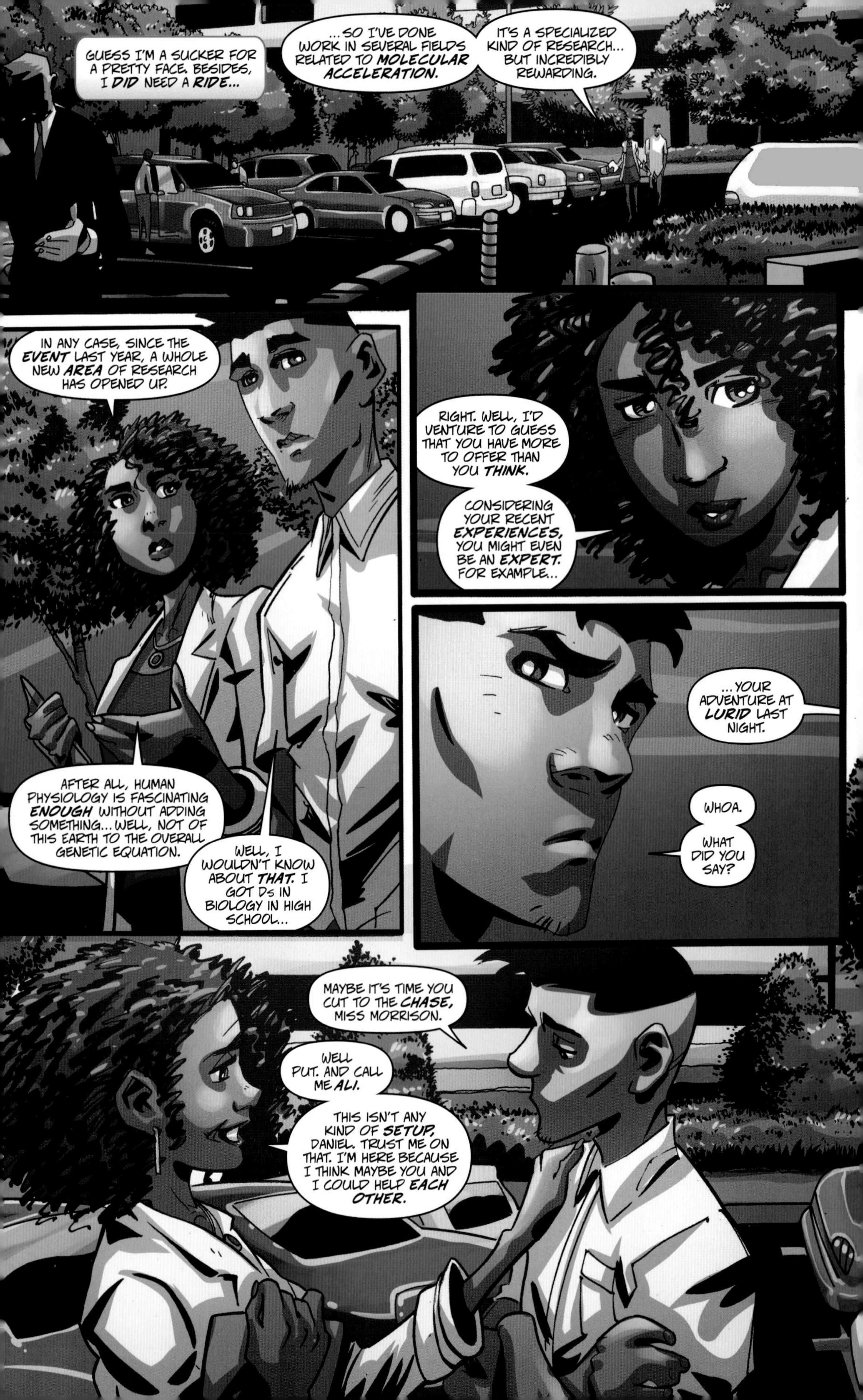
GUESS I'M A SUCKER FOR A PRETTY FACE. BESIDES, I DID NEED A RIDE...
...SO I'VE DONE WORK IN SEVERAL FIELDS RELATED TO MOLECULAR ACCELERATION.
IT'S A SPECIALIZED KIND OF RESEARCH... BUT INCREDIBLY REWARDING.
IN ANY CASE, SINCE THE EVENT LAST YEAR, A WHOLE NEW AREA OF RESEARCH HAS OPENED UP.
AFTER ALL, HUMAN PHYSIOLOGY IS FASCINATING ENOUGH WITHOUT ADDING SOMETHING... WELL, NOT OF THIS EARTH TO THE OVERALL GENETIC EQUATION.
WELL, I WOULDN'T KNOW ABOUT THAT. I GOT Ds IN BIOLOGY IN HIGH SCHOOL...
RIGHT. WELL, I'D VENTURE TO GUESS THAT YOU HAVE MORE TO OFFER THAN YOU THINK.
CONSIDERING YOUR RECENT EXPERIENCES, YOU MIGHT EVEN BE AN EXPERT. FOR EXAMPLE...
...YOUR ADVENTURE AT LURID LAST NIGHT.
WHOA.
WHAT DID YOU SAY?
MAYBE IT'S TIME YOU CUT TO THE CHASE, MISS MORRISON.
WELL PUT. AND CALL ME ALI.
THIS ISN'T ANY KIND OF SETUP, DANIEL. TRUST ME ON THAT. I'M HERE BECAUSE I THINK MAYBE YOU AND I COULD HELP EACH OTHER.

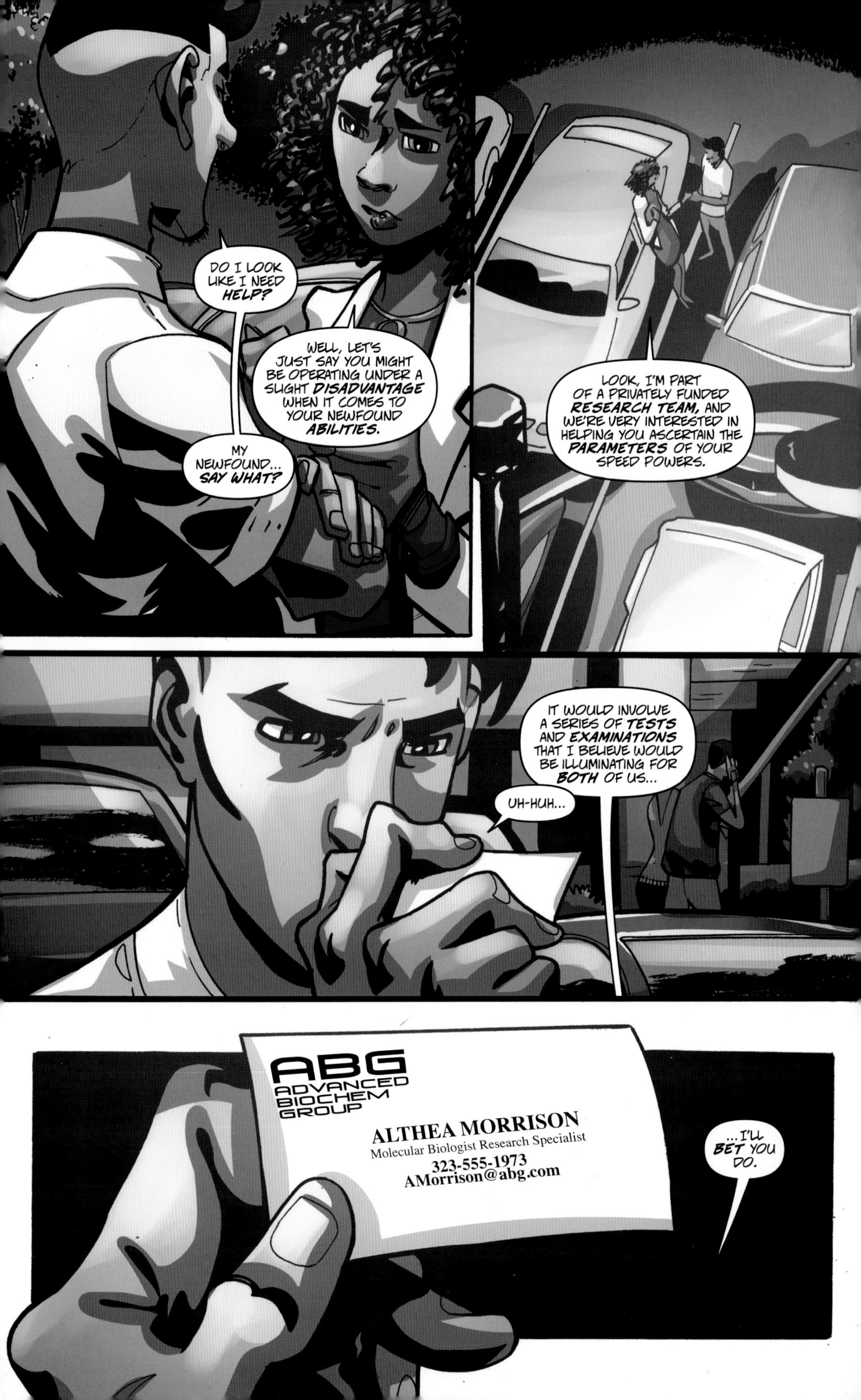
DO I LOOK LIKE I NEED HELP?
WELL, LET'S JUST SAY YOU MIGHT BE OPERATING UNDER A SLIGHT DISADVANTAGE WHEN IT COMES TO YOUR NEWFOUND ABILITIES.
MY NEWFOUND... SAY WHAT?
LOOK, I'M PART OF A PRIVATELY FUNDED RESEARCH TEAM, AND WE'RE VERY INTERESTED IN HELPING YOU ASCERTAIN THE PARAMETERS OF YOUR SPEED POWERS.
IT WOULD INVOLVE A SERIES OF TESTS AND EXAMINATIONS THAT I BELIEVE WOULD BE ILLUMINATING FOR BOTH OF US...
UH-HUH...
ABG ADVANCED BIOCHEM GROUP
ALTHEA MORRISON
Molecular Biologist Research Specialist
323-555-1973
AMorrison@abg.com
...I'LL BET YOU DO.

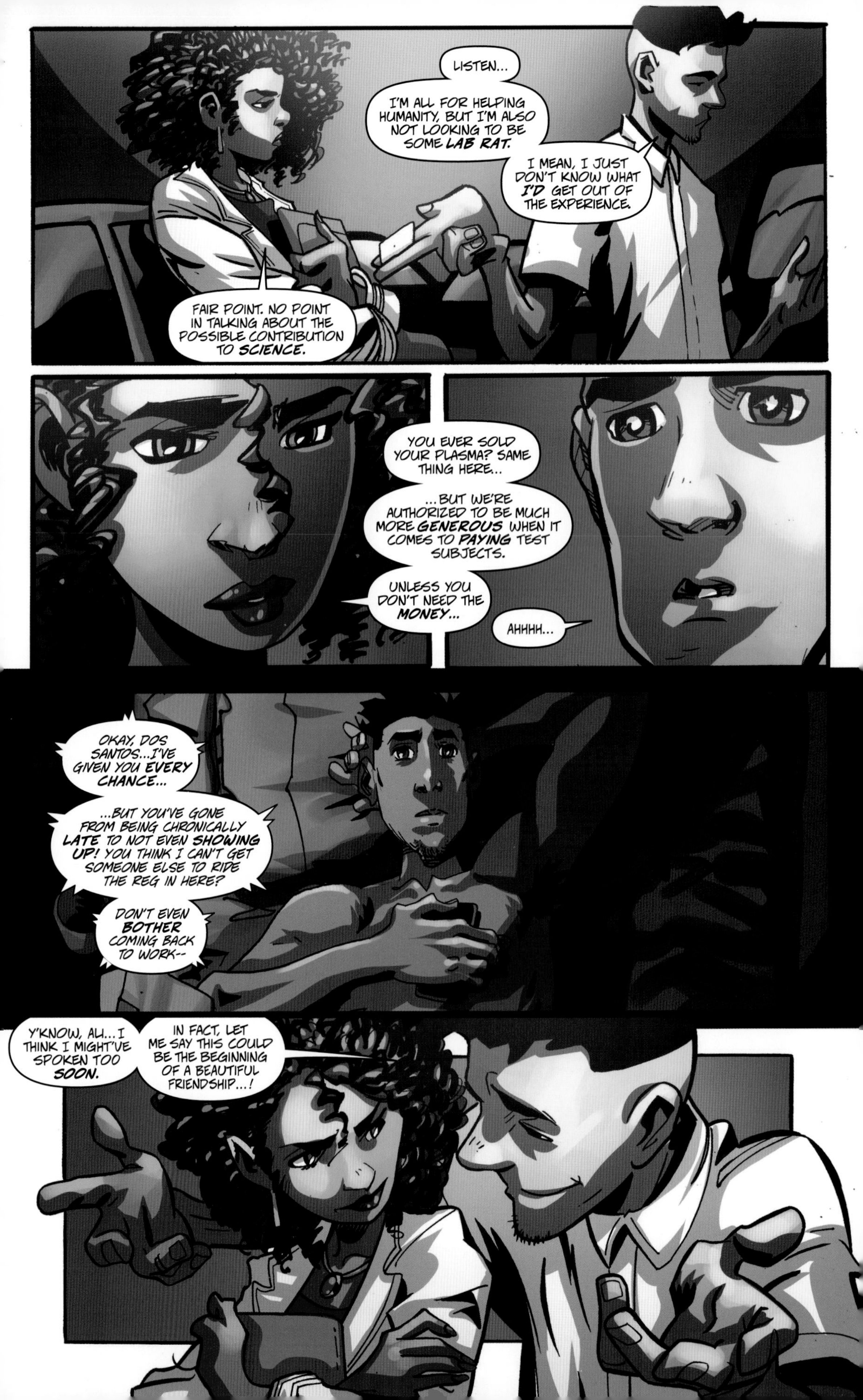
LISTEN...
I'M ALL FOR HELPING HUMANITY, BUT I'M ALSO NOT LOOKING TO BE SOME LAB RAT.
I MEAN, I JUST DON'T KNOW WHAT I'D GET OUT OF THE EXPERIENCE.
FAIR POINT. NO POINT IN TALKING ABOUT THE POSSIBLE CONTRIBUTION TO SCIENCE.
YOU EVER SOLD YOUR PLASMA? SAME THING HERE...
...BUT WE'RE AUTHORIZED TO BE MUCH MORE GENEROUS WHEN IT COMES TO PAYING TEST SUBJECTS.
UNLESS YOU DON'T NEED THE MONEY...
AHHHH...
OKAY, DOS SANTOS...I'VE GIVEN YOU EVERY CHANCE...
...BUT YOU'VE GONE FROM BEING CHRONICALLY LATE TO NOT EVEN SHOWING UP! YOU THINK I CAN'T GET SOMEONE ELSE TO RIDE THE REG IN HERE?
DON'T EVEN BOTHER COMING BACK TO WORK--
Y'KNOW, ALI...I THINK I MIGHT'VE SPOKEN TOO SOON.
IN FACT, LET ME SAY THIS COULD BE THE BEGINNING OF A BEAUTIFUL FRIENDSHIP...!

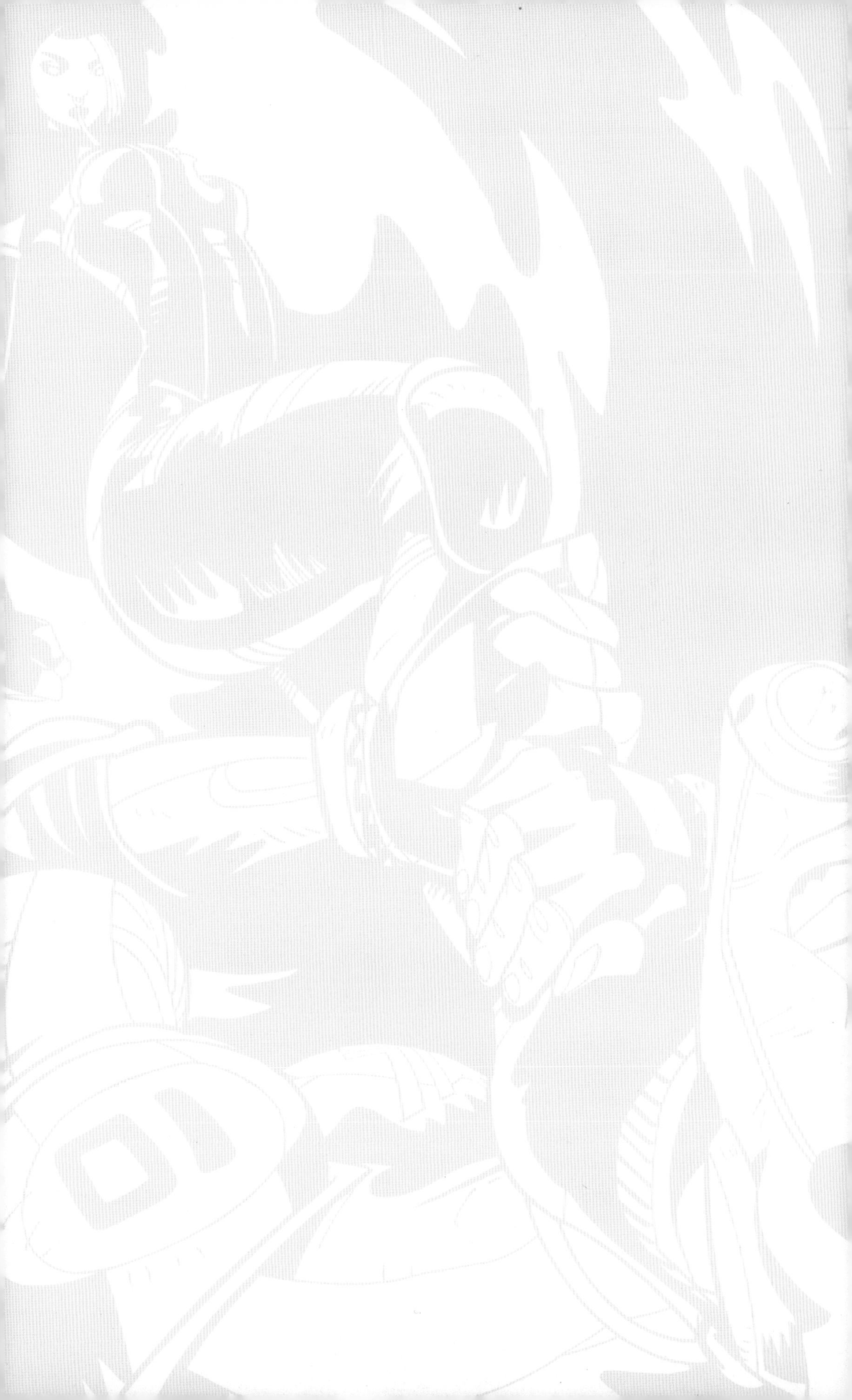

CHAPTER THREE

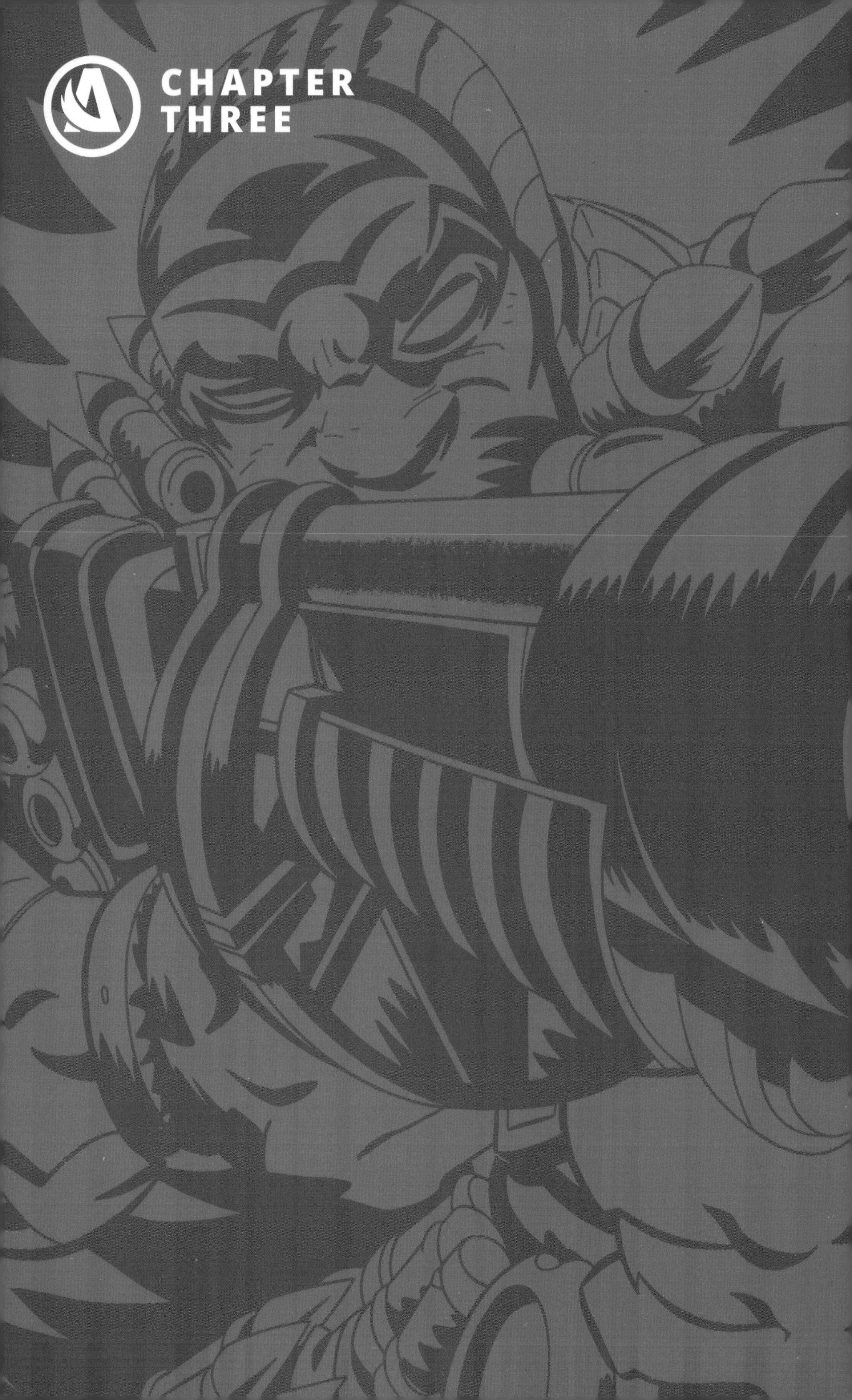

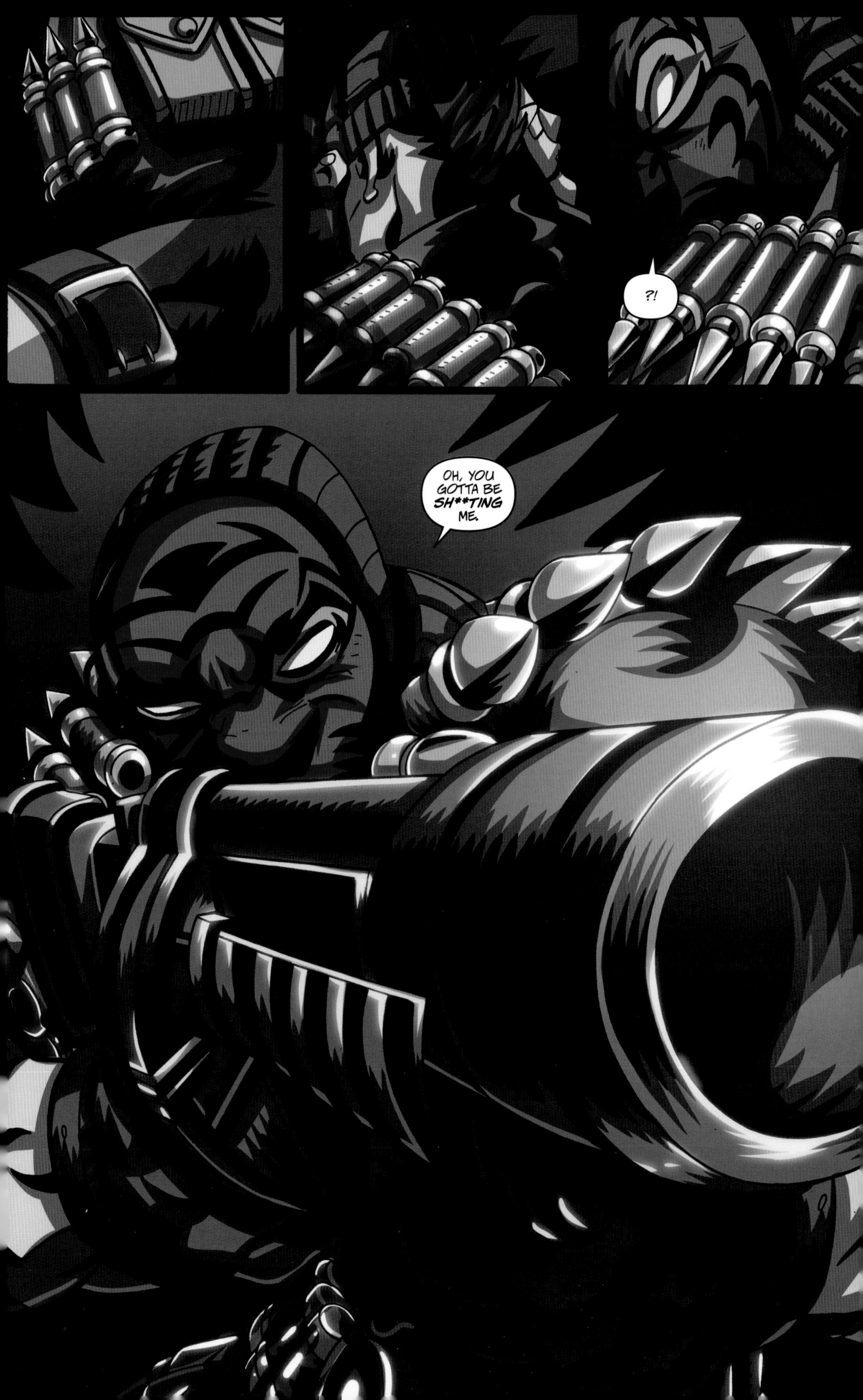
?!
OH, YOU GOTTA BE SH**TING ME.

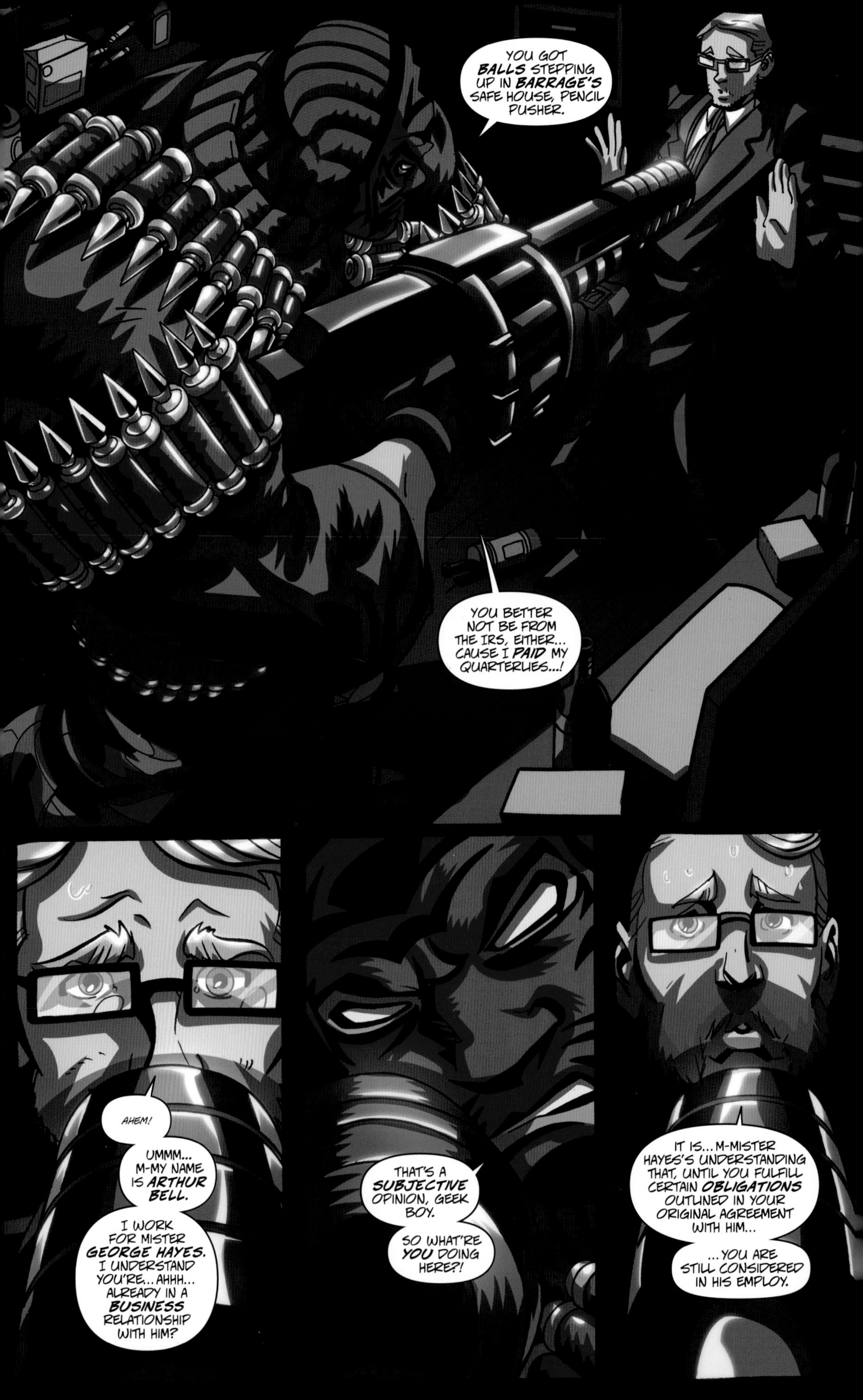
YOU GOT BALLS STEPPING UP IN BARRAGE'S SAFE HOUSE, PENCIL PUSHER.
YOU BETTER NOT BE FROM THE IRS, EITHER... CAUSE I PAID MY QUARTERLIES...!
AHEM!
UMMM... M-MY NAME IS ARTHUR BELL.
I WORK FOR MISTER GEORGE HAYES. I UNDERSTAND YOU'RE... AHHH... ALREADY IN A BUSINESS RELATIONSHIP WITH HIM?
THAT'S A SUBJECTIVE OPINION, GEEK BOY.
SO WHAT'RE YOU DOING HERE?!
IT IS... M-MISTER HAYES'S UNDERSTANDING THAT, UNTIL YOU FULFILL CERTAIN OBLIGATIONS OUTLINED IN YOUR ORIGINAL AGREEMENT WITH HIM...
...YOU ARE STILL CONSIDERED IN HIS EMPLOY.

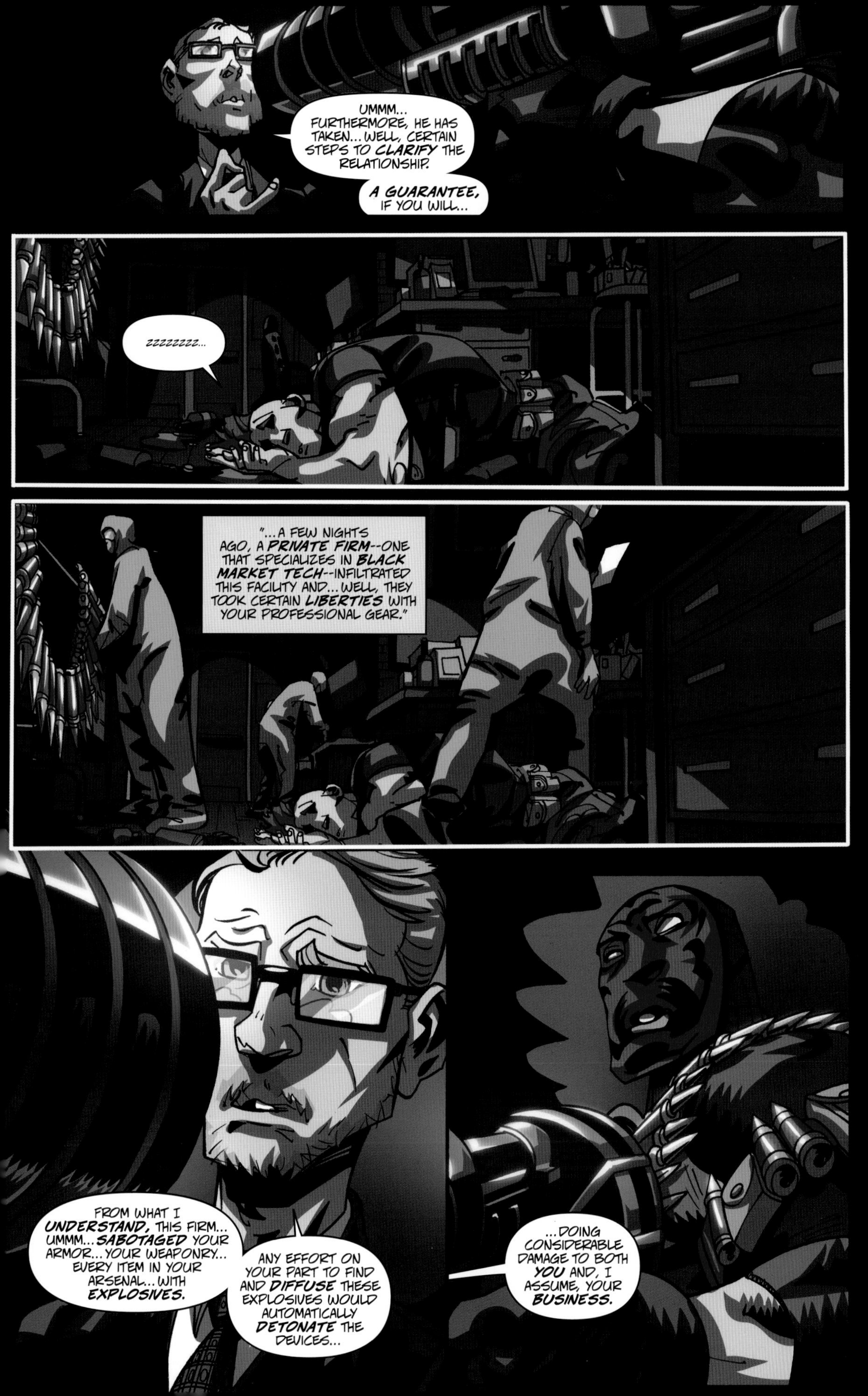
UMMM... FURTHERMORE, HE HAS TAKEN... WELL, CERTAIN STEPS TO CLARIFY THE RELATIONSHIP.
A GUARANTEE, IF YOU WILL...
zzzzzzzz...
"...A FEW NIGHTS AGO, A PRIVATE FIRM--ONE THAT SPECIALIZES IN BLACK MARKET TECH--INFILTRATED THIS FACILITY AND... WELL, THEY TOOK CERTAIN LIBERTIES WITH YOUR PROFESSIONAL GEAR."
FROM WHAT I UNDERSTAND, THIS FIRM... UMMM... SABOTAGED YOUR ARMOR... YOUR WEAPONRY... EVERY ITEM IN YOUR ARSENAL... WITH EXPLOSIVES.
ANY EFFORT ON YOUR PART TO FIND AND DIFFUSE THESE EXPLOSIVES WOULD AUTOMATICALLY DETONATE THE DEVICES...
...DOING CONSIDERABLE DAMAGE TO BOTH YOU AND, I ASSUME, YOUR BUSINESS.

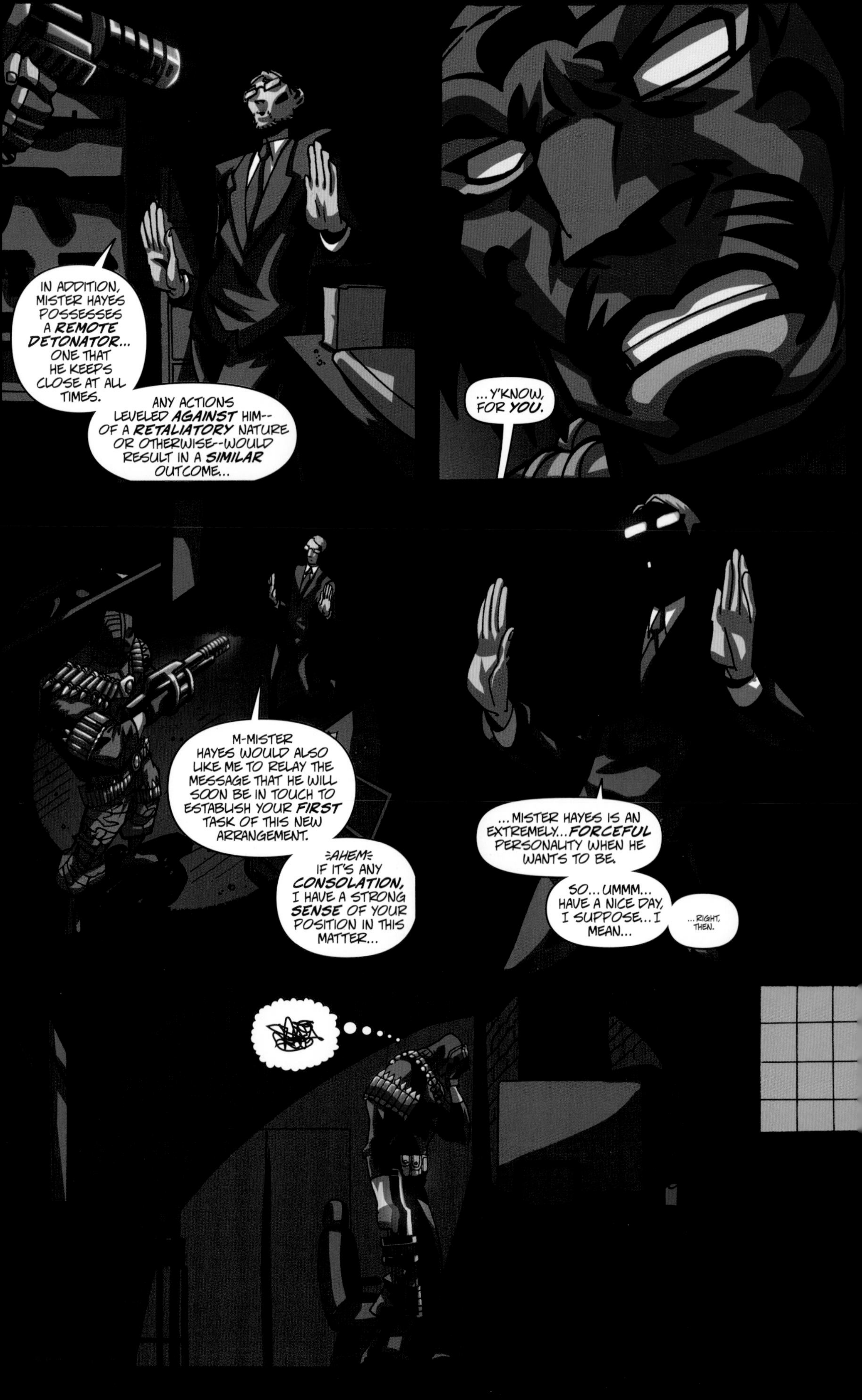
IN ADDITION, MISTER HAYES POSSESSES A **REMOTE DETONATOR**... ONE THAT HE KEEPS CLOSE AT ALL TIMES.
ANY ACTIONS LEVELED **AGAINST** HIM--OF A **RETALIATORY** NATURE OR OTHERWISE--WOULD RESULT IN A **SIMILAR** OUTCOME...
...Y'KNOW, FOR **YOU**.
M-MISTER HAYES WOULD ALSO LIKE ME TO RELAY THE MESSAGE THAT HE WILL SOON BE IN TOUCH TO ESTABLISH YOUR **FIRST** TASK OF THIS NEW ARRANGEMENT.
AHEM
IF IT'S ANY **CONSOLATION**, I HAVE A STRONG **SENSE** OF YOUR POSITION IN THIS MATTER...
...MISTER HAYES IS AN EXTREMELY...**FORCEFUL** PERSONALITY WHEN HE WANTS TO BE.
SO... UMMM... HAVE A NICE DAY, I SUPPOSE... I MEAN...
...RIGHT, THEN.

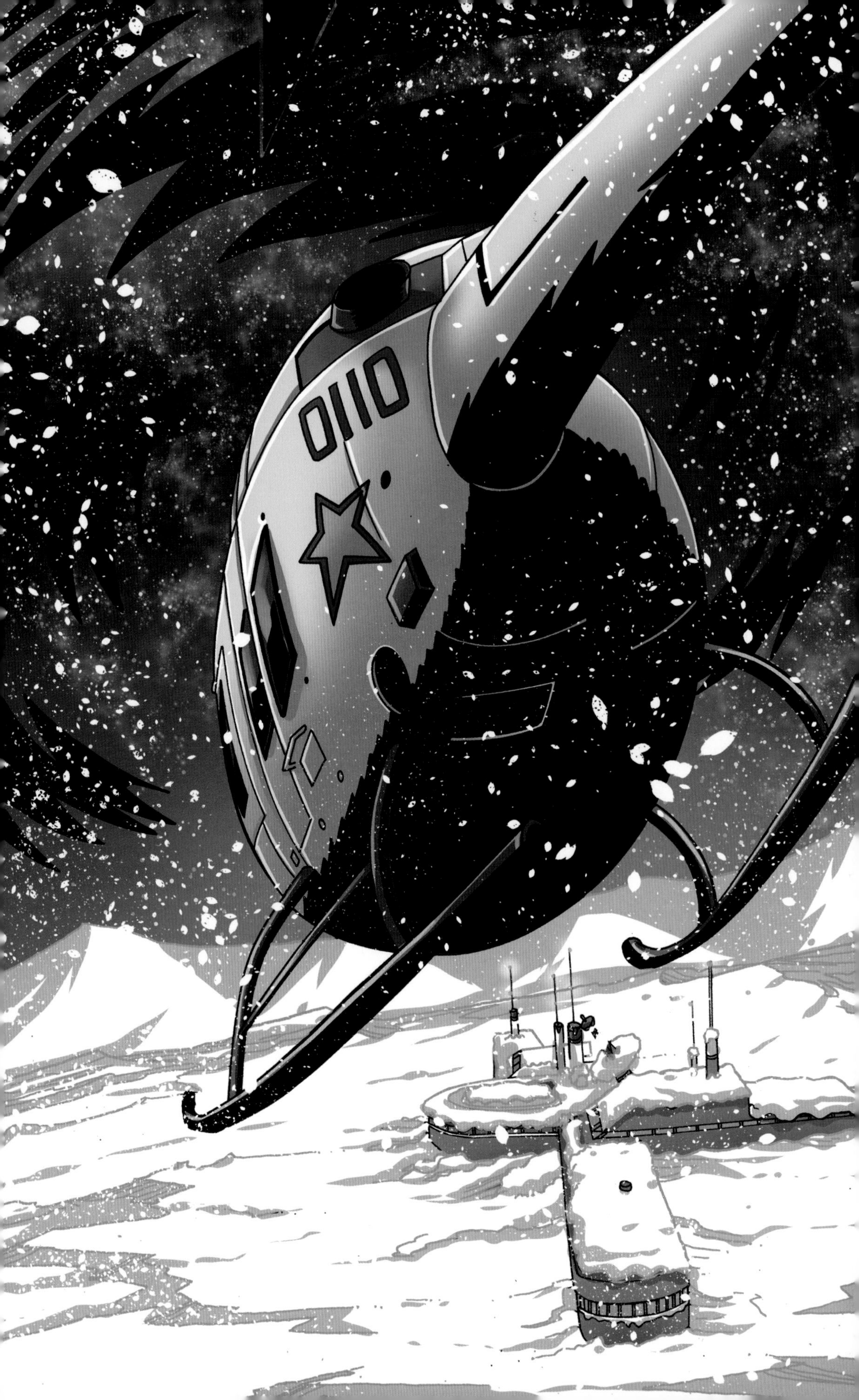
0110

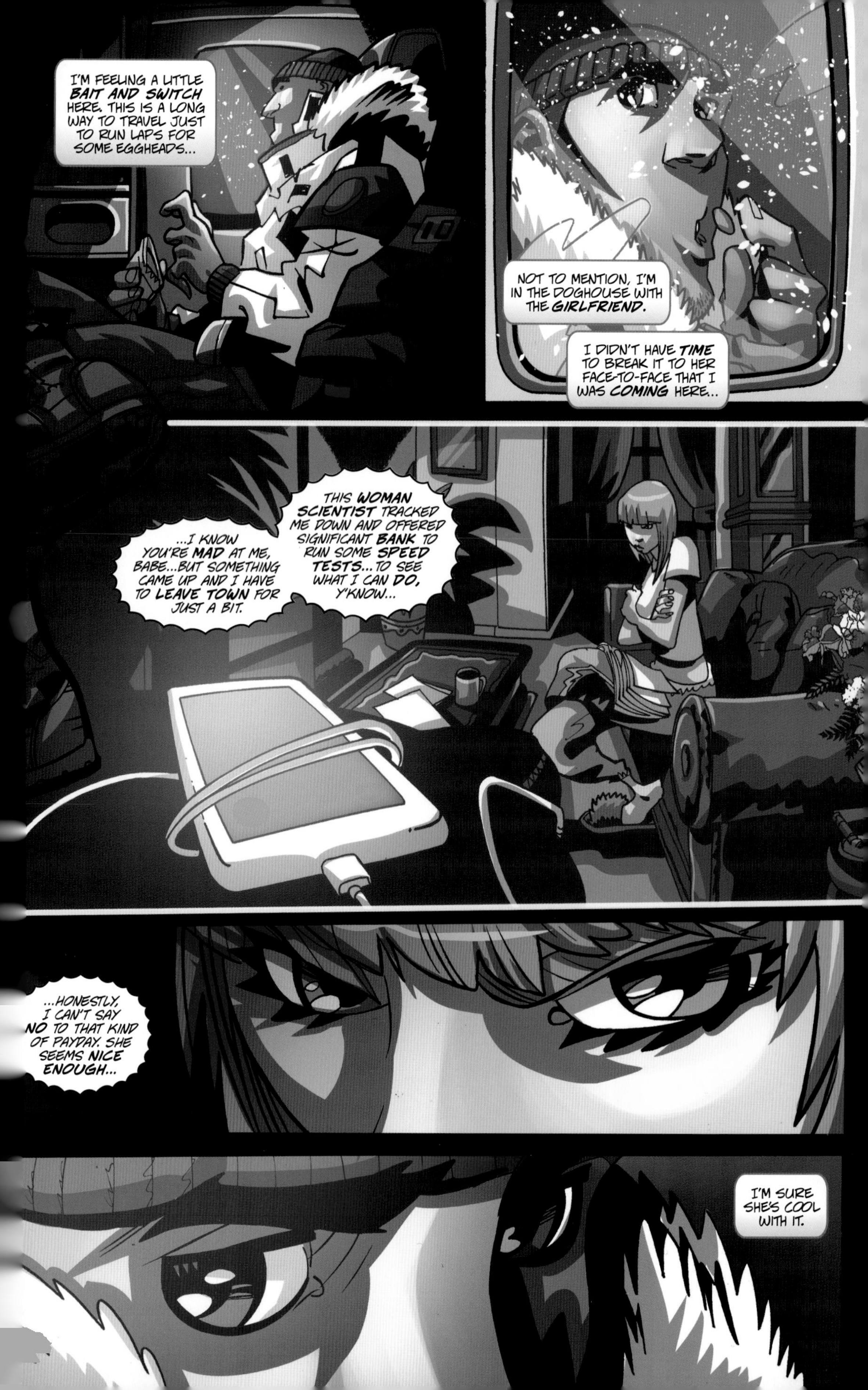
I'M FEELING A LITTLE BAIT AND SWITCH HERE. THIS IS A LONG WAY TO TRAVEL JUST TO RUN LAPS FOR SOME EGGHEADS...
NOT TO MENTION, I'M IN THE DOGHOUSE WITH THE GIRLFRIEND.
I DIDN'T HAVE TIME TO BREAK IT TO HER FACE-TO-FACE THAT I WAS COMING HERE...
...I KNOW YOU'RE MAD AT ME, BABE...BUT SOMETHING CAME UP AND I HAVE TO LEAVE TOWN FOR JUST A BIT.
THIS WOMAN SCIENTIST TRACKED ME DOWN AND OFFERED SIGNIFICANT BANK TO RUN SOME SPEED TESTS...TO SEE WHAT I CAN DO, Y'KNOW...
...HONESTLY, I CAN'T SAY NO TO THAT KIND OF PAYDAY. SHE SEEMS NICE ENOUGH...
I'M SURE SHE'S COOL WITH IT.

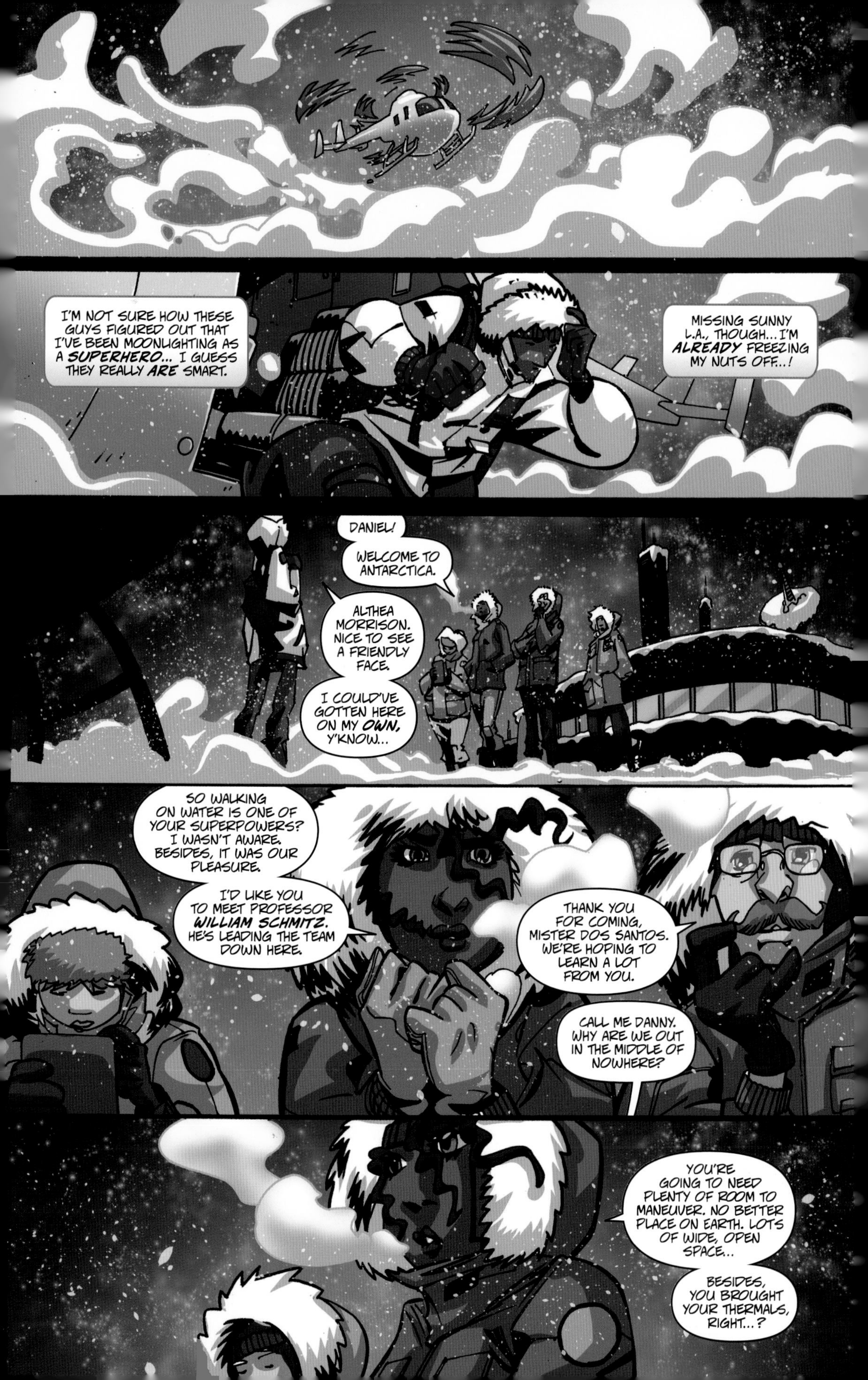
I'M NOT SURE HOW THESE GUYS FIGURED OUT THAT I'VE BEEN MOONLIGHTING AS A SUPERHERO... I GUESS THEY REALLY ARE SMART.
MISSING SUNNY L.A., THOUGH... I'M ALREADY FREEZING MY NUTS OFF...!
DANIEL!
WELCOME TO ANTARCTICA.
ALTHEA MORRISON. NICE TO SEE A FRIENDLY FACE.
I COULD'VE GOTTEN HERE ON MY OWN, Y'KNOW...
SO WALKING ON WATER IS ONE OF YOUR SUPERPOWERS? I WASN'T AWARE. BESIDES, IT WAS OUR PLEASURE.
I'D LIKE YOU TO MEET PROFESSOR WILLIAM SCHMITZ. HE'S LEADING THE TEAM DOWN HERE.
THANK YOU FOR COMING, MISTER DOS SANTOS. WE'RE HOPING TO LEARN A LOT FROM YOU.
CALL ME DANNY. WHY ARE WE OUT IN THE MIDDLE OF NOWHERE?
YOU'RE GOING TO NEED PLENTY OF ROOM TO MANEUVER. NO BETTER PLACE ON EARTH. LOTS OF WIDE, OPEN SPACE...
BESIDES, YOU BROUGHT YOUR THERMALS, RIGHT...?

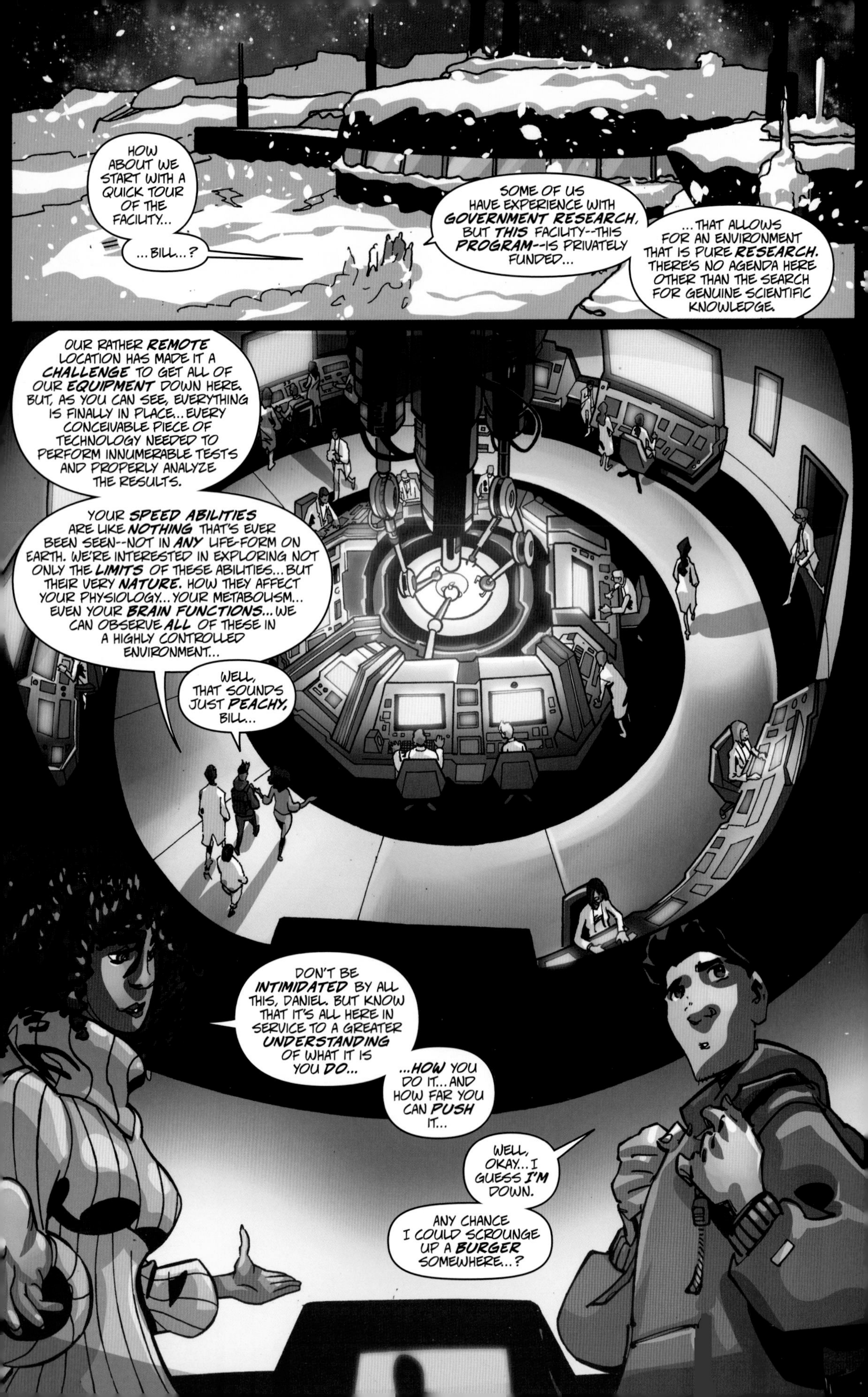
HOW ABOUT WE START WITH A QUICK TOUR OF THE FACILITY...
...BILL...?
SOME OF US HAVE EXPERIENCE WITH GOVERNMENT RESEARCH, BUT THIS FACILITY--THIS PROGRAM--IS PRIVATELY FUNDED...
...THAT ALLOWS FOR AN ENVIRONMENT THAT IS PURE RESEARCH. THERE'S NO AGENDA HERE OTHER THAN THE SEARCH FOR GENUINE SCIENTIFIC KNOWLEDGE.
OUR RATHER REMOTE LOCATION HAS MADE IT A CHALLENGE TO GET ALL OF OUR EQUIPMENT DOWN HERE. BUT, AS YOU CAN SEE, EVERYTHING IS FINALLY IN PLACE...EVERY CONCEIVABLE PIECE OF TECHNOLOGY NEEDED TO PERFORM INNUMERABLE TESTS AND PROPERLY ANALYZE THE RESULTS.
YOUR SPEED ABILITIES ARE LIKE NOTHING THAT'S EVER BEEN SEEN--NOT IN ANY LIFE-FORM ON EARTH. WE'RE INTERESTED IN EXPLORING NOT ONLY THE LIMITS OF THESE ABILITIES...BUT THEIR VERY NATURE. HOW THEY AFFECT YOUR PHYSIOLOGY...YOUR METABOLISM... EVEN YOUR BRAIN FUNCTIONS...WE CAN OBSERVE ALL OF THESE IN A HIGHLY CONTROLLED ENVIRONMENT...
WELL, THAT SOUNDS JUST PEACHY, BILL...
DON'T BE INTIMIDATED BY ALL THIS, DANIEL. BUT KNOW THAT IT'S ALL HERE IN SERVICE TO A GREATER UNDERSTANDING OF WHAT IT IS YOU DO...
...HOW YOU DO IT...AND HOW FAR YOU CAN PUSH IT...
WELL, OKAY...I GUESS I'M DOWN.
ANY CHANCE I COULD SCROUNGE UP A BURGER SOMEWHERE...?

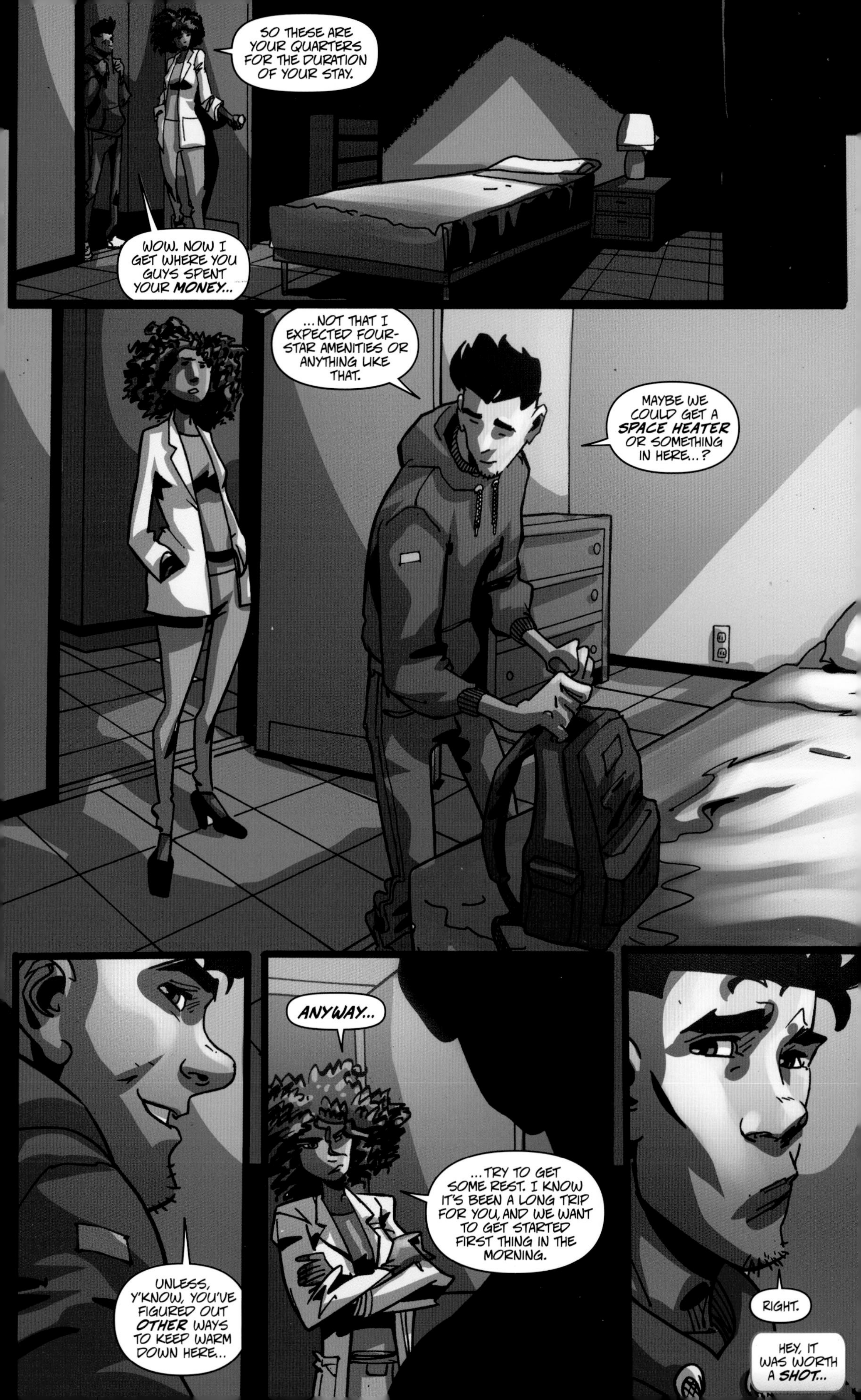
SO THESE ARE YOUR QUARTERS FOR THE DURATION OF YOUR STAY.
WOW. NOW I GET WHERE YOU GUYS SPENT YOUR MONEY...
...NOT THAT I EXPECTED FOUR-STAR AMENITIES OR ANYTHING LIKE THAT.
MAYBE WE COULD GET A SPACE HEATER OR SOMETHING IN HERE...?
UNLESS, Y'KNOW, YOU'VE FIGURED OUT OTHER WAYS TO KEEP WARM DOWN HERE...
ANYWAY...
...TRY TO GET SOME REST. I KNOW IT'S BEEN A LONG TRIP FOR YOU, AND WE WANT TO GET STARTED FIRST THING IN THE MORNING.
RIGHT.
HEY, IT WAS WORTH A SHOT...

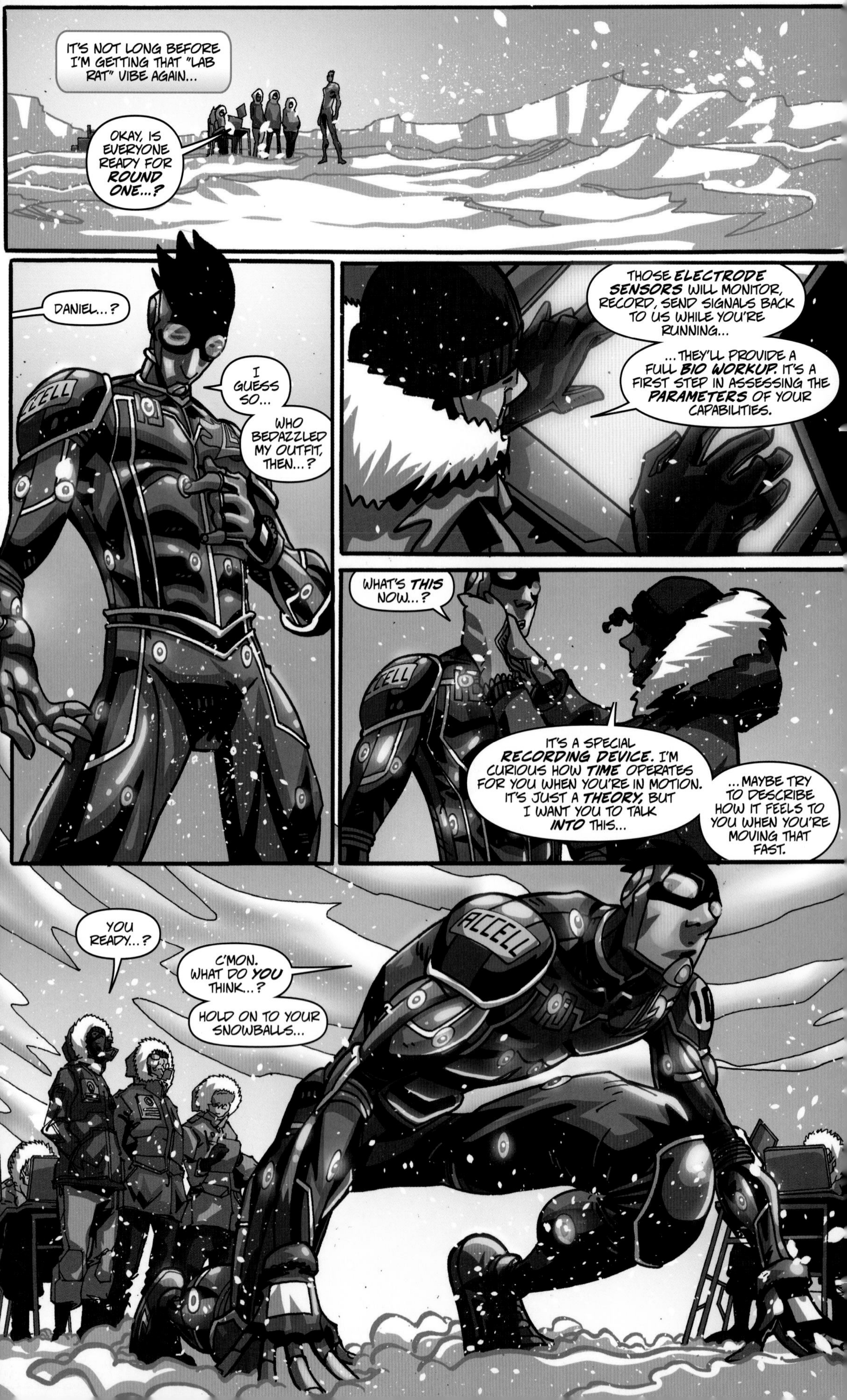
IT'S NOT LONG BEFORE I'M GETTING THAT "LAB RAT" VIBE AGAIN...
OKAY, IS EVERYONE READY FOR ROUND ONE...?
DANIEL...?
I GUESS SO...
WHO BEDAZZLED MY OUTFIT, THEN...?
THOSE ELECTRODE SENSORS WILL MONITOR, RECORD, SEND SIGNALS BACK TO US WHILE YOU'RE RUNNING...
...THEY'LL PROVIDE A FULL BIO WORKUP. IT'S A FIRST STEP IN ASSESSING THE PARAMETERS OF YOUR CAPABILITIES.
WHAT'S THIS NOW...?
IT'S A SPECIAL RECORDING DEVICE. I'M CURIOUS HOW TIME OPERATES FOR YOU WHEN YOU'RE IN MOTION. IT'S JUST A THEORY, BUT I WANT YOU TO TALK INTO THIS...
...MAYBE TRY TO DESCRIBE HOW IT FEELS TO YOU WHEN YOU'RE MOVING THAT FAST.
YOU READY...?
C'MON. WHAT DO YOU THINK...?
HOLD ON TO YOUR SNOWBALLS...

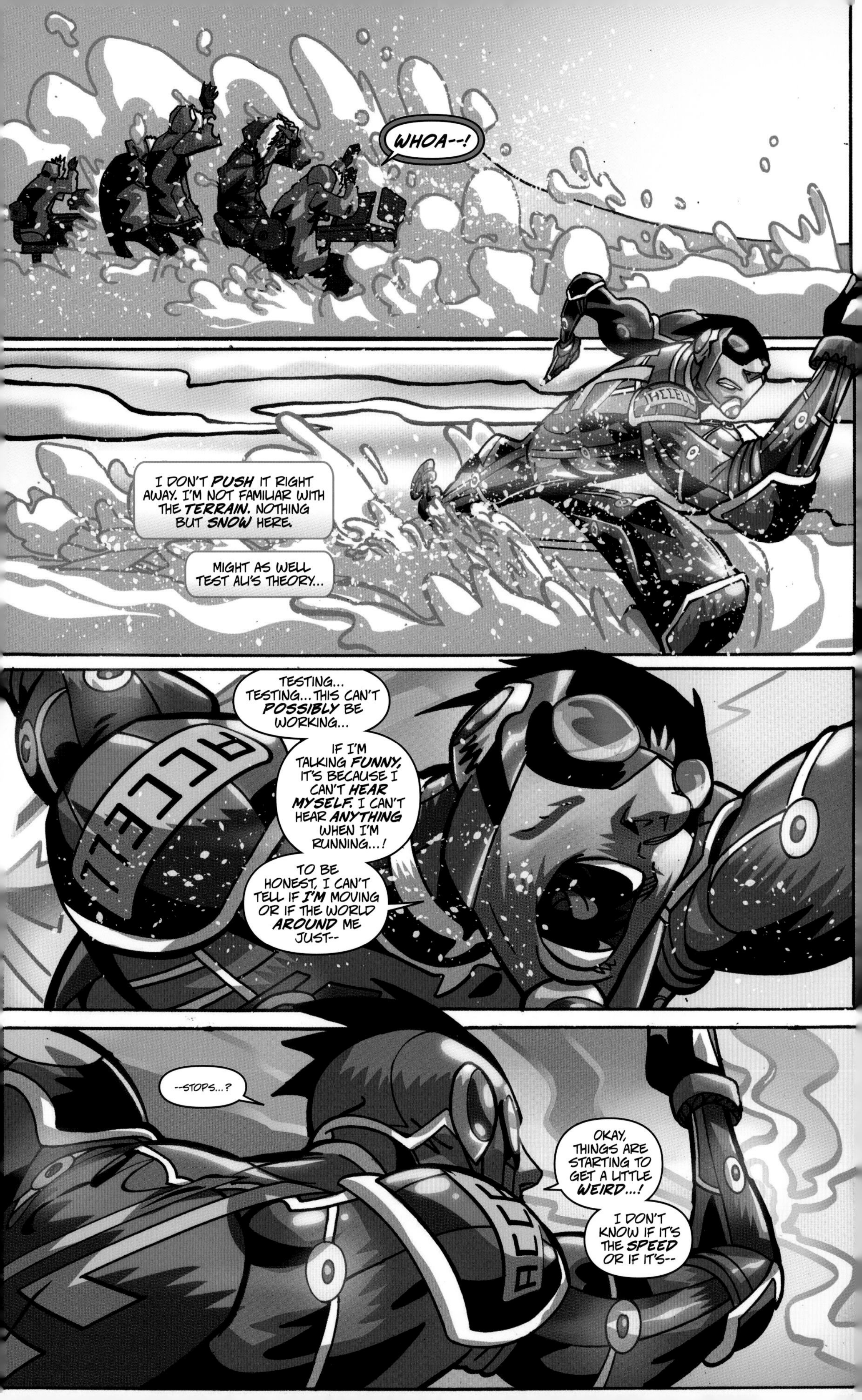
WHOA--!
I DON'T PUSH IT RIGHT AWAY. I'M NOT FAMILIAR WITH THE TERRAIN. NOTHING BUT SNOW HERE.
MIGHT AS WELL TEST ALI'S THEORY...
TESTING... TESTING... THIS CAN'T POSSIBLY BE WORKING...
IF I'M TALKING FUNNY, IT'S BECAUSE I CAN'T HEAR MYSELF. I CAN'T HEAR ANYTHING WHEN I'M RUNNING...!
TO BE HONEST, I CAN'T TELL IF I'M MOVING OR IF THE WORLD AROUND ME JUST--
--STOPS...?
OKAY, THINGS ARE STARTING TO GET A LITTLE WEIRD...!
I DON'T KNOW IF IT'S THE SPEED OR IF IT'S--

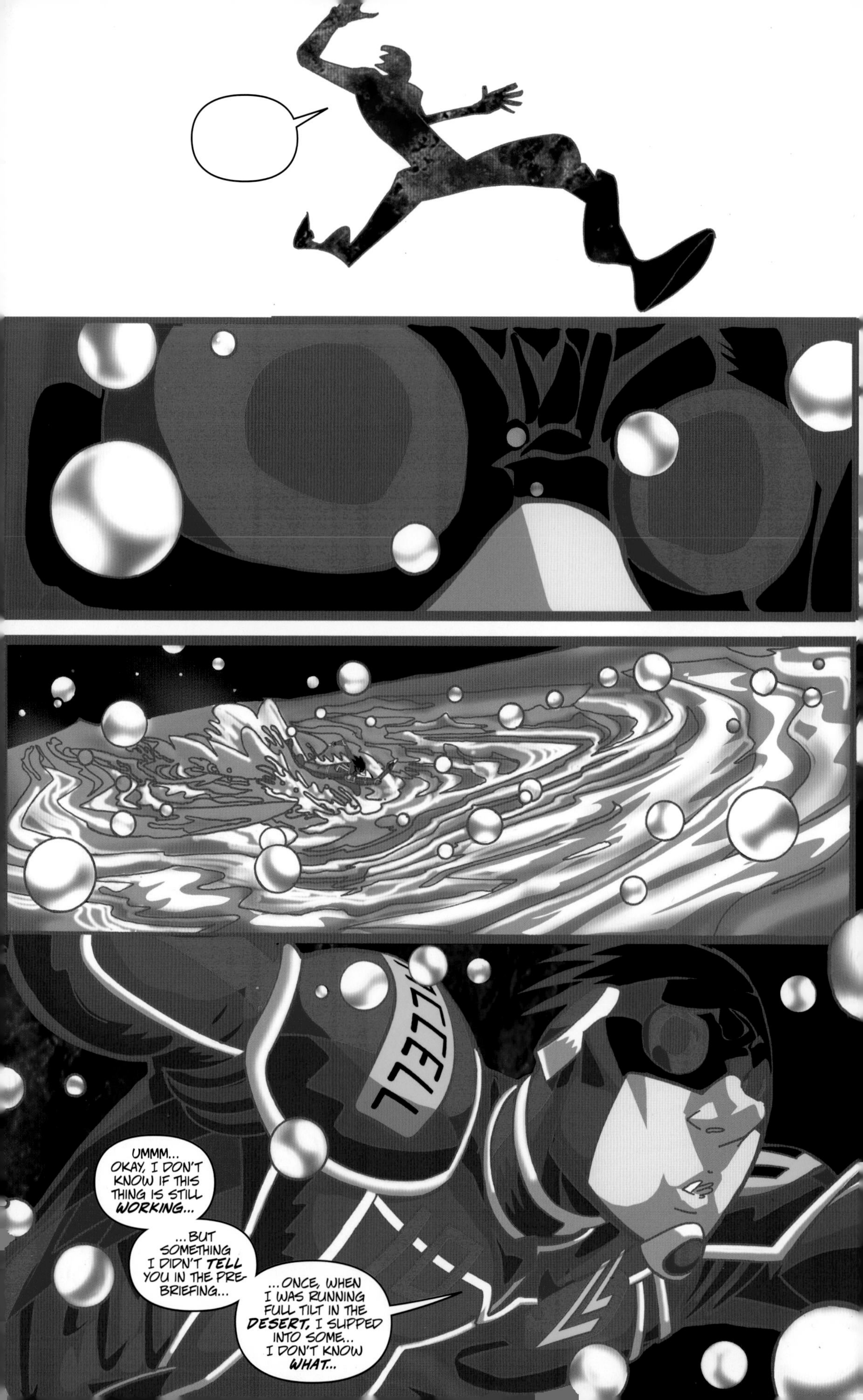

CCELL
UMMM... OKAY, I DON'T KNOW IF THIS THING IS STILL WORKING...
...BUT SOMETHING I DIDN'T TELL YOU IN THE PRE-BRIEFING...
...ONCE, WHEN I WAS RUNNING FULL TILT IN THE DESERT, I SLIPPED INTO SOME... I DON'T KNOW WHAT...

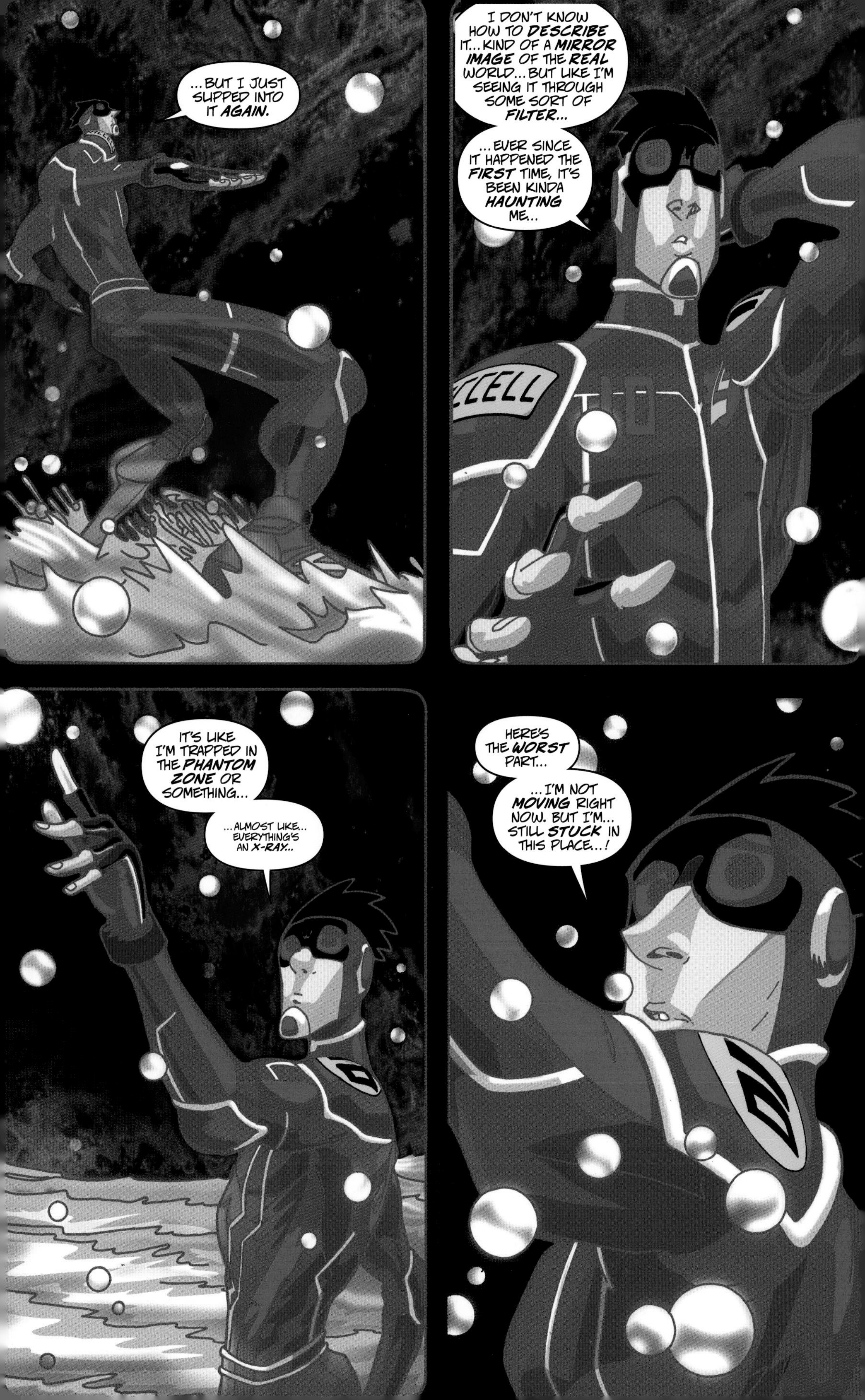
...BUT I JUST SLIPPED INTO IT AGAIN.
I DON'T KNOW HOW TO DESCRIBE IT... KIND OF A MIRROR IMAGE OF THE REAL WORLD... BUT LIKE I'M SEEING IT THROUGH SOME SORT OF FILTER...
...EVER SINCE IT HAPPENED THE FIRST TIME, IT'S BEEN KINDA HAUNTING ME...
IT'S LIKE I'M TRAPPED IN THE PHANTOM ZONE OR SOMETHING...
...ALMOST LIKE... EVERYTHING'S AN X-RAY...
HERE'S THE WORST PART...
...I'M NOT MOVING RIGHT NOW. BUT I'M... STILL STUCK IN THIS PLACE...!

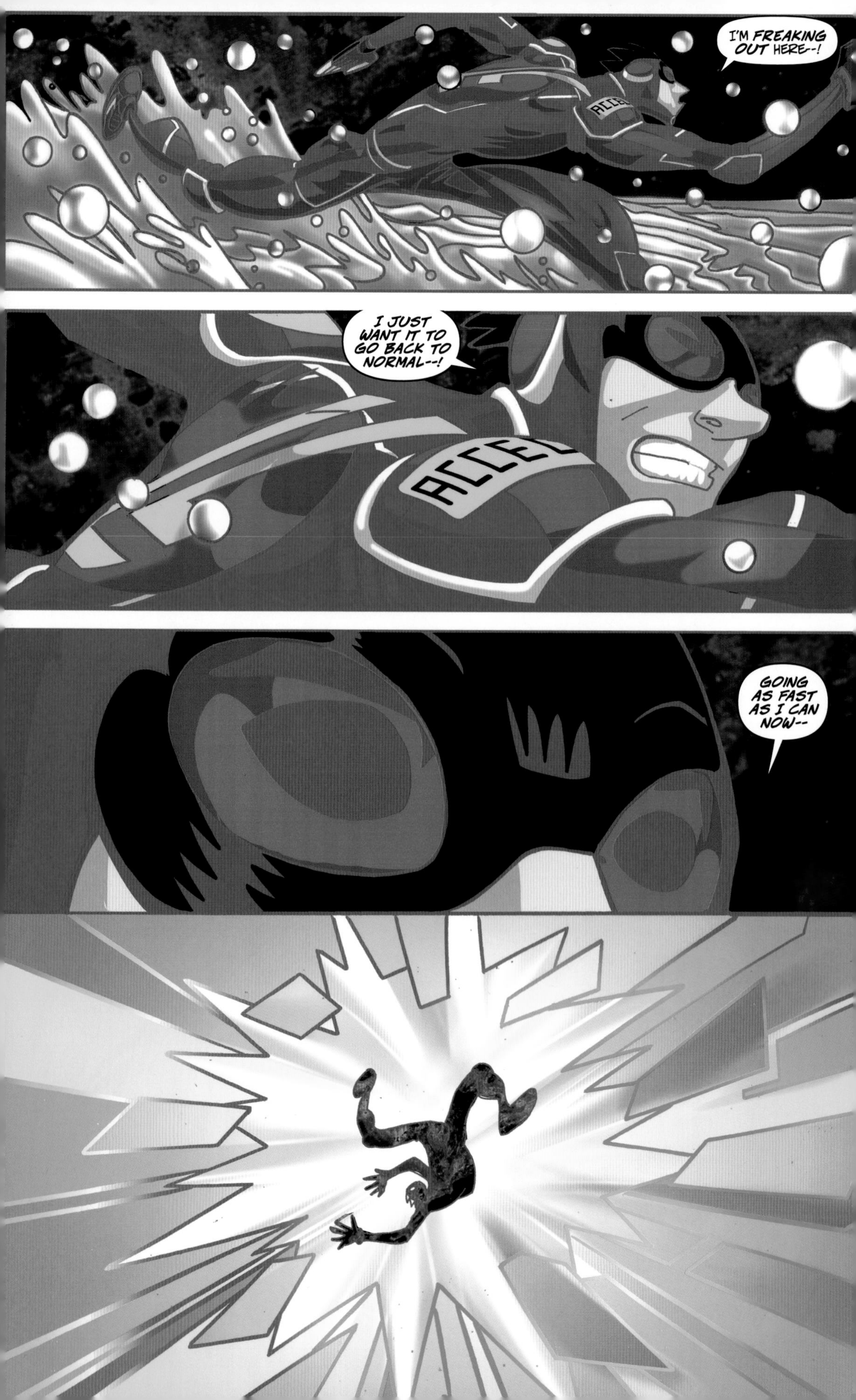
I'M FREAKING OUT HERE--!
I JUST WANT IT TO GO BACK TO NORMAL--!
GOING AS FAST AS I CAN NOW--

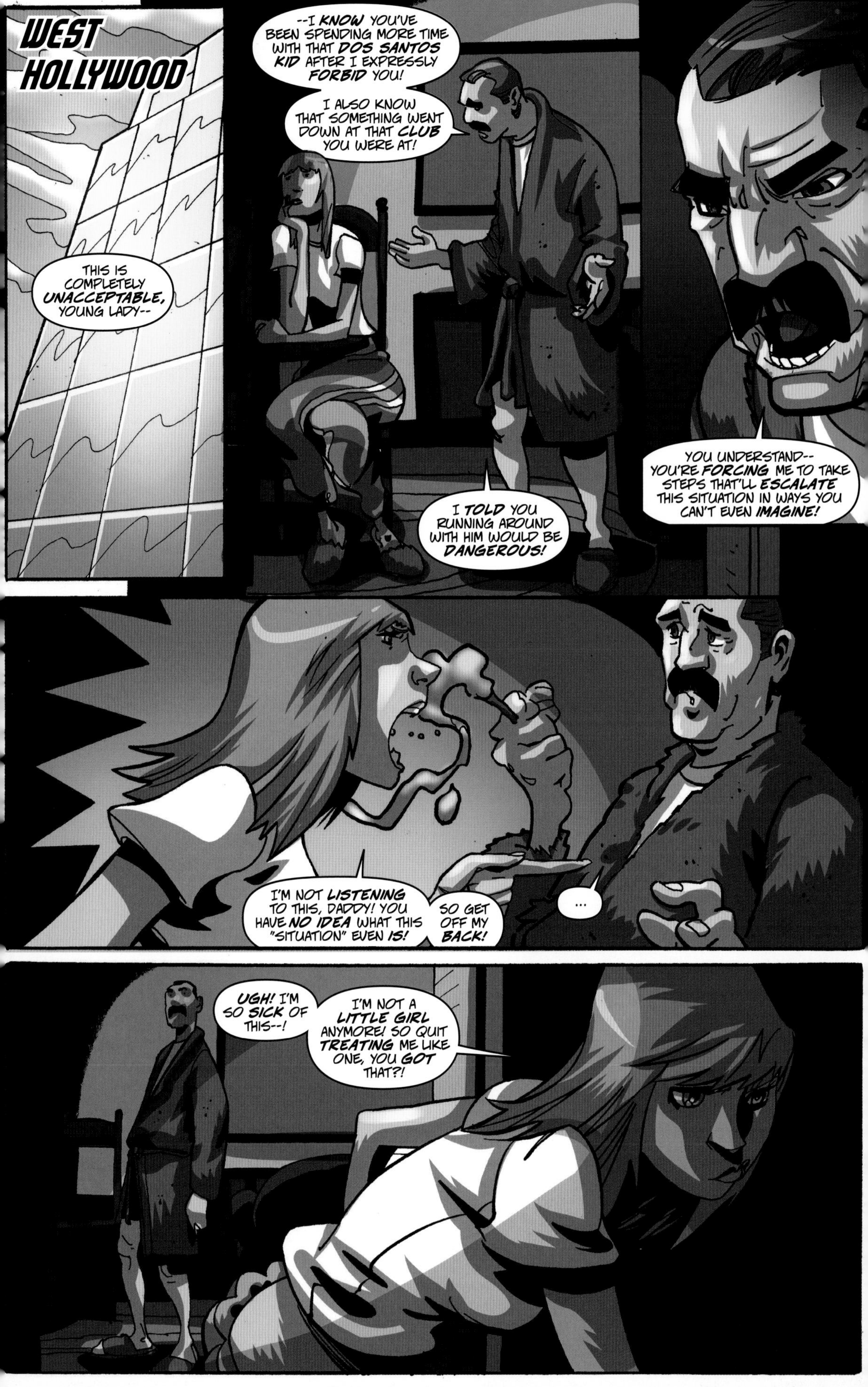
WEST HOLLYWOOD
THIS IS COMPLETELY UNACCEPTABLE, YOUNG LADY--
--I KNOW YOU'VE BEEN SPENDING MORE TIME WITH THAT DOS SANTOS KID AFTER I EXPRESSLY FORBID YOU!
I ALSO KNOW THAT SOMETHING WENT DOWN AT THAT CLUB YOU WERE AT!
I TOLD YOU RUNNING AROUND WITH HIM WOULD BE DANGEROUS!
YOU UNDERSTAND-- YOU'RE FORCING ME TO TAKE STEPS THAT'LL ESCALATE THIS SITUATION IN WAYS YOU CAN'T EVEN IMAGINE!
I'M NOT LISTENING TO THIS, DADDY! YOU HAVE NO IDEA WHAT THIS "SITUATION" EVEN IS!
SO GET OFF MY BACK!
...
UGH! I'M SO SICK OF THIS--!
I'M NOT A LITTLE GIRL ANYMORE! SO QUIT TREATING ME LIKE ONE, YOU GOT THAT?!

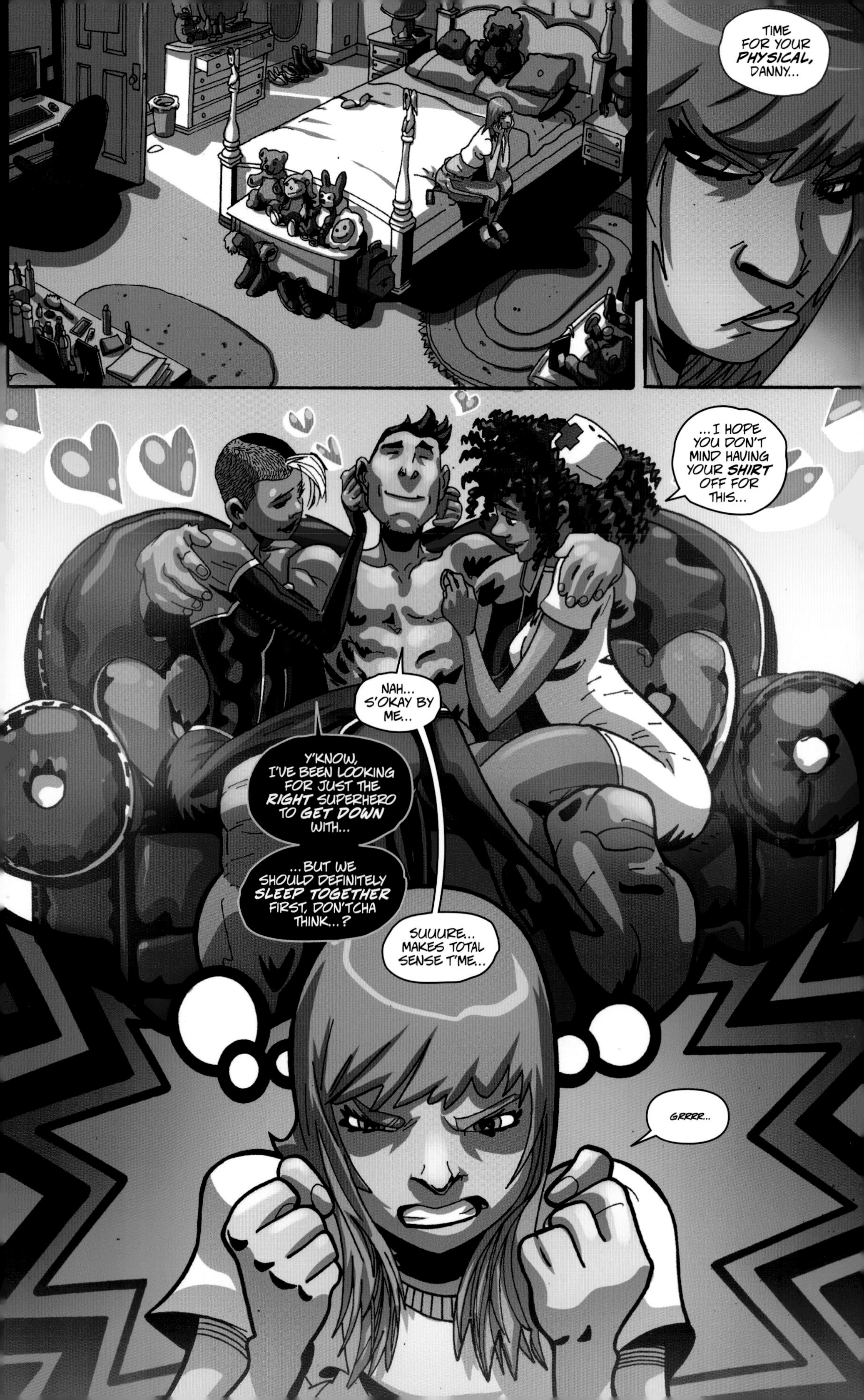
TIME FOR YOUR PHYSICAL, DANNY...
...I HOPE YOU DON'T MIND HAVING YOUR SHIRT OFF FOR THIS...
NAH... S'OKAY BY ME...
Y'KNOW, I'VE BEEN LOOKING FOR JUST THE RIGHT SUPERHERO TO GET DOWN WITH...
...BUT WE SHOULD DEFINITELY SLEEP TOGETHER FIRST, DON'TCHA THINK...?
SUUURE... MAKES TOTAL SENSE T'ME...
GRRRR...

ANY
SIGN OF
HIM?

NOT YET.
JUST KEEP
FOLLOWING
THE TRAIL--

--HE'S
GOT TO BE
AT THE END
OF IT.

YUP.
LOOK DOWN
THERE...!

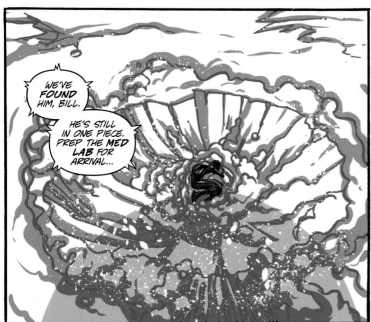

WE'VE
FOUND
HIM, BILL.

HE'S STILL
IN ONE PIECE.
PREP THE MED
LAB FOR
ARRIVAL...

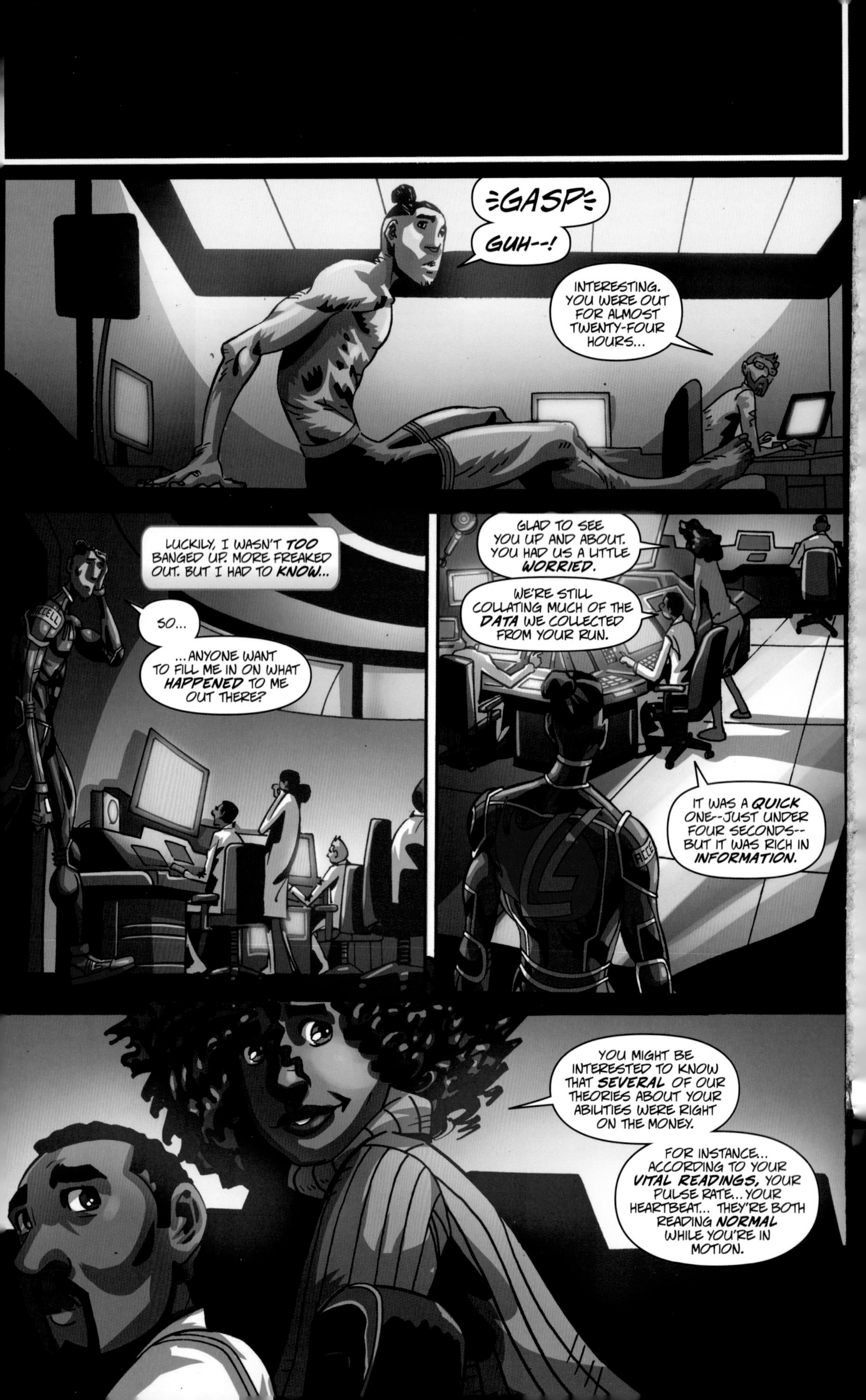

GASP
GUH--!
INTERESTING. YOU WERE OUT FOR ALMOST TWENTY-FOUR HOURS...
LUCKILY, I WASN'T TOO BANGED UP. MORE FREAKED OUT. BUT I HAD TO KNOW...
SO...
...ANYONE WANT TO FILL ME IN ON WHAT HAPPENED TO ME OUT THERE?
GLAD TO SEE YOU UP AND ABOUT. YOU HAD US A LITTLE WORRIED.
WE'RE STILL COLLATING MUCH OF THE DATA WE COLLECTED FROM YOUR RUN.
IT WAS A QUICK ONE--JUST UNDER FOUR SECONDS--BUT IT WAS RICH IN INFORMATION.
YOU MIGHT BE INTERESTED TO KNOW THAT SEVERAL OF OUR THEORIES ABOUT YOUR ABILITIES WERE RIGHT ON THE MONEY.
FOR INSTANCE... ACCORDING TO YOUR VITAL READINGS, YOUR PULSE RATE... YOUR HEARTBEAT... THEY'RE BOTH READING NORMAL WHILE YOU'RE IN MOTION.

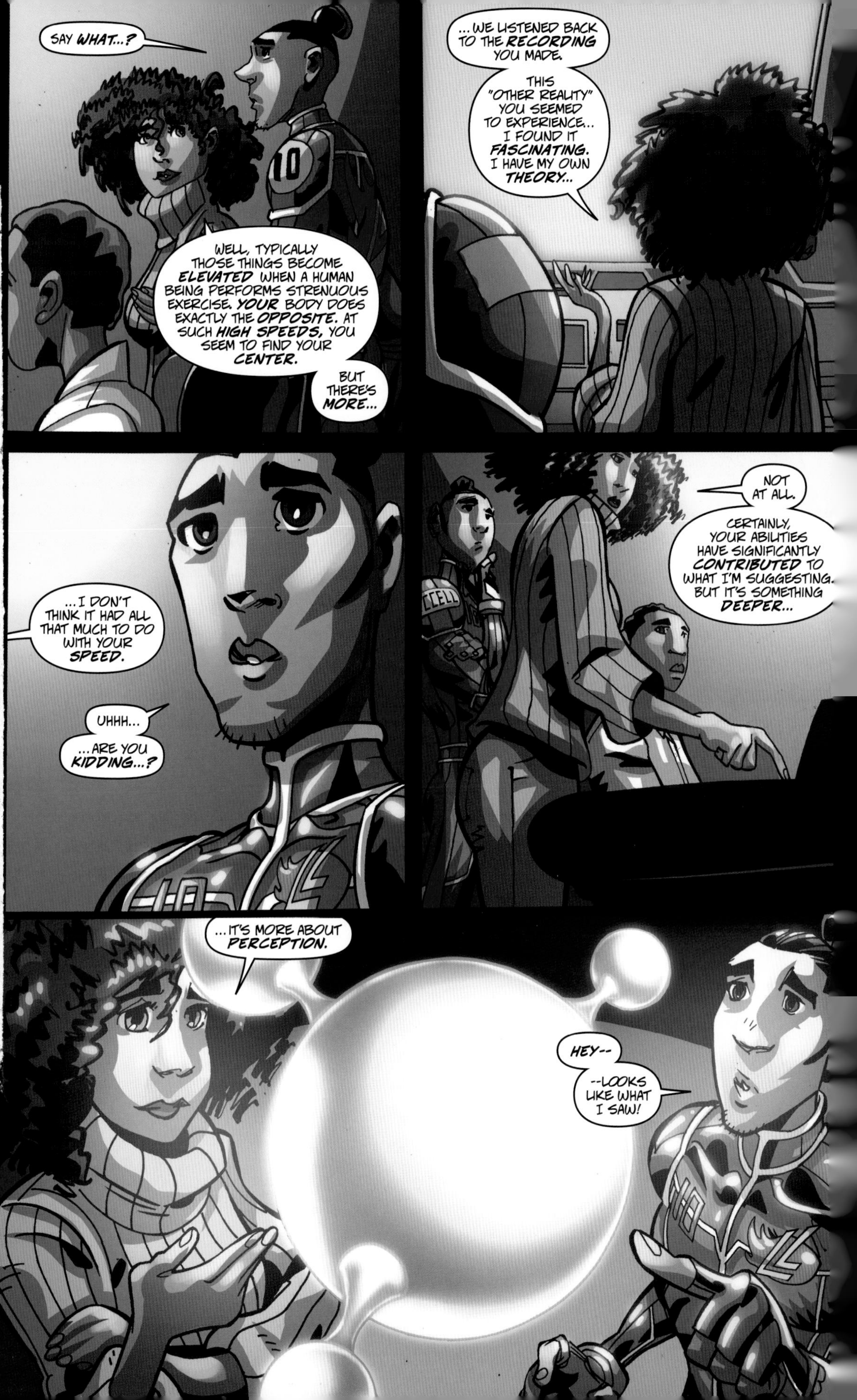
SAY WHAT...?
WELL, TYPICALLY THOSE THINGS BECOME ELEVATED WHEN A HUMAN BEING PERFORMS STRENUOUS EXERCISE. YOUR BODY DOES EXACTLY THE OPPOSITE. AT SUCH HIGH SPEEDS, YOU SEEM TO FIND YOUR CENTER.
BUT THERE'S MORE...
...WE LISTENED BACK TO THE RECORDING YOU MADE.
THIS "OTHER REALITY" YOU SEEMED TO EXPERIENCE... I FOUND IT FASCINATING. I HAVE MY OWN THEORY...
...I DON'T THINK IT HAD ALL THAT MUCH TO DO WITH YOUR SPEED.
UHHH...
...ARE YOU KIDDING...?
NOT AT ALL.
CERTAINLY, YOUR ABILITIES HAVE SIGNIFICANTLY CONTRIBUTED TO WHAT I'M SUGGESTING. BUT IT'S SOMETHING DEEPER...
...IT'S MORE ABOUT PERCEPTION.
HEY--
--LOOKS LIKE WHAT I SAW!

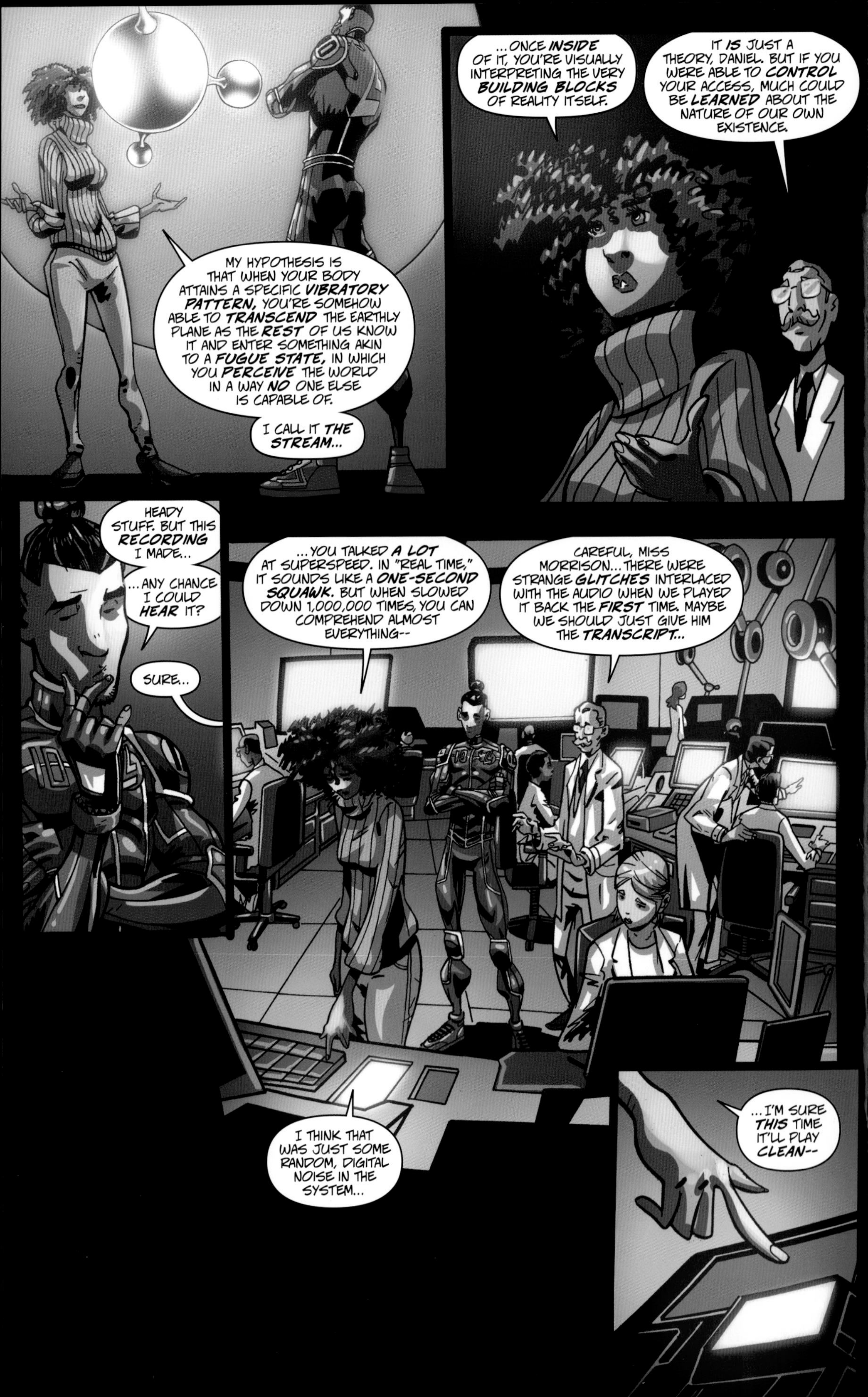
MY HYPOTHESIS IS THAT WHEN YOUR BODY ATTAINS A SPECIFIC VIBRATORY PATTERN, YOU'RE SOMEHOW ABLE TO TRANSCEND THE EARTHLY PLANE AS THE REST OF US KNOW IT AND ENTER SOMETHING AKIN TO A FUGUE STATE, IN WHICH YOU PERCEIVE THE WORLD IN A WAY NO ONE ELSE IS CAPABLE OF.
I CALL IT THE STREAM...
...ONCE INSIDE OF IT, YOU'RE VISUALLY INTERPRETING THE VERY BUILDING BLOCKS OF REALITY ITSELF.
IT IS JUST A THEORY, DANIEL. BUT IF YOU WERE ABLE TO CONTROL YOUR ACCESS, MUCH COULD BE LEARNED ABOUT THE NATURE OF OUR OWN EXISTENCE.
HEADY STUFF. BUT THIS RECORDING I MADE...
...ANY CHANCE I COULD HEAR IT?
SURE...
...YOU TALKED A LOT AT SUPERSPEED. IN "REAL TIME," IT SOUNDS LIKE A ONE-SECOND SQUAWK. BUT WHEN SLOWED DOWN 1,000,000 TIMES, YOU CAN COMPREHEND ALMOST EVERYTHING--
CAREFUL, MISS MORRISON... THERE WERE STRANGE GLITCHES INTERLACED WITH THE AUDIO WHEN WE PLAYED IT BACK THE FIRST TIME. MAYBE WE SHOULD JUST GIVE HIM THE TRANSCRIPT...
I THINK THAT WAS JUST SOME RANDOM, DIGITAL NOISE IN THE SYSTEM...
...I'M SURE THIS TIME IT'LL PLAY CLEAN--

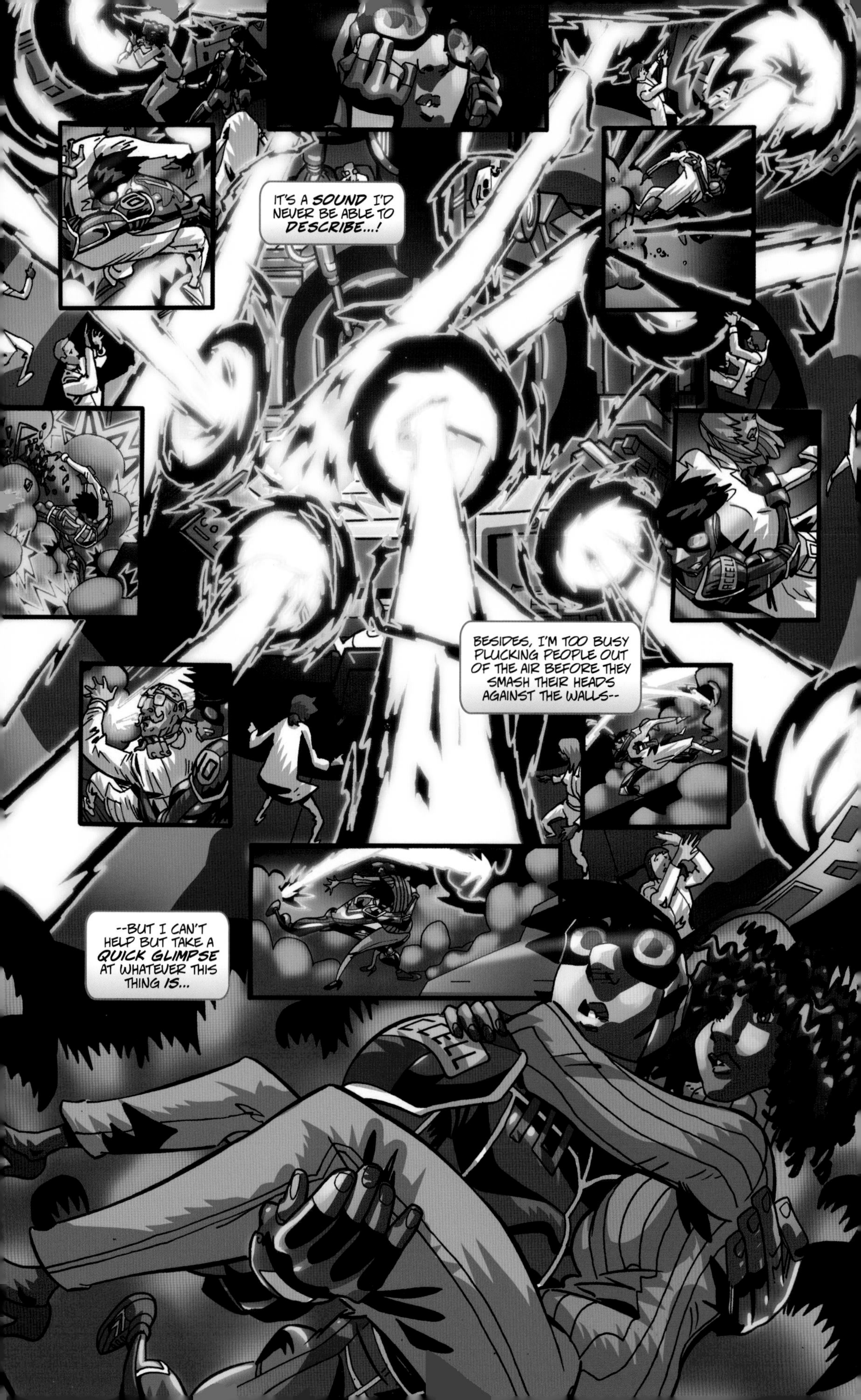
IT'S A SOUND I'D NEVER BE ABLE TO DESCRIBE...!
BESIDES, I'M TOO BUSY PLUCKING PEOPLE OUT OF THE AIR BEFORE THEY SMASH THEIR HEADS AGAINST THE WALLS--
--BUT I CAN'T HELP BUT TAKE A QUICK GLIMPSE AT WHATEVER THIS THING IS...

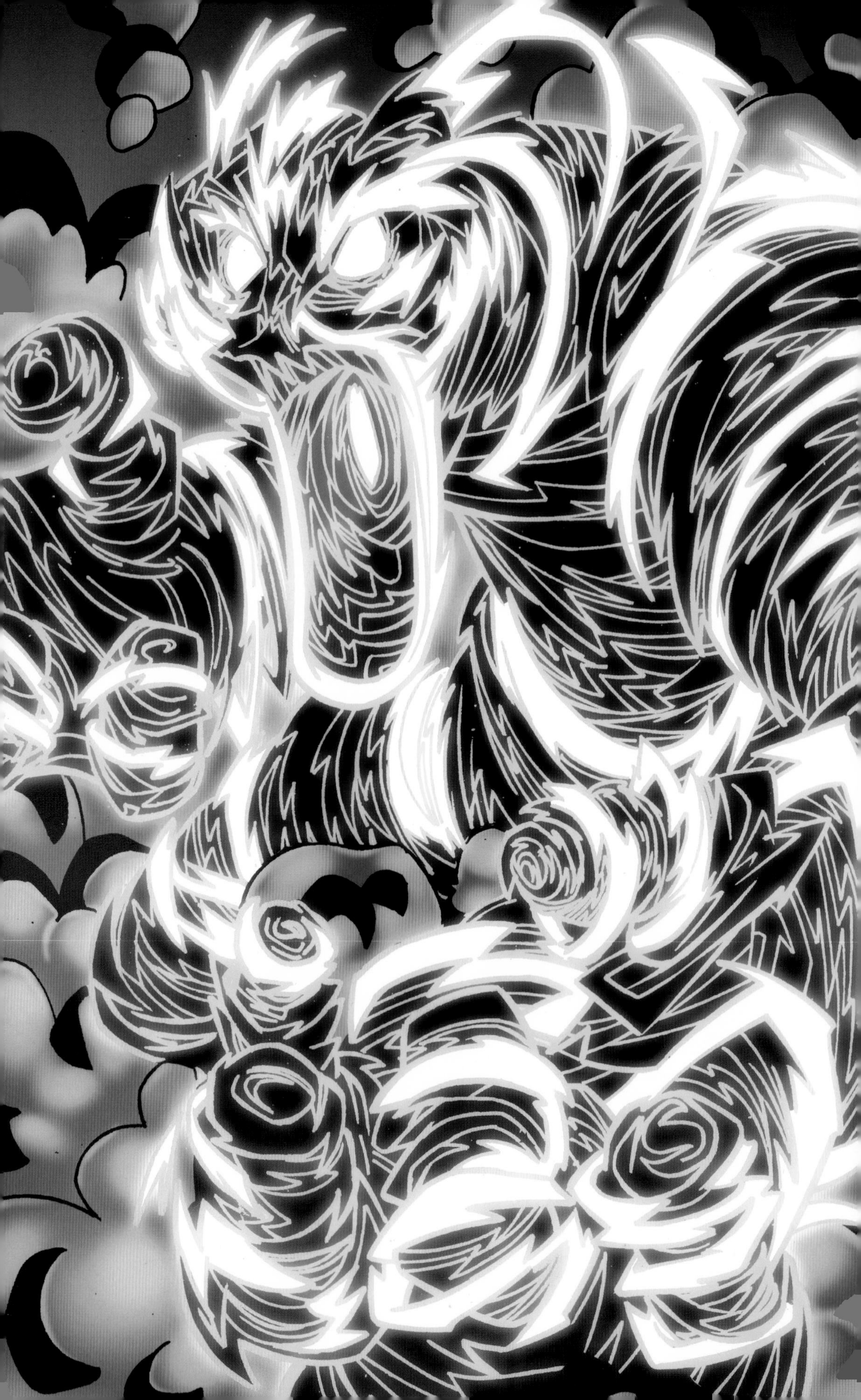

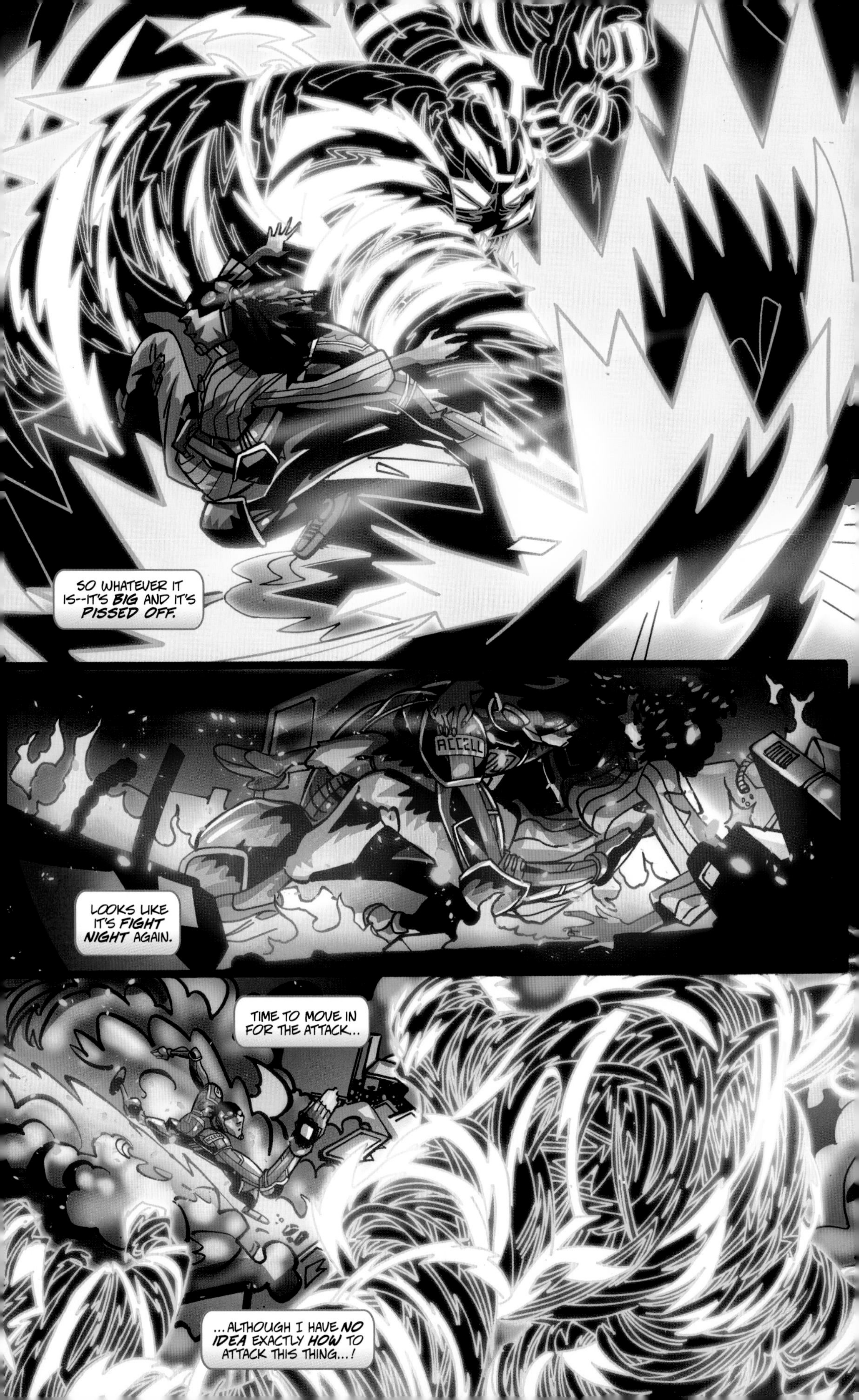

SO WHATEVER IT IS--IT'S BIG AND IT'S PISSED OFF.
LOOKS LIKE IT'S FIGHT NIGHT AGAIN.
TIME TO MOVE IN FOR THE ATTACK...
...ALTHOUGH I HAVE NO IDEA EXACTLY HOW TO ATTACK THIS THING...!

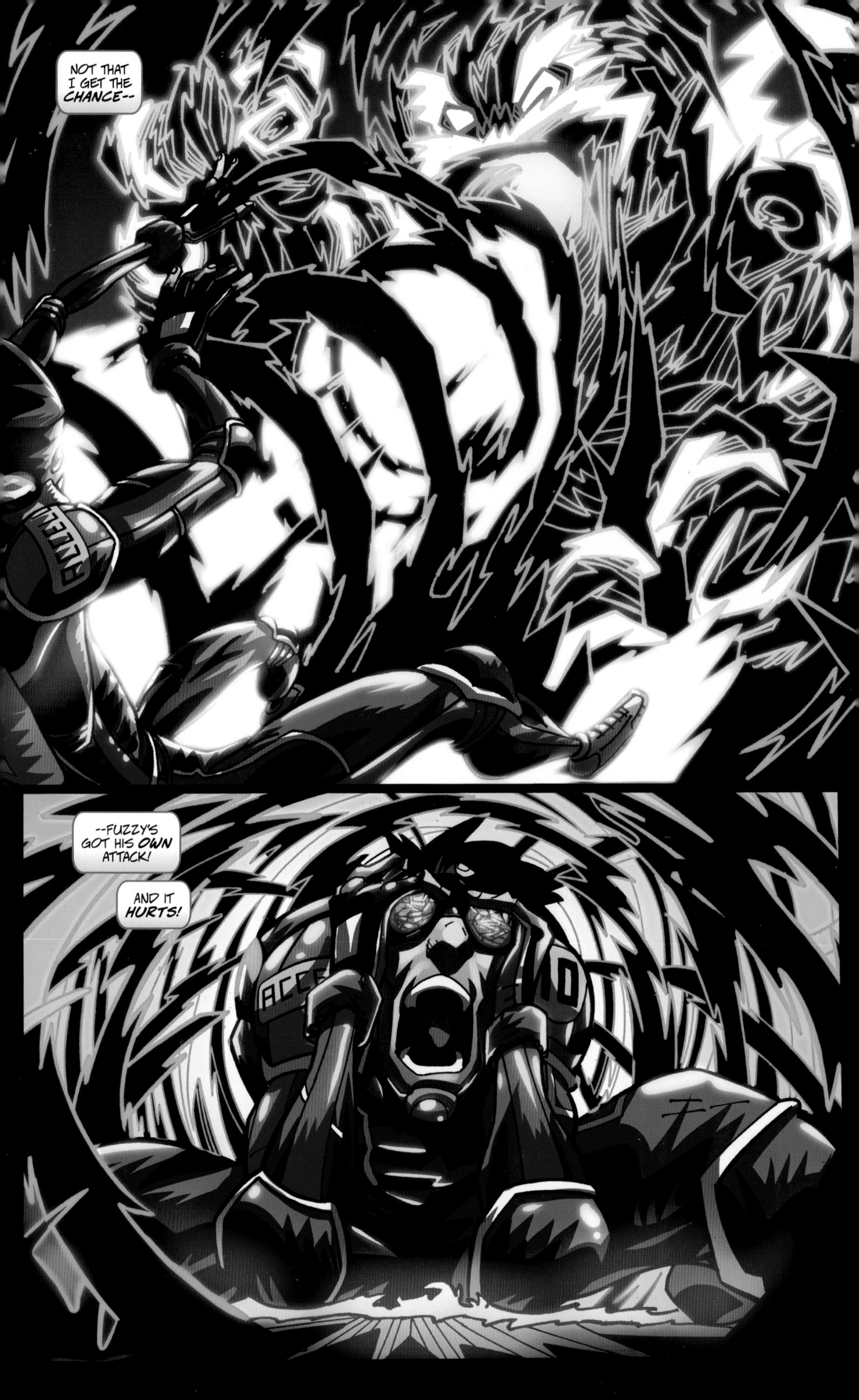
NOT THAT I GET THE *CHANCE*--
--FUZZY'S GOT HIS *OWN* ATTACK!
AND IT *HURTS!*

CHAPTER FOUR

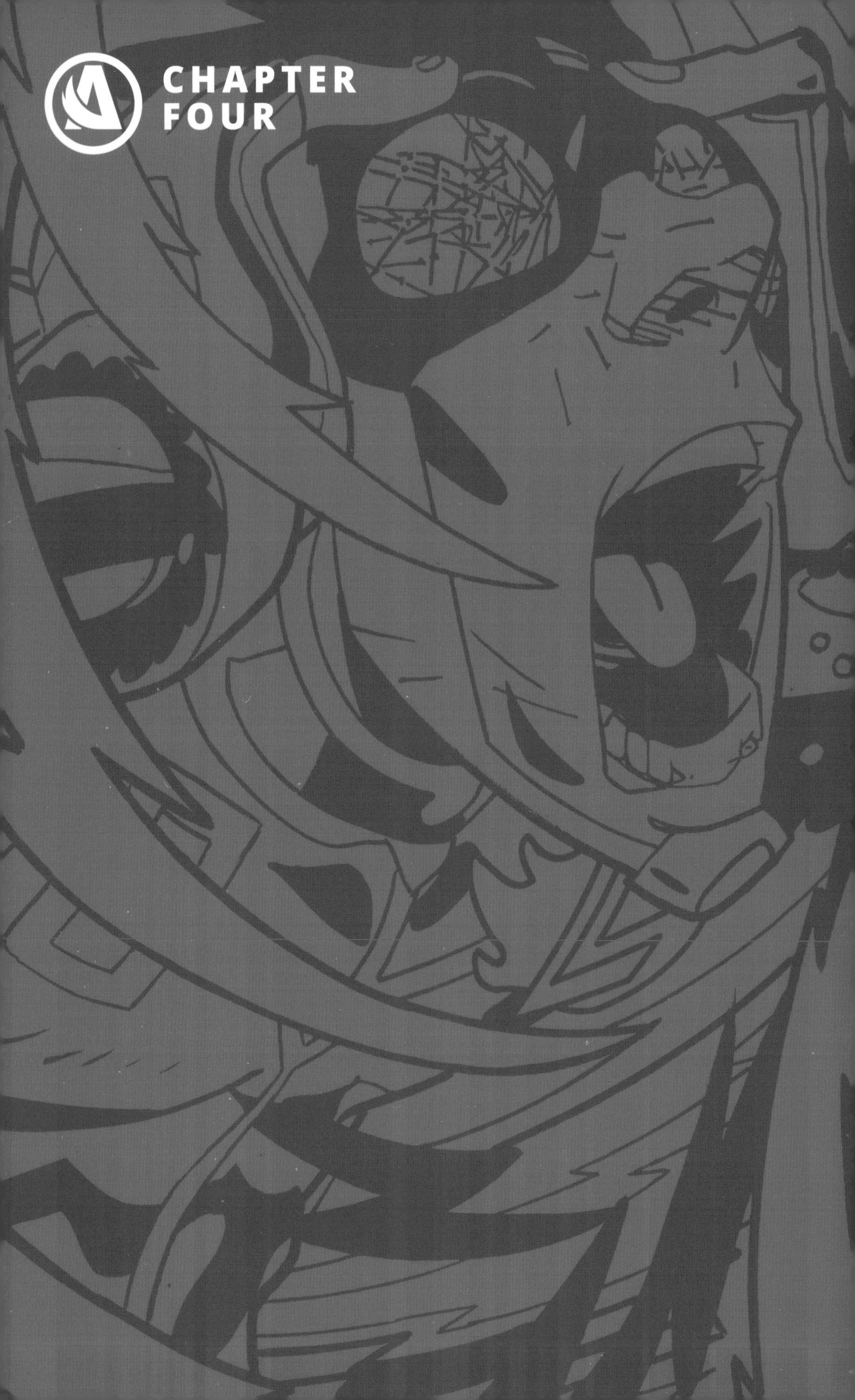

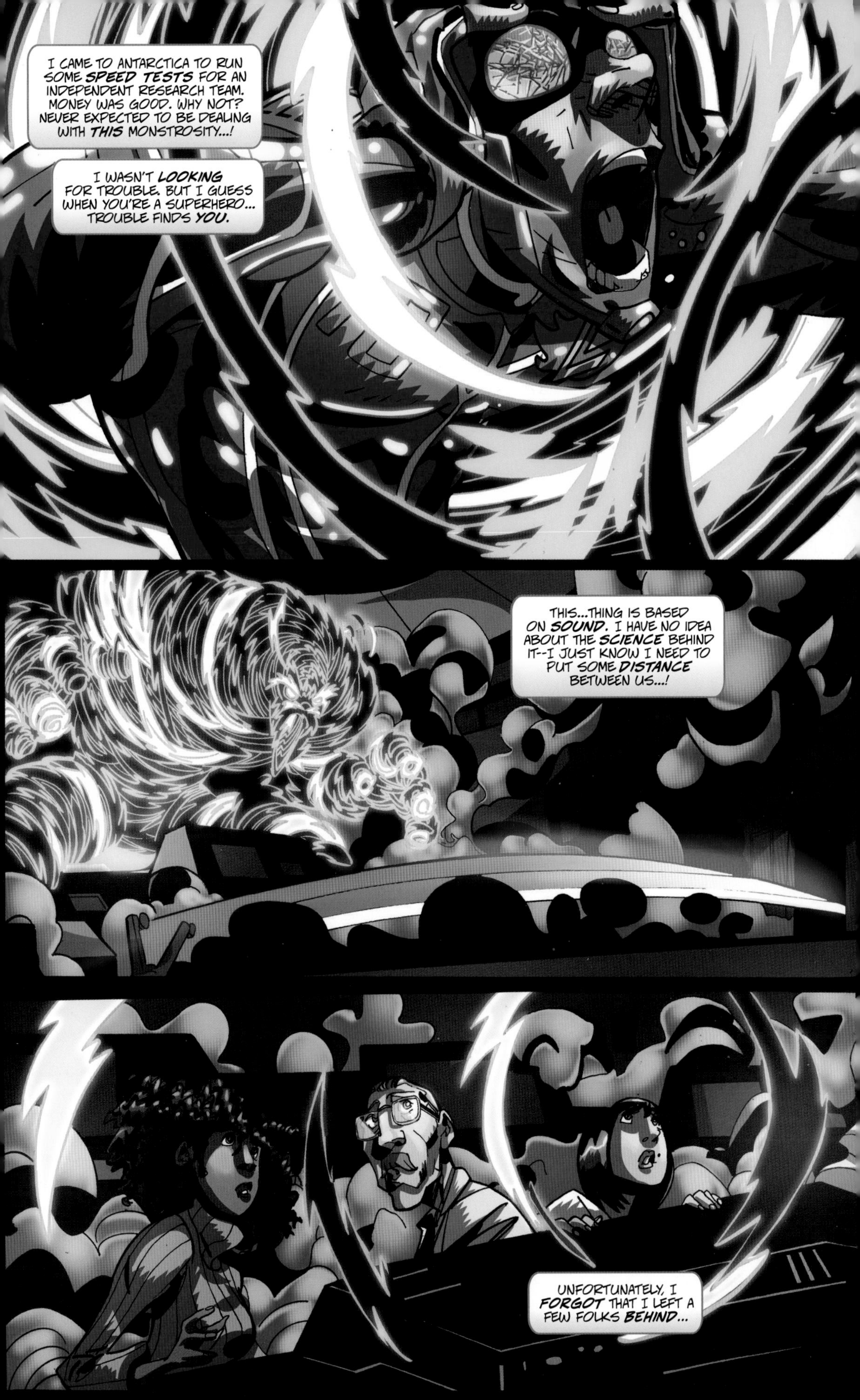
I CAME TO ANTARCTICA TO RUN SOME SPEED TESTS FOR AN INDEPENDENT RESEARCH TEAM. MONEY WAS GOOD. WHY NOT? NEVER EXPECTED TO BE DEALING WITH THIS MONSTROSITY...!
I WASN'T LOOKING FOR TROUBLE. BUT I GUESS WHEN YOU'RE A SUPERHERO... TROUBLE FINDS YOU.
THIS...THING IS BASED ON SOUND. I HAVE NO IDEA ABOUT THE SCIENCE BEHIND IT--I JUST KNOW I NEED TO PUT SOME DISTANCE BETWEEN US...!
UNFORTUNATELY, I FORGOT THAT I LEFT A FEW FOLKS BEHIND...

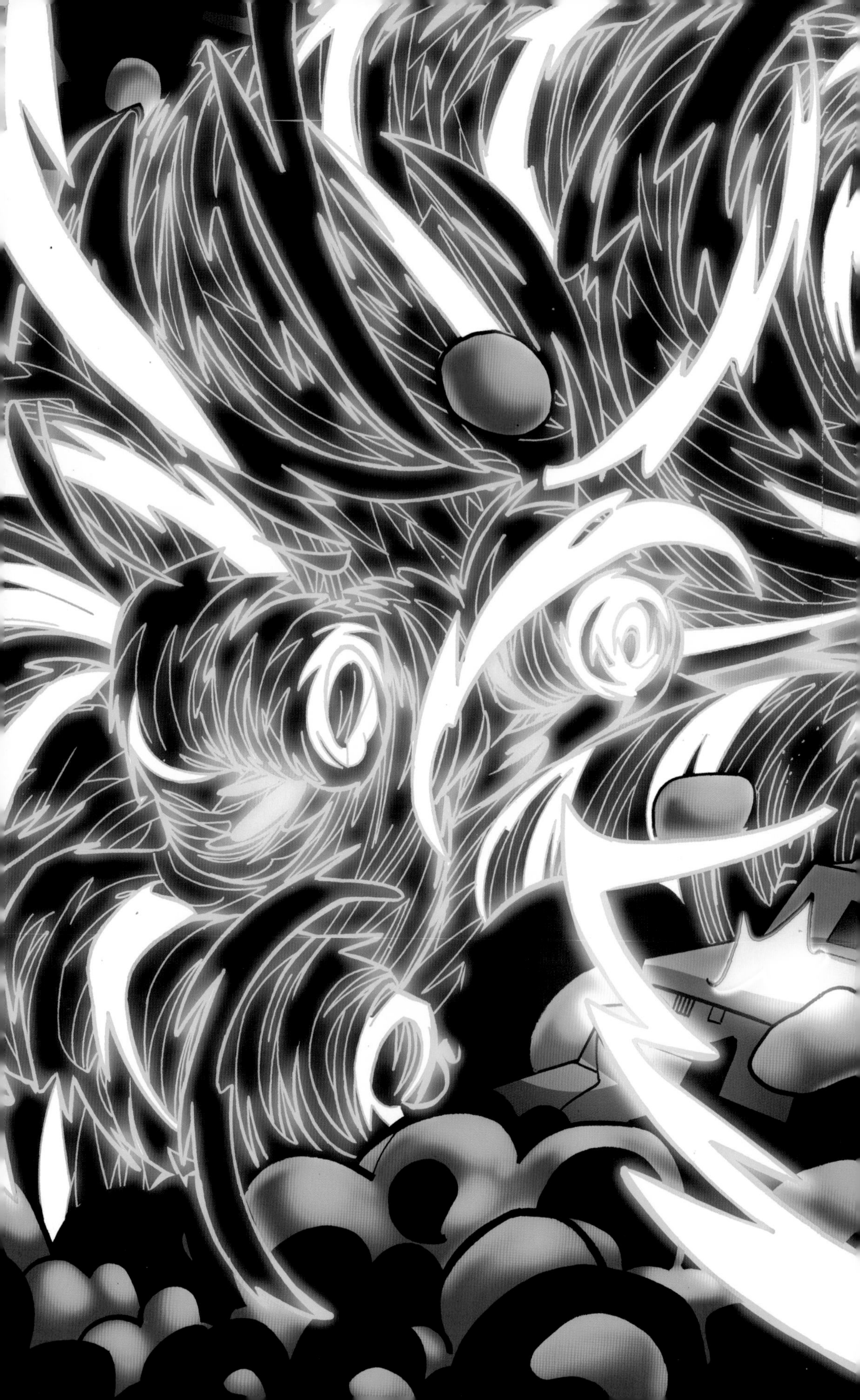

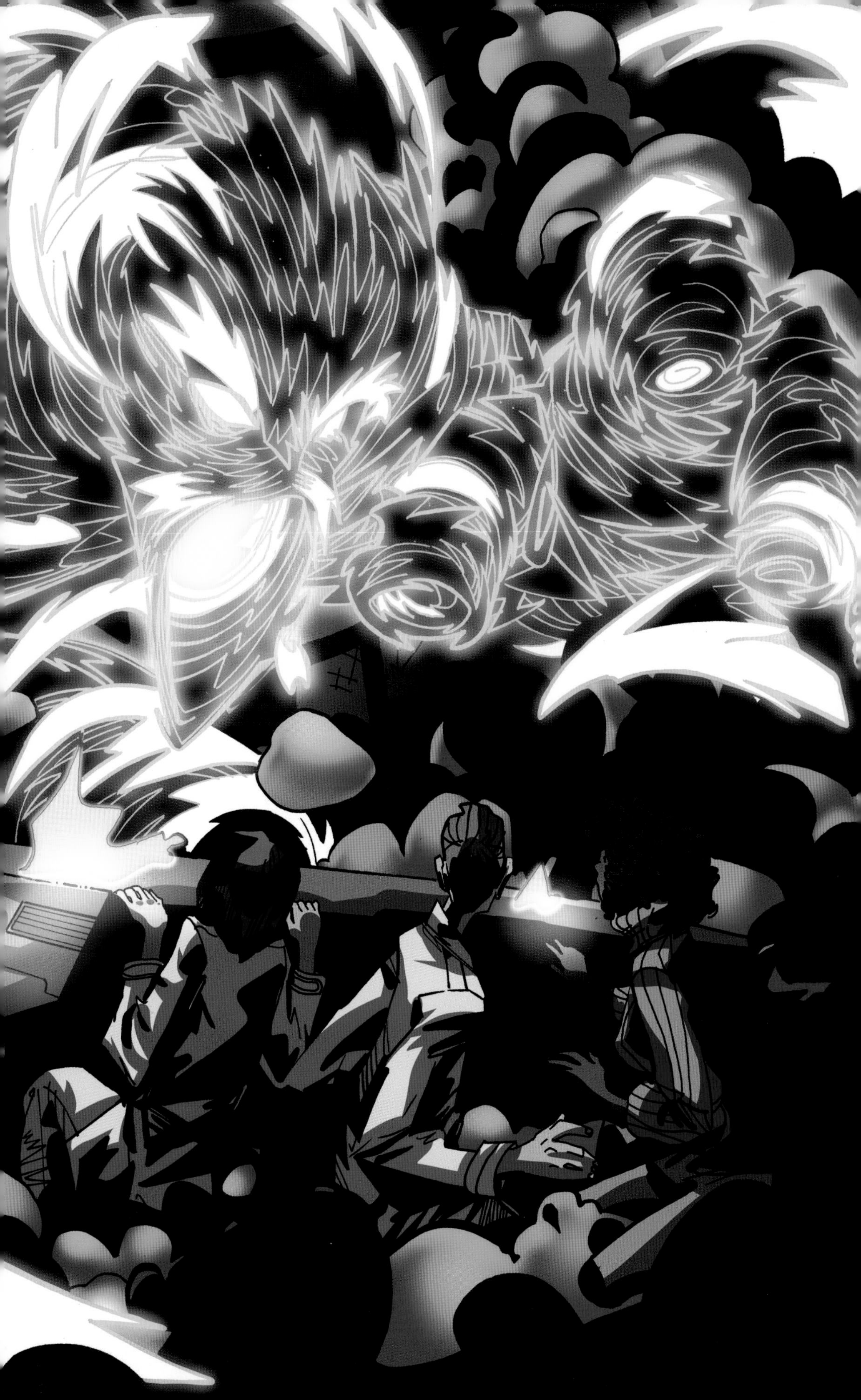

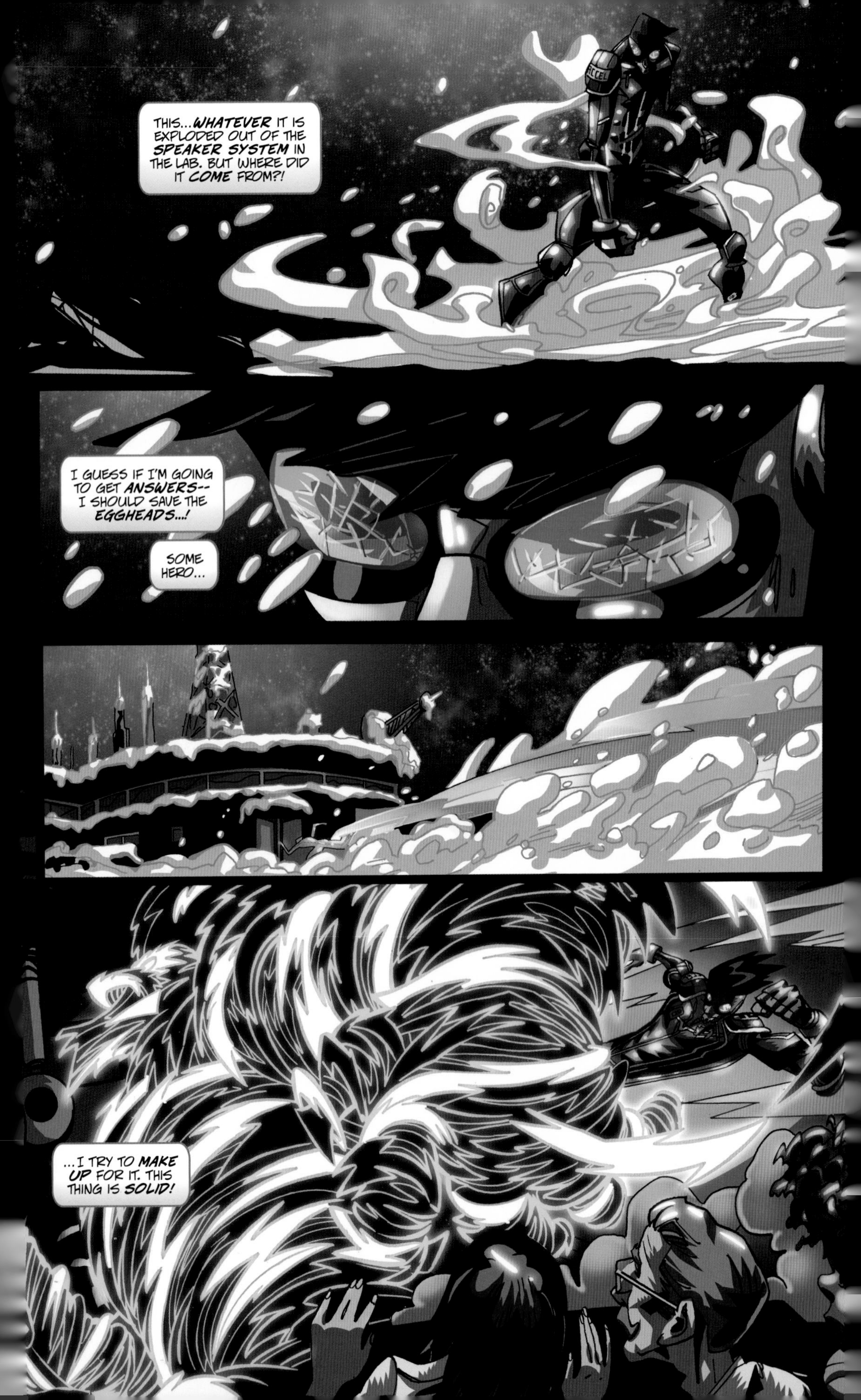
THIS...WHATEVER IT IS EXPLODED OUT OF THE SPEAKER SYSTEM IN THE LAB. BUT WHERE DID IT COME FROM?!
I GUESS IF I'M GOING TO GET ANSWERS-- I SHOULD SAVE THE EGGHEADS...!
SOME HERO...
...I TRY TO MAKE UP FOR IT. THIS THING IS SOLID!

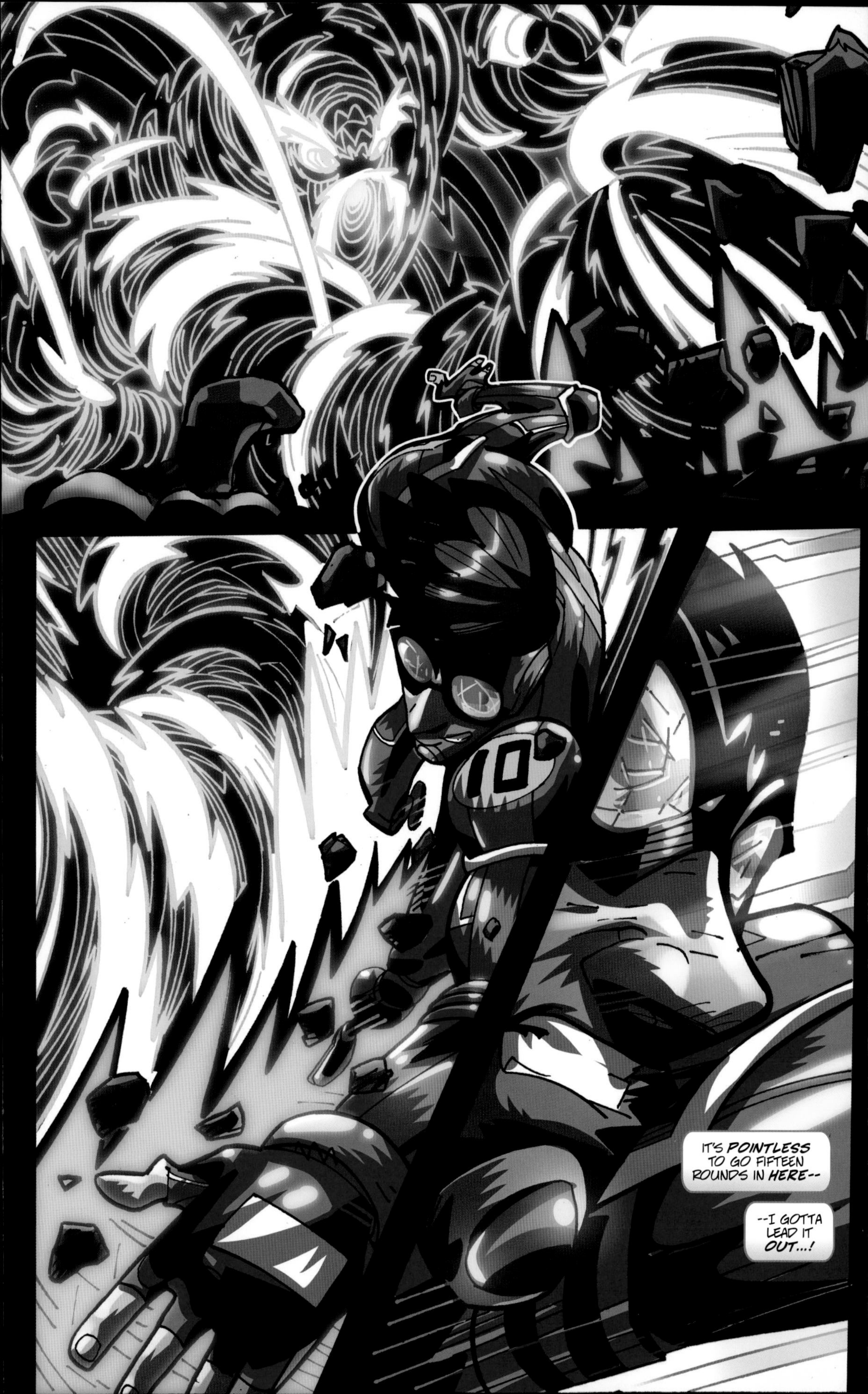
IT'S POINTLESS TO GO FIFTEEN ROUNDS IN HERE--
--I GOTTA LEAD IT OUT...!

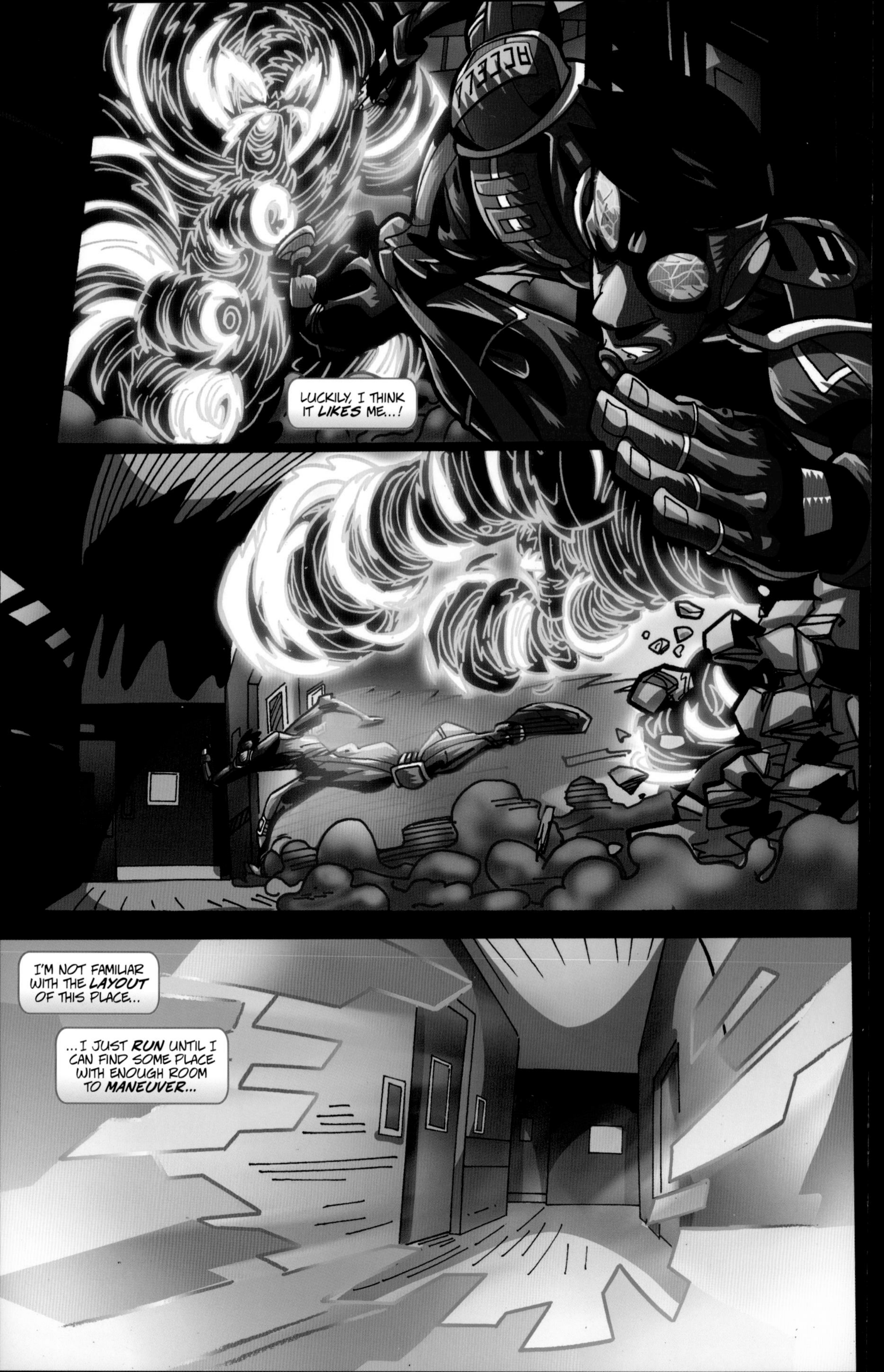
LUCKILY, I THINK IT LIKES ME...!
I'M NOT FAMILIAR WITH THE LAYOUT OF THIS PLACE...
...I JUST RUN UNTIL I CAN FIND SOME PLACE WITH ENOUGH ROOM TO MANEUVER...

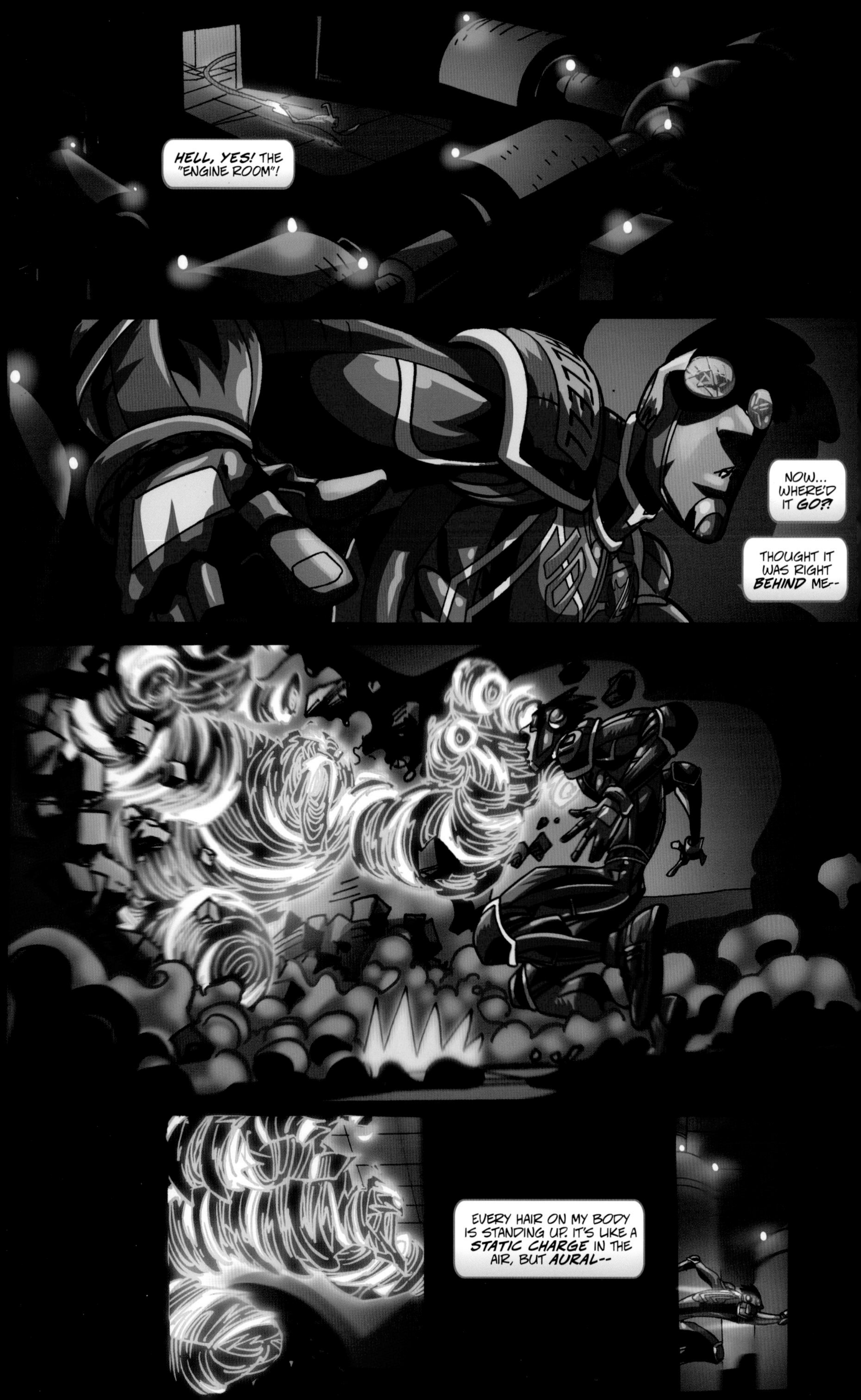
HELL, YES! THE "ENGINE ROOM"!
NOW... WHERE'D IT GO?!
THOUGHT IT WAS RIGHT BEHIND ME--
EVERY HAIR ON MY BODY IS STANDING UP. IT'S LIKE A STATIC CHARGE IN THE AIR, BUT AURAL--

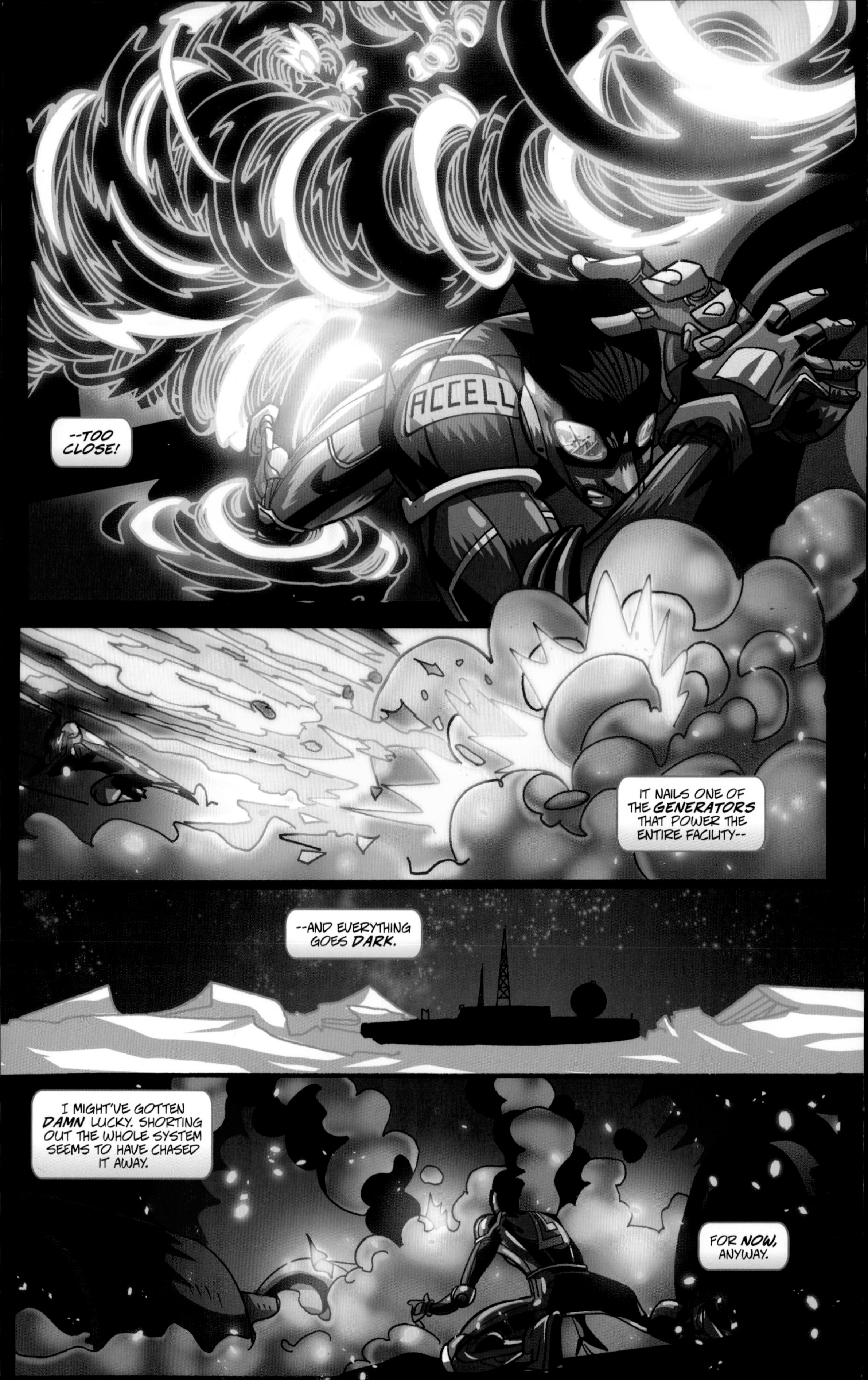
--TOO CLOSE!
ACCELL
IT NAILS ONE OF THE GENERATORS THAT POWER THE ENTIRE FACILITY--
--AND EVERYTHING GOES DARK.
I MIGHT'VE GOTTEN DAMN LUCKY. SHORTING OUT THE WHOLE SYSTEM SEEMS TO HAVE CHASED IT AWAY.
FOR NOW, ANYWAY.

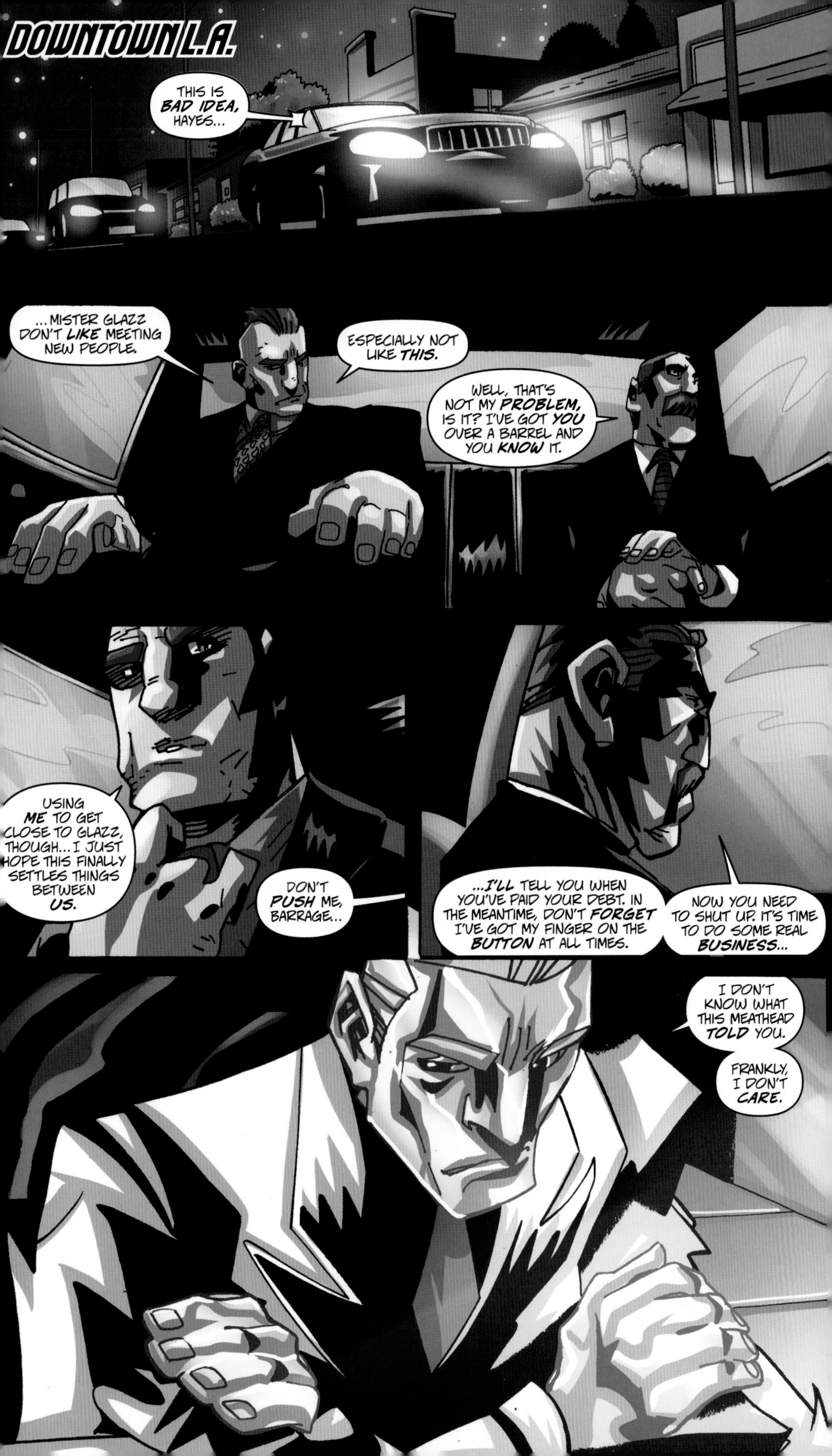
DOWNTOWN L.A.
THIS IS BAD IDEA, HAYES...
...MISTER GLAZZ DON'T LIKE MEETING NEW PEOPLE.
ESPECIALLY NOT LIKE THIS.
WELL, THAT'S NOT MY PROBLEM, IS IT? I'VE GOT YOU OVER A BARREL AND YOU KNOW IT.
USING ME TO GET CLOSE TO GLAZZ, THOUGH... I JUST HOPE THIS FINALLY SETTLES THINGS BETWEEN US.
DON'T PUSH ME, BARRAGE...
...I'LL TELL YOU WHEN YOU'VE PAID YOUR DEBT. IN THE MEANTIME, DON'T FORGET I'VE GOT MY FINGER ON THE BUTTON AT ALL TIMES.
NOW YOU NEED TO SHUT UP. IT'S TIME TO DO SOME REAL BUSINESS...
I DON'T KNOW WHAT THIS MEATHEAD TOLD YOU.
FRANKLY, I DON'T CARE.

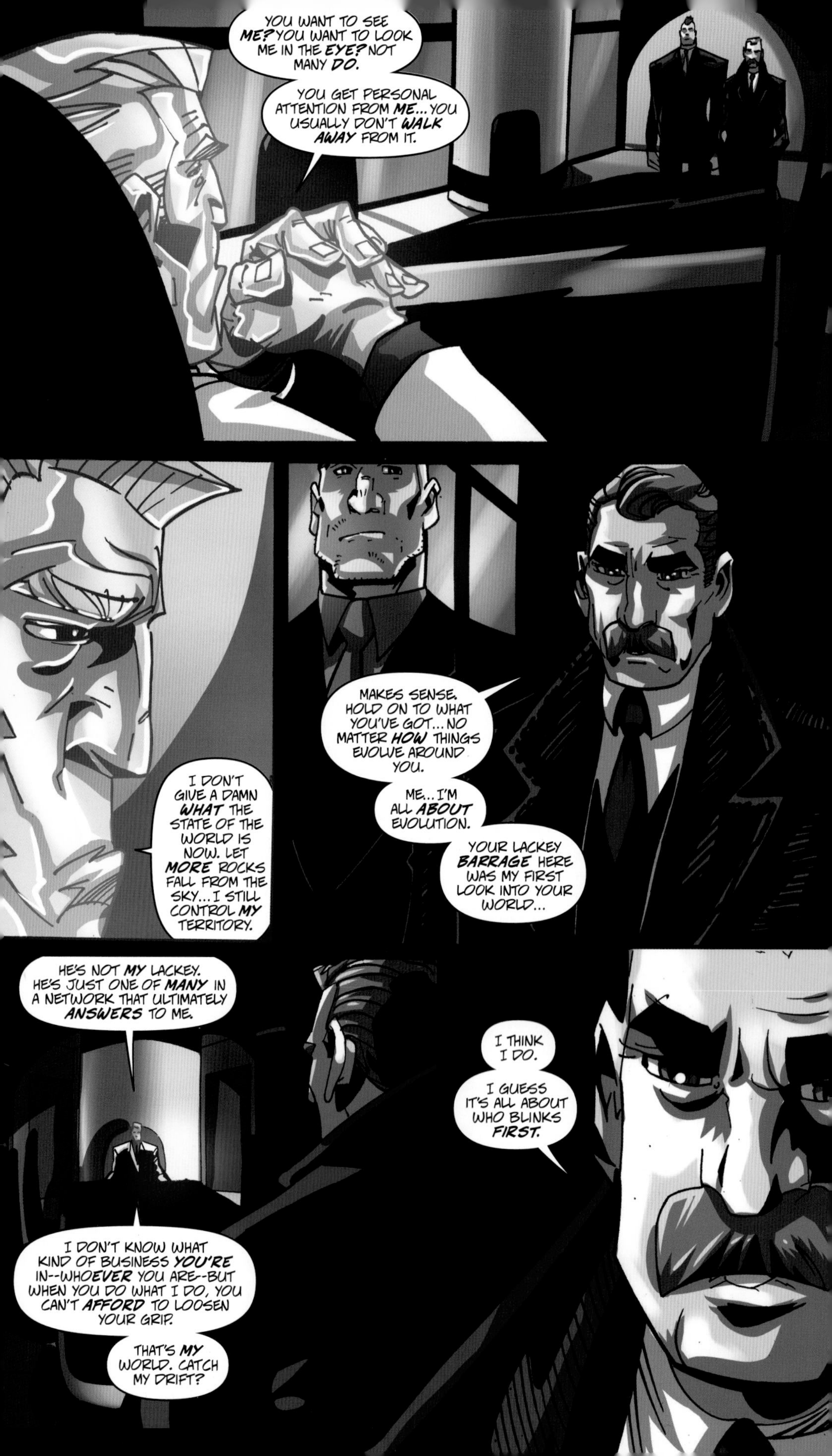
YOU WANT TO SEE ME? YOU WANT TO LOOK ME IN THE EYE? NOT MANY DO.
YOU GET PERSONAL ATTENTION FROM ME... YOU USUALLY DON'T WALK AWAY FROM IT.
I DON'T GIVE A DAMN WHAT THE STATE OF THE WORLD IS NOW. LET MORE ROCKS FALL FROM THE SKY... I STILL CONTROL MY TERRITORY.
MAKES SENSE. HOLD ON TO WHAT YOU'VE GOT... NO MATTER HOW THINGS EVOLVE AROUND YOU.
ME... I'M ALL ABOUT EVOLUTION.
YOUR LACKEY BARRAGE HERE WAS MY FIRST LOOK INTO YOUR WORLD...
HE'S NOT MY LACKEY. HE'S JUST ONE OF MANY IN A NETWORK THAT ULTIMATELY ANSWERS TO ME.
I DON'T KNOW WHAT KIND OF BUSINESS YOU'RE IN--WHOEVER YOU ARE--BUT WHEN YOU DO WHAT I DO, YOU CAN'T AFFORD TO LOOSEN YOUR GRIP.
THAT'S MY WORLD. CATCH MY DRIFT?
I THINK I DO.
I GUESS IT'S ALL ABOUT WHO BLINKS FIRST.

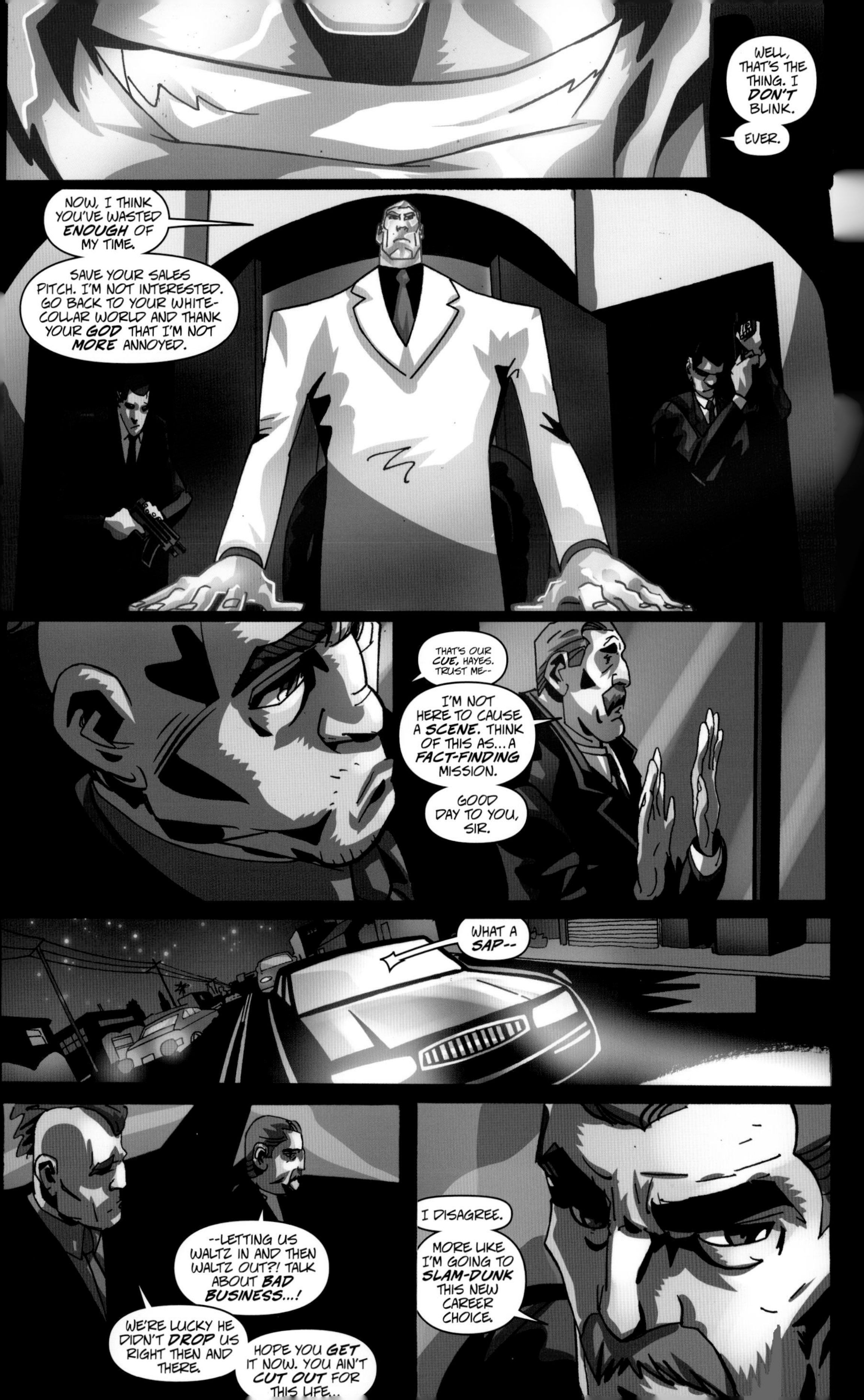

WELL, THAT'S THE THING. I DON'T BLINK.
EVER.
NOW, I THINK YOU'VE WASTED ENOUGH OF MY TIME.
SAVE YOUR SALES PITCH. I'M NOT INTERESTED. GO BACK TO YOUR WHITE-COLLAR WORLD AND THANK YOUR GOD THAT I'M NOT MORE ANNOYED.
THAT'S OUR CUE, HAYES. TRUST ME--
I'M NOT HERE TO CAUSE A SCENE. THINK OF THIS AS...A FACT-FINDING MISSION.
GOOD DAY TO YOU, SIR.
WHAT A SAP--
--LETTING US WALTZ IN AND THEN WALTZ OUT?! TALK ABOUT BAD BUSINESS...!
WE'RE LUCKY HE DIDN'T DROP US RIGHT THEN AND THERE.
HOPE YOU GET IT NOW. YOU AIN'T CUT OUT FOR THIS LIFE...
I DISAGREE.
MORE LIKE I'M GOING TO SLAM-DUNK THIS NEW CAREER CHOICE.

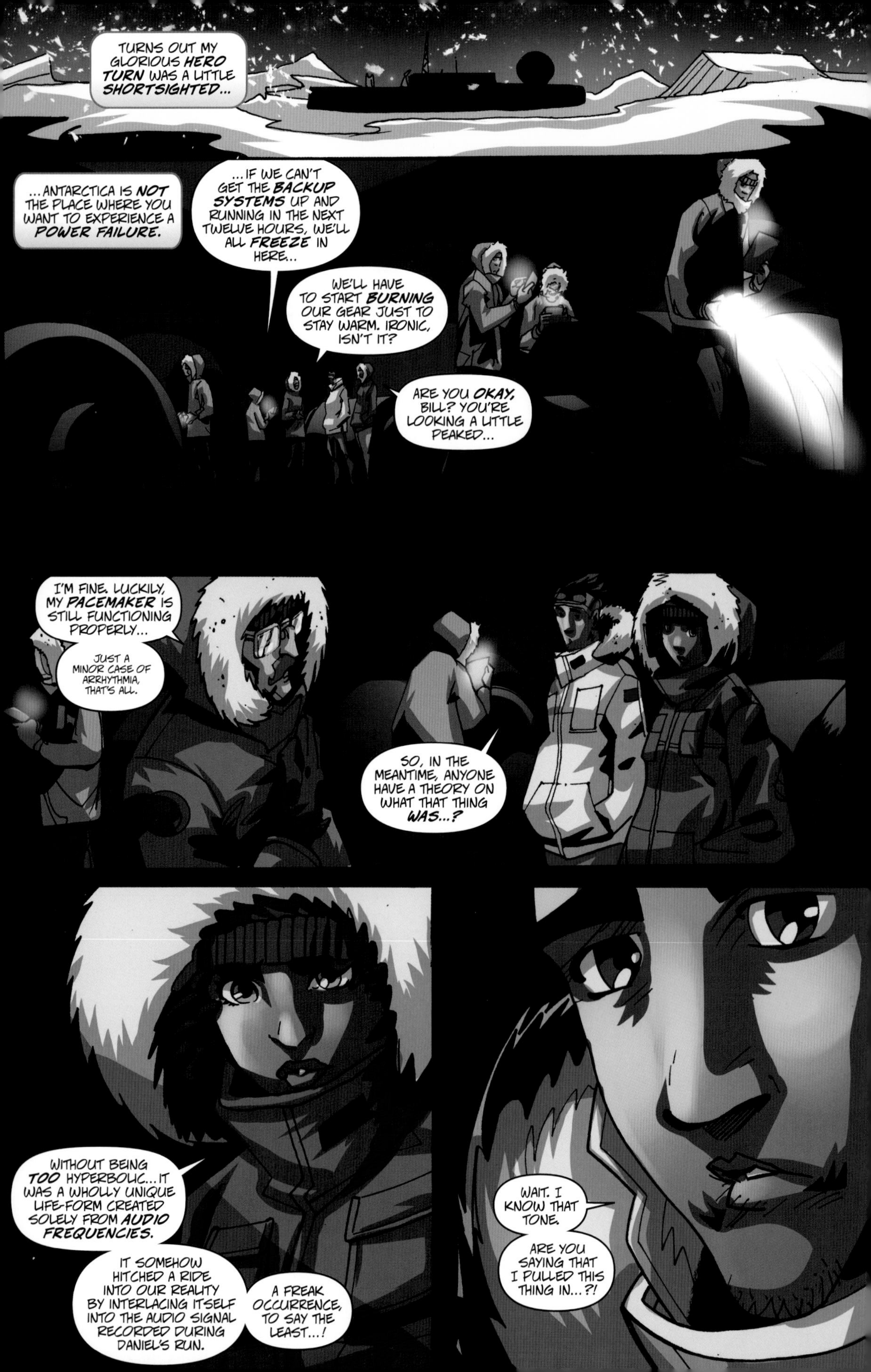
TURNS OUT MY GLORIOUS HERO TURN WAS A LITTLE SHORTSIGHTED...
...ANTARCTICA IS NOT THE PLACE WHERE YOU WANT TO EXPERIENCE A POWER FAILURE.
...IF WE CAN'T GET THE BACKUP SYSTEMS UP AND RUNNING IN THE NEXT TWELVE HOURS, WE'LL ALL FREEZE IN HERE...
WE'LL HAVE TO START BURNING OUR GEAR JUST TO STAY WARM. IRONIC, ISN'T IT?
ARE YOU OKAY, BILL? YOU'RE LOOKING A LITTLE PEAKED...
I'M FINE. LUCKILY, MY PACEMAKER IS STILL FUNCTIONING PROPERLY...
JUST A MINOR CASE OF ARRHYTHMIA, THAT'S ALL.
SO, IN THE MEANTIME, ANYONE HAVE A THEORY ON WHAT THAT THING WAS...?
WITHOUT BEING TOO HYPERBOLIC... IT WAS A WHOLLY UNIQUE LIFE-FORM CREATED SOLELY FROM AUDIO FREQUENCIES.
IT SOMEHOW HITCHED A RIDE INTO OUR REALITY BY INTERLACING ITSELF INTO THE AUDIO SIGNAL RECORDED DURING DANIEL'S RUN.
A FREAK OCCURRENCE, TO SAY THE LEAST...!
WAIT. I KNOW THAT TONE.
ARE YOU SAYING THAT I PULLED THIS THING IN...?!

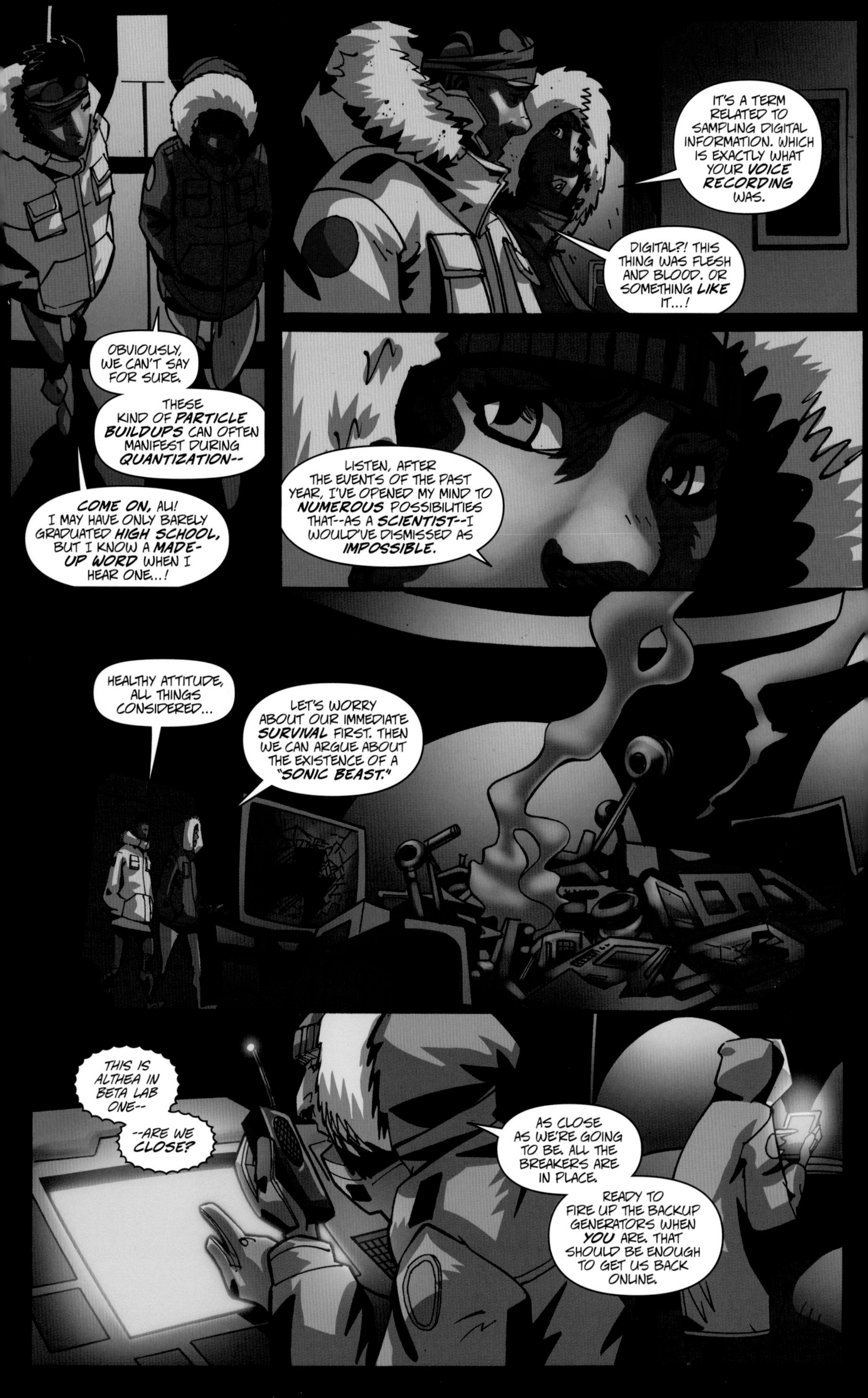
IT'S A TERM RELATED TO SAMPLING DIGITAL INFORMATION. WHICH IS EXACTLY WHAT YOUR VOICE RECORDING WAS.
DIGITAL?! THIS THING WAS FLESH AND BLOOD. OR SOMETHING LIKE IT...!
OBVIOUSLY, WE CAN'T SAY FOR SURE.
THESE KIND OF PARTICLE BUILDUPS CAN OFTEN MANIFEST DURING QUANTIZATION--
COME ON, ALI! I MAY HAVE ONLY BARELY GRADUATED HIGH SCHOOL, BUT I KNOW A MADE-UP WORD WHEN I HEAR ONE...!
LISTEN, AFTER THE EVENTS OF THE PAST YEAR, I'VE OPENED MY MIND TO NUMEROUS POSSIBILITIES THAT--AS A SCIENTIST--I WOULD'VE DISMISSED AS IMPOSSIBLE.
HEALTHY ATTITUDE, ALL THINGS CONSIDERED...
LET'S WORRY ABOUT OUR IMMEDIATE SURVIVAL FIRST. THEN WE CAN ARGUE ABOUT THE EXISTENCE OF A "SONIC BEAST."
THIS IS ALTHEA IN BETA LAB ONE--
--ARE WE CLOSE?
AS CLOSE AS WE'RE GOING TO BE. ALL THE BREAKERS ARE IN PLACE.
READY TO FIRE UP THE BACKUP GENERATORS WHEN YOU ARE. THAT SHOULD BE ENOUGH TO GET US BACK ONLINE.

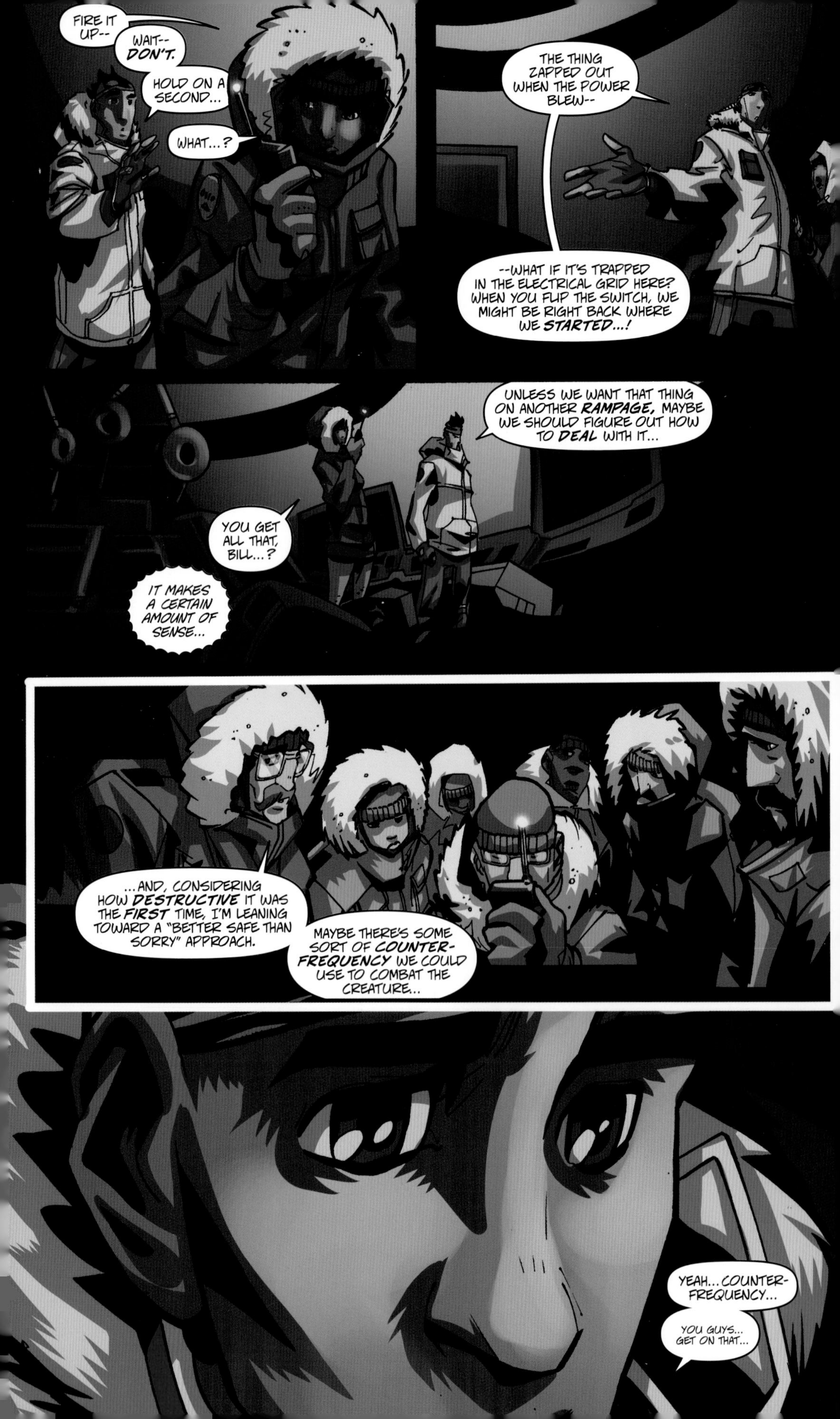
FIRE IT UP--
WAIT-- DON'T.
HOLD ON A SECOND...
WHAT...?
THE THING ZAPPED OUT WHEN THE POWER BLEW--
--WHAT IF IT'S TRAPPED IN THE ELECTRICAL GRID HERE? WHEN YOU FLIP THE SWITCH, WE MIGHT BE RIGHT BACK WHERE WE STARTED...!
UNLESS WE WANT THAT THING ON ANOTHER RAMPAGE, MAYBE WE SHOULD FIGURE OUT HOW TO DEAL WITH IT...
YOU GET ALL THAT, BILL...?
IT MAKES A CERTAIN AMOUNT OF SENSE...
...AND, CONSIDERING HOW DESTRUCTIVE IT WAS THE FIRST TIME, I'M LEANING TOWARD A "BETTER SAFE THAN SORRY" APPROACH.
MAYBE THERE'S SOME SORT OF COUNTER-FREQUENCY WE COULD USE TO COMBAT THE CREATURE...
YEAH... COUNTER-FREQUENCY...
YOU GUYS... GET ON THAT...

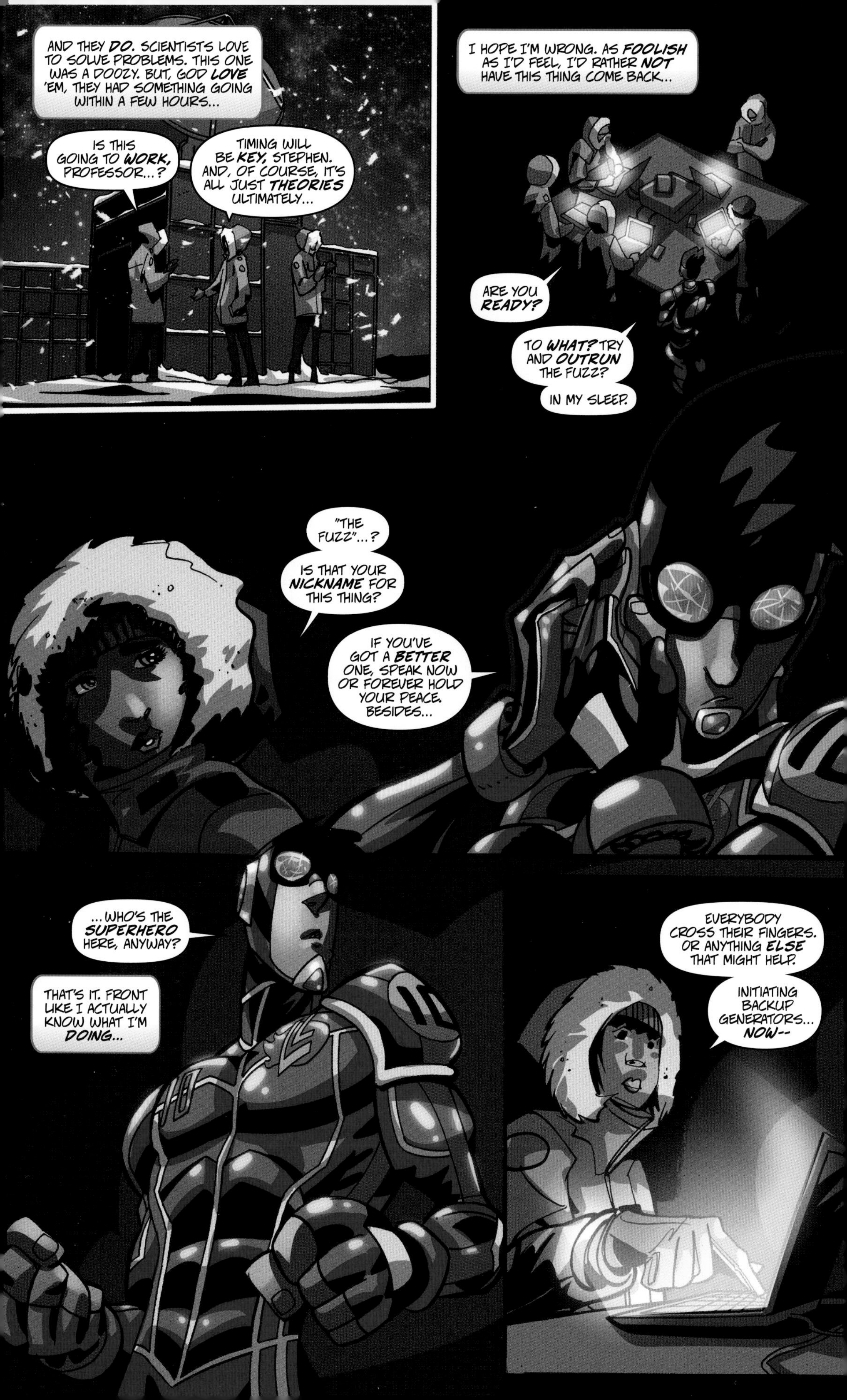
AND THEY DO. SCIENTISTS LOVE TO SOLVE PROBLEMS. THIS ONE WAS A DOOZY. BUT, GOD LOVE 'EM, THEY HAD SOMETHING GOING WITHIN A FEW HOURS...
IS THIS GOING TO WORK, PROFESSOR...?
TIMING WILL BE KEY, STEPHEN. AND, OF COURSE, IT'S ALL JUST THEORIES ULTIMATELY...
I HOPE I'M WRONG. AS FOOLISH AS I'D FEEL, I'D RATHER NOT HAVE THIS THING COME BACK...
ARE YOU READY?
TO WHAT? TRY AND OUTRUN THE FUZZ?
IN MY SLEEP.
"THE FUZZ"...?
IS THAT YOUR NICKNAME FOR THIS THING?
IF YOU'VE GOT A BETTER ONE, SPEAK NOW OR FOREVER HOLD YOUR PEACE. BESIDES...
...WHO'S THE SUPERHERO HERE, ANYWAY?
THAT'S IT. FRONT LIKE I ACTUALLY KNOW WHAT I'M DOING...
EVERYBODY CROSS THEIR FINGERS. OR ANYTHING ELSE THAT MIGHT HELP.
INITIATING BACKUP GENERATORS... NOW--

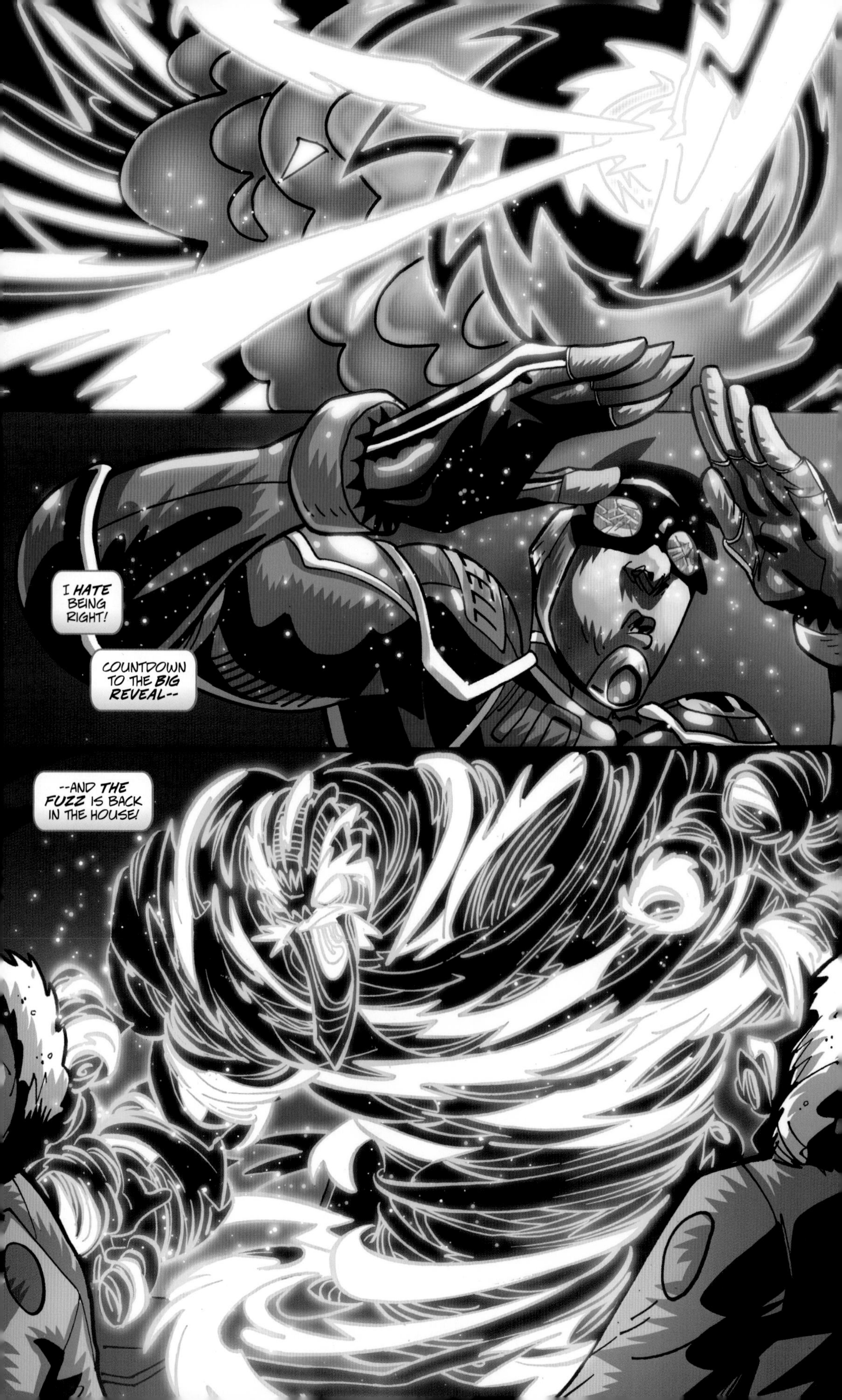

I HATE BEING RIGHT!
COUNTDOWN TO THE BIG REVEAL--
--AND THE FUZZ IS BACK IN THE HOUSE!

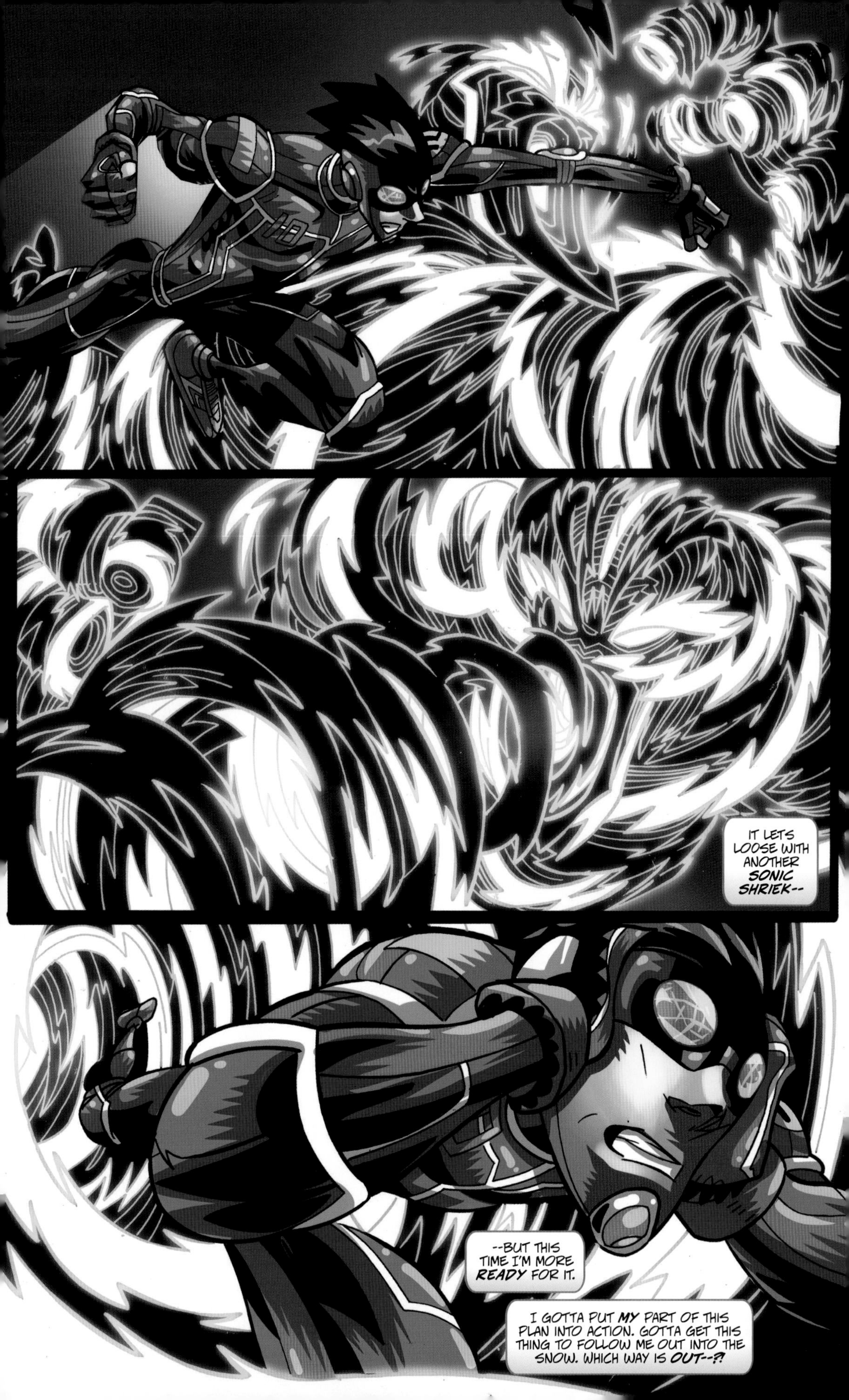
IT LETS LOOSE WITH ANOTHER **SONIC SHRIEK**--
--BUT THIS TIME I'M MORE **READY** FOR IT.
I GOTTA PUT **MY** PART OF THIS PLAN INTO ACTION. GOTTA GET THIS THING TO FOLLOW ME OUT INTO THE SNOW. WHICH WAY IS **OUT**--?!

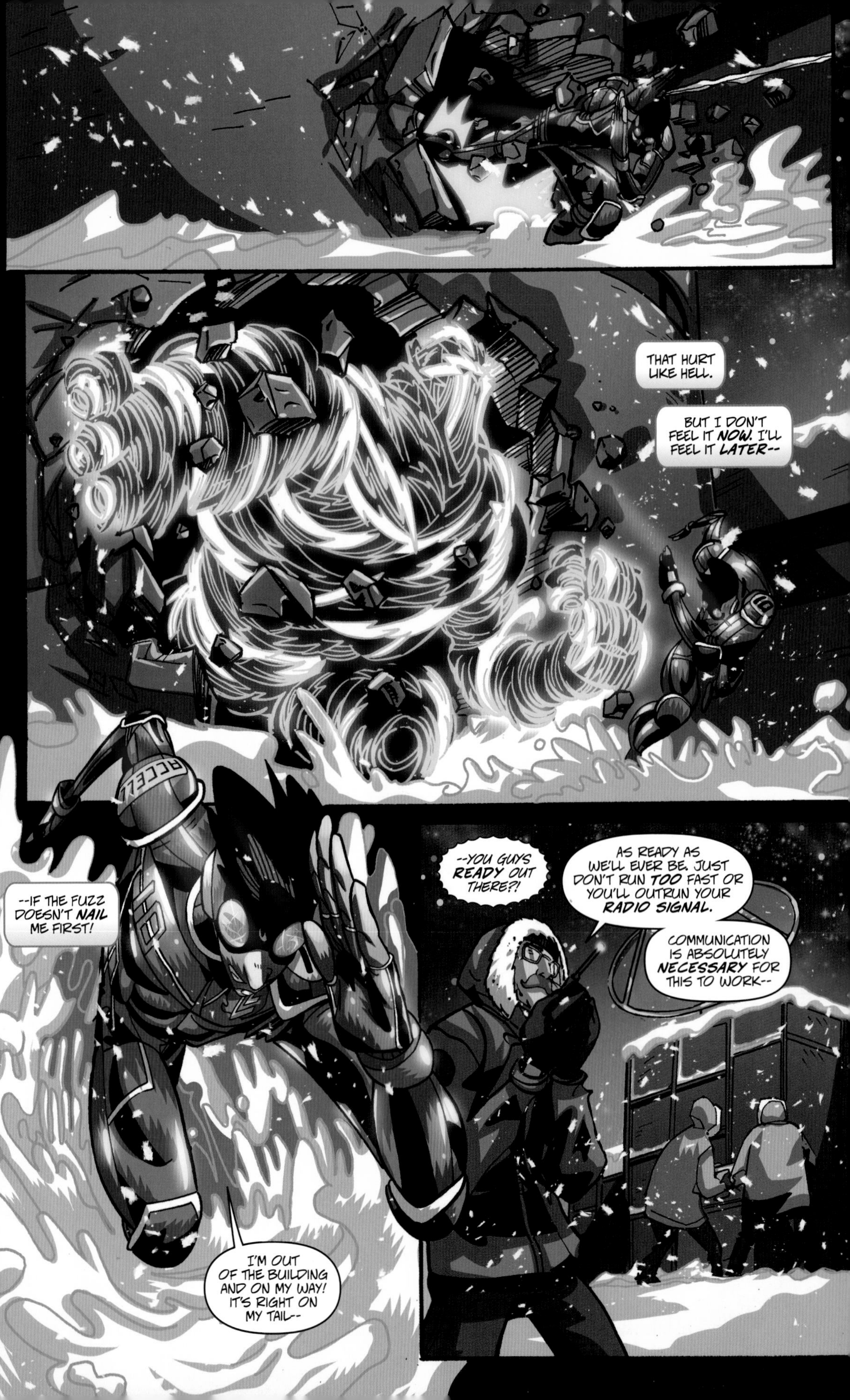
THAT HURT LIKE HELL.
BUT I DON'T FEEL IT NOW. I'LL FEEL IT LATER--
--IF THE FUZZ DOESN'T NAIL ME FIRST!
I'M OUT OF THE BUILDING AND ON MY WAY! IT'S RIGHT ON MY TAIL--
--YOU GUYS READY OUT THERE?!
AS READY AS WE'LL EVER BE. JUST DON'T RUN TOO FAST OR YOU'LL OUTRUN YOUR RADIO SIGNAL.
COMMUNICATION IS ABSOLUTELY NECESSARY FOR THIS TO WORK--

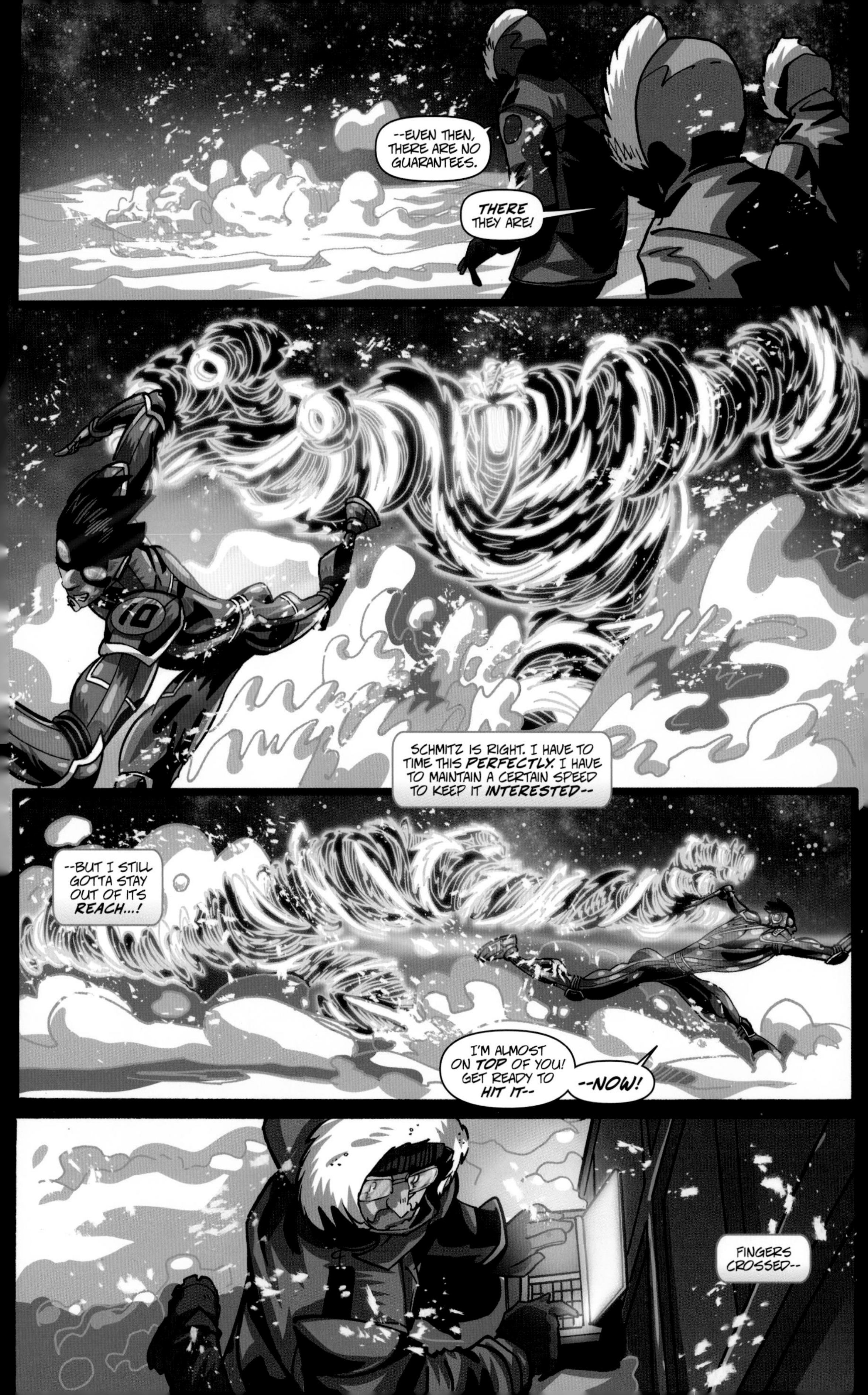
--EVEN THEN, THERE ARE NO GUARANTEES.
THERE THEY ARE!
SCHMITZ IS RIGHT. I HAVE TO TIME THIS PERFECTLY. I HAVE TO MAINTAIN A CERTAIN SPEED TO KEEP IT INTERESTED--
--BUT I STILL GOTTA STAY OUT OF ITS REACH...!
I'M ALMOST ON TOP OF YOU! GET READY TO HIT IT--
--NOW!
FINGERS CROSSED--

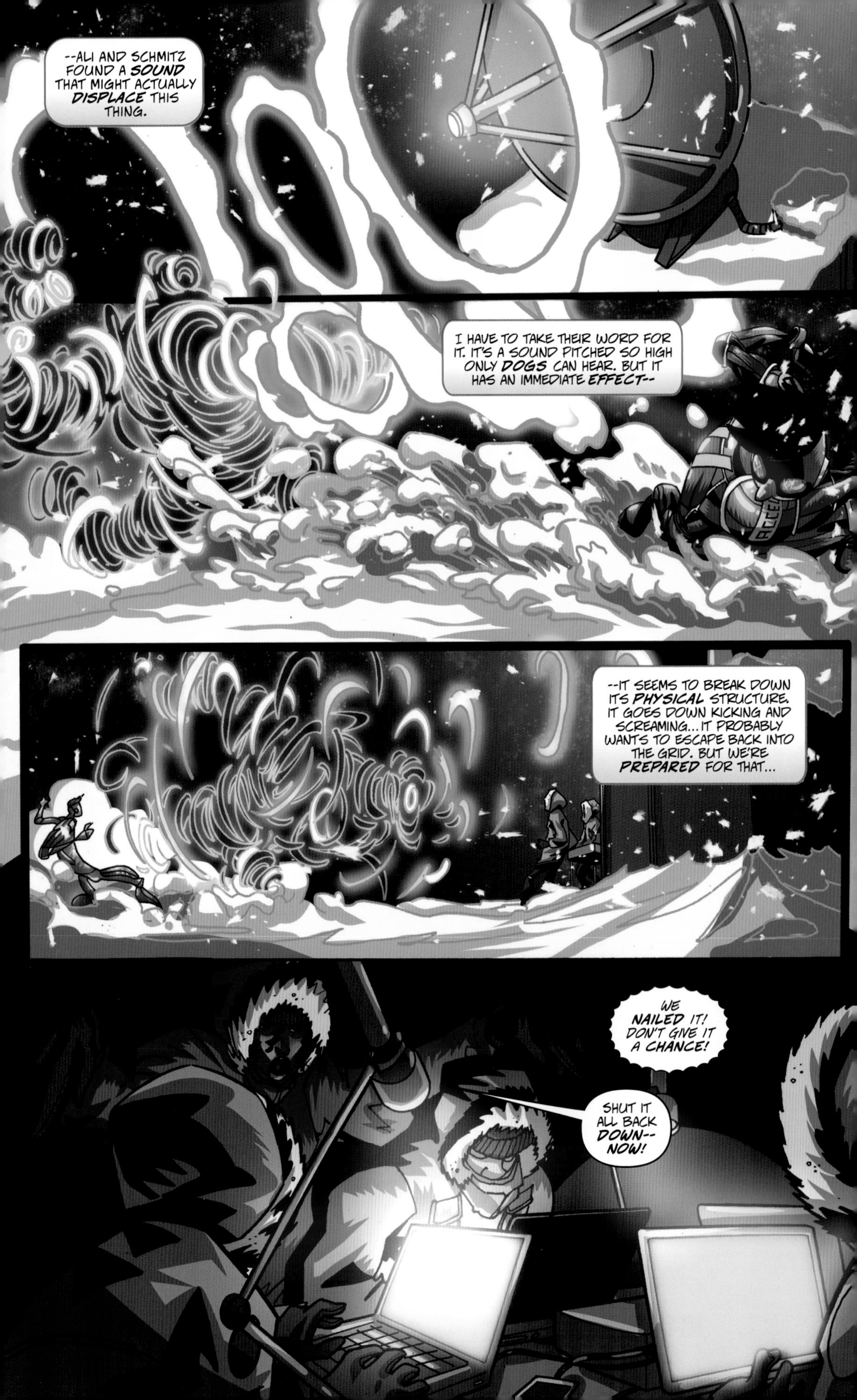
--ALI AND SCHMITZ FOUND A SOUND THAT MIGHT ACTUALLY DISPLACE THIS THING.
I HAVE TO TAKE THEIR WORD FOR IT. IT'S A SOUND PITCHED SO HIGH ONLY DOGS CAN HEAR. BUT IT HAS AN IMMEDIATE EFFECT--
--IT SEEMS TO BREAK DOWN ITS PHYSICAL STRUCTURE. IT GOES DOWN KICKING AND SCREAMING... IT PROBABLY WANTS TO ESCAPE BACK INTO THE GRID. BUT WE'RE PREPARED FOR THAT...
WE NAILED IT! DON'T GIVE IT A CHANCE!
SHUT IT ALL BACK DOWN-- NOW!

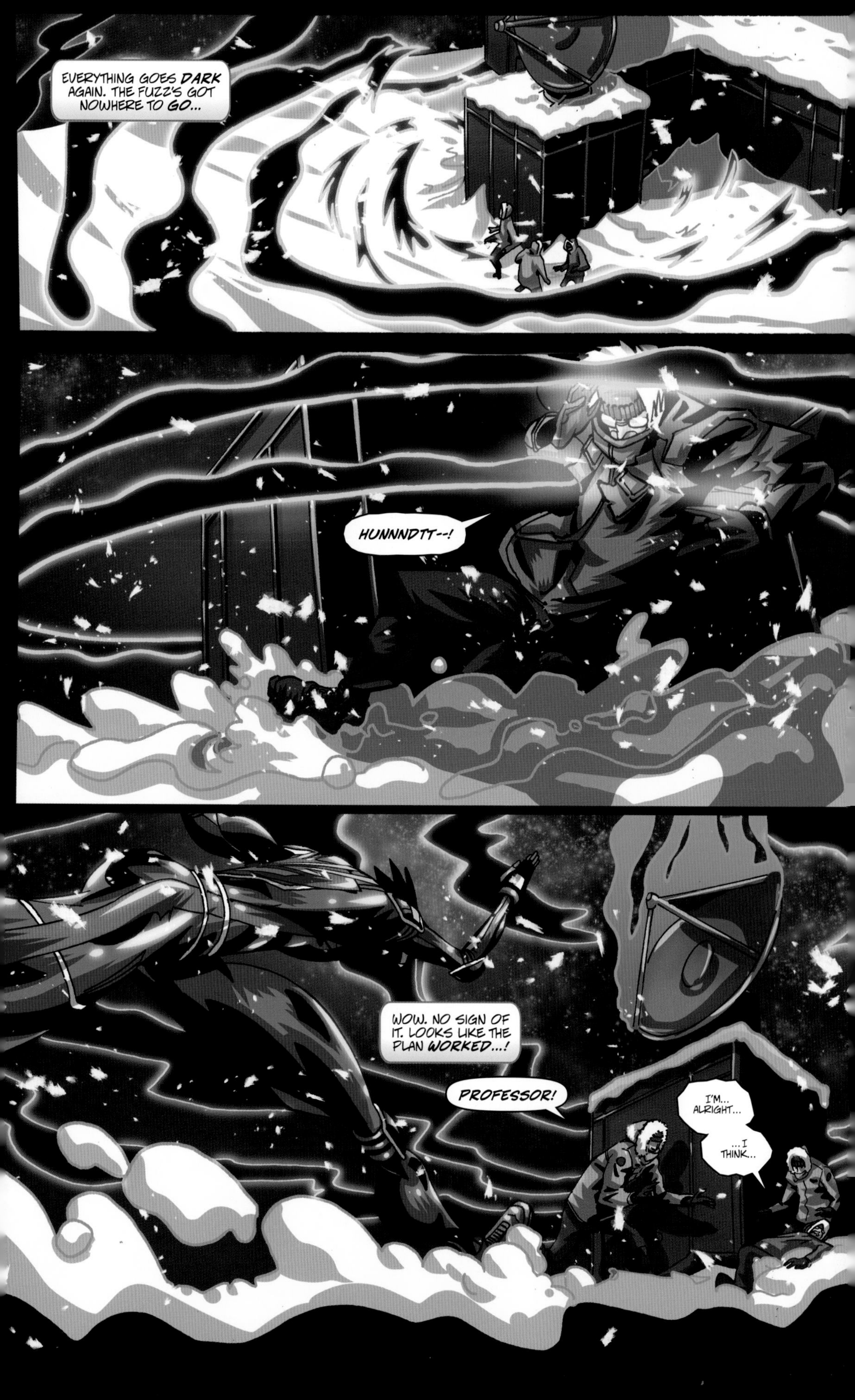
EVERYTHING GOES DARK AGAIN. THE FUZZ'S GOT NOWHERE TO GO...
HUNNNDTT--!
WOW. NO SIGN OF IT. LOOKS LIKE THE PLAN WORKED...!
PROFESSOR!
I'M... ALRIGHT...
...I THINK...

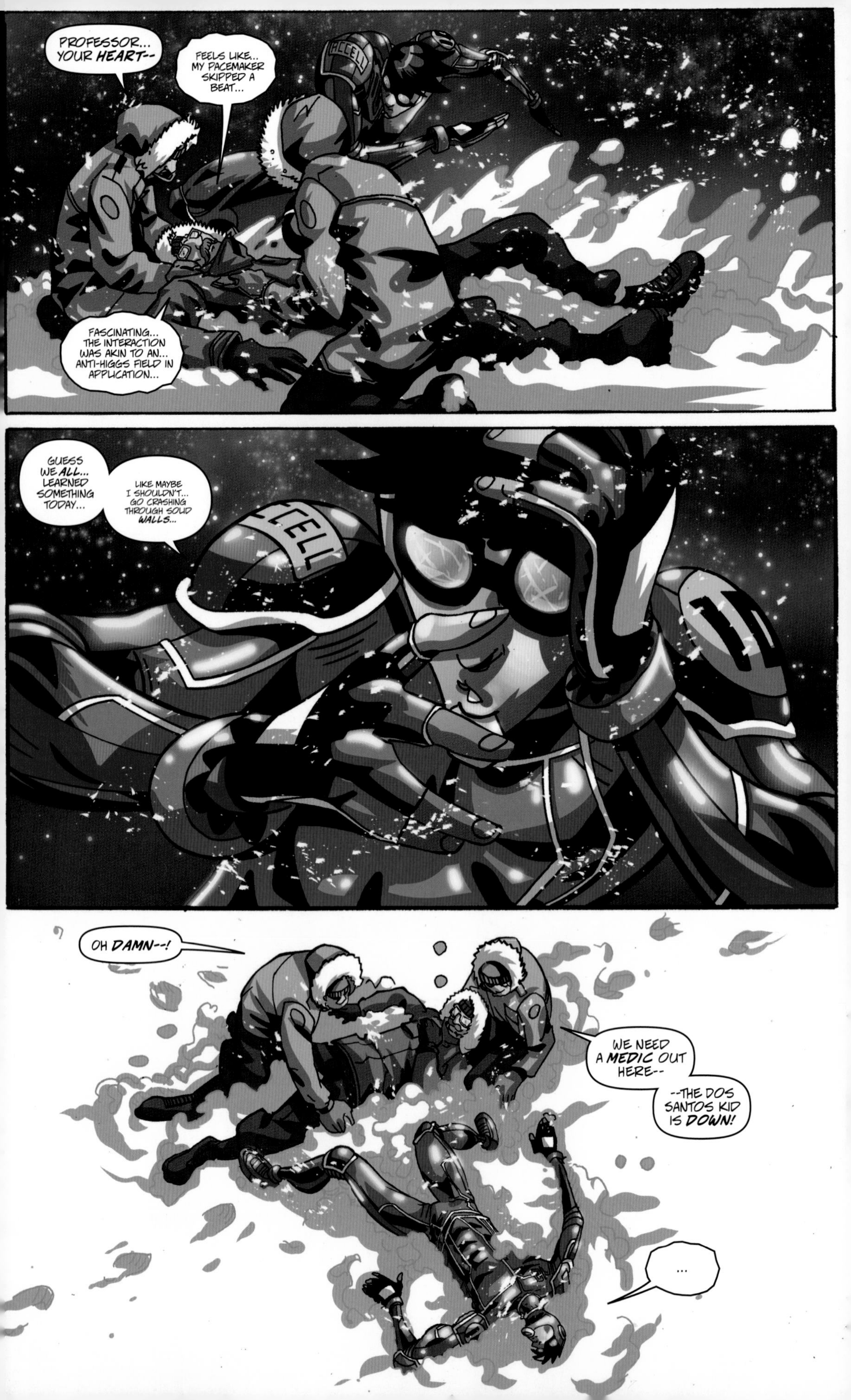
PROFESSOR... YOUR HEART--
FEELS LIKE... MY PACEMAKER SKIPPED A BEAT...
FASCINATING... THE INTERACTION WAS AKIN TO AN... ANTI-HIGGS FIELD IN APPLICATION...
GUESS WE ALL... LEARNED SOMETHING TODAY...
LIKE MAYBE I SHOULDN'T... GO CRASHING THROUGH SOLID WALLS...
OH DAMN--!
WE NEED A MEDIC OUT HERE--
--THE DOS SANTOS KID IS DOWN!
...

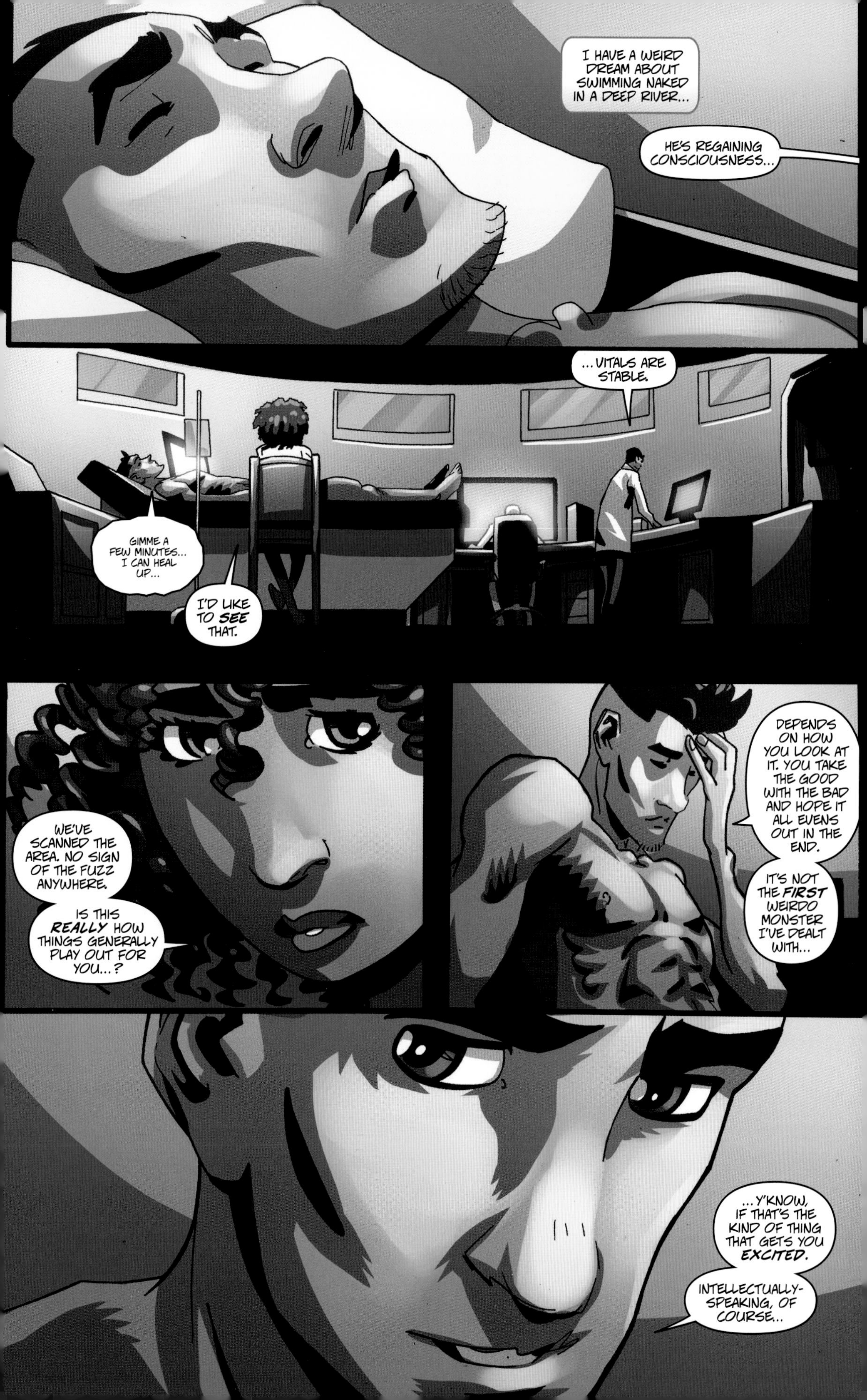

I HAVE A WEIRD DREAM ABOUT SWIMMING NAKED IN A DEEP RIVER...
HE'S REGAINING CONSCIOUSNESS...
...VITALS ARE STABLE.
GIMME A FEW MINUTES... I CAN HEAL UP...
I'D LIKE TO **SEE** THAT.
WE'VE SCANNED THE AREA. NO SIGN OF THE FUZZ ANYWHERE.
IS THIS **REALLY** HOW THINGS GENERALLY PLAY OUT FOR YOU...?
DEPENDS ON HOW YOU LOOK AT IT. YOU TAKE THE GOOD WITH THE BAD AND HOPE IT ALL EVENS OUT IN THE END.
IT'S NOT THE ***FIRST*** WEIRDO MONSTER I'VE DEALT WITH...
...Y'KNOW, IF THAT'S THE KIND OF THING THAT GETS YOU ***EXCITED.***
INTELLECTUALLY-SPEAKING, OF COURSE...

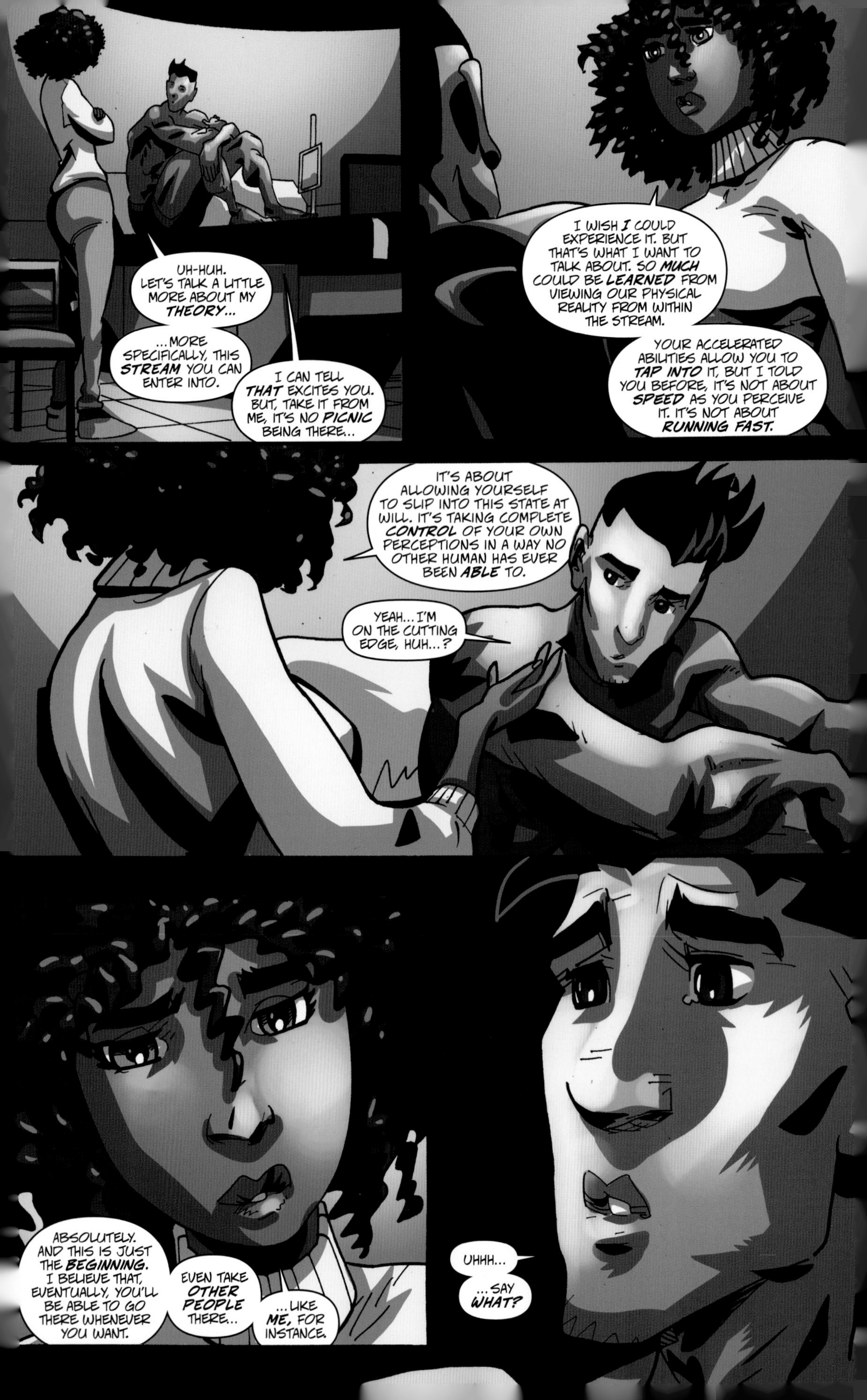
UH-HUH. LET'S TALK A LITTLE MORE ABOUT MY *THEORY*...
...MORE SPECIFICALLY, THIS *STREAM* YOU CAN ENTER INTO.
I CAN TELL *THAT* EXCITES YOU. BUT, TAKE IT FROM ME, IT'S NO *PICNIC* BEING THERE...
I WISH *I* COULD EXPERIENCE IT. BUT THAT'S WHAT I WANT TO TALK ABOUT. SO *MUCH* COULD BE *LEARNED* FROM VIEWING OUR PHYSICAL REALITY FROM WITHIN THE STREAM.
YOUR ACCELERATED ABILITIES ALLOW YOU TO *TAP INTO* IT, BUT I TOLD YOU BEFORE, IT'S NOT ABOUT *SPEED* AS YOU PERCEIVE IT. IT'S NOT ABOUT *RUNNING FAST.*
IT'S ABOUT ALLOWING YOURSELF TO SLIP INTO THIS STATE AT WILL. IT'S TAKING COMPLETE *CONTROL* OF YOUR OWN PERCEPTIONS IN A WAY NO OTHER HUMAN HAS EVER BEEN *ABLE* TO.
YEAH... I'M ON THE CUTTING EDGE, HUH...?
ABSOLUTELY. AND THIS IS JUST THE *BEGINNING.* I BELIEVE THAT, EVENTUALLY, YOU'LL BE ABLE TO GO THERE WHENEVER YOU WANT.
EVEN TAKE *OTHER PEOPLE* THERE...
...LIKE *ME,* FOR INSTANCE.
UHHH...
...SAY *WHAT?*

CHAPTER FIVE

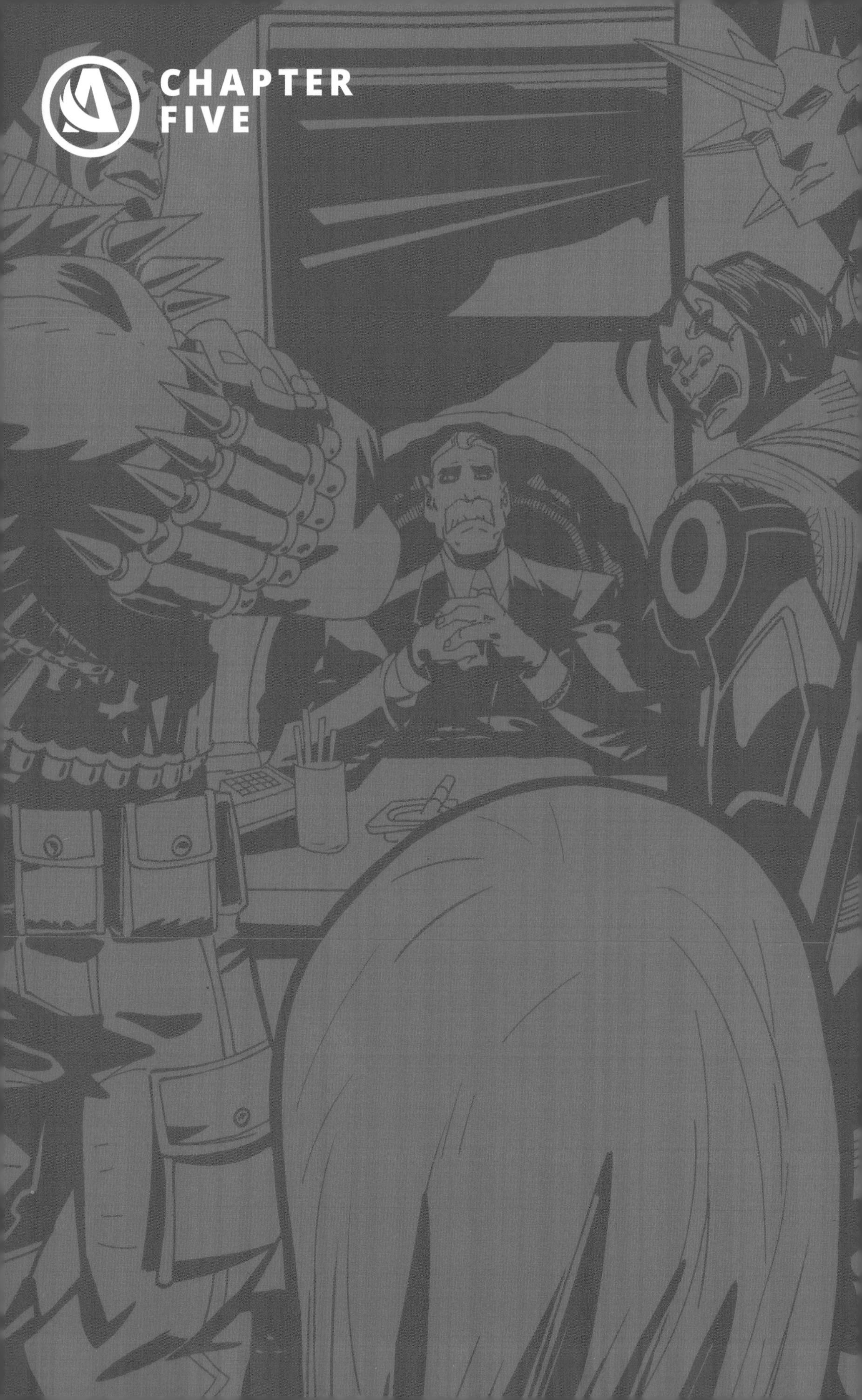

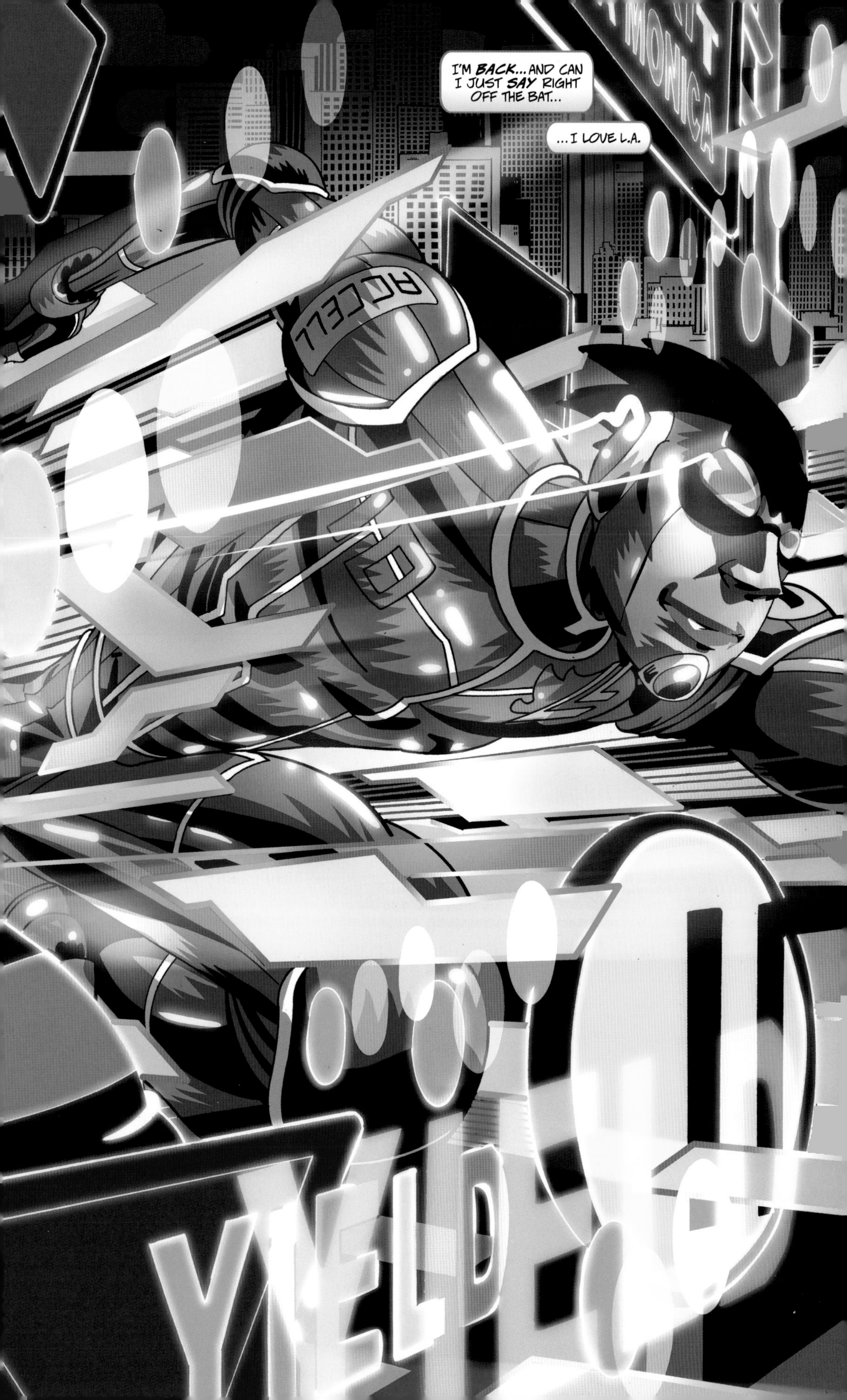
I'M BACK... AND CAN I JUST SAY RIGHT OFF THE BAT...
...I LOVE L.A.
MONICA
ACCELL
YIELD

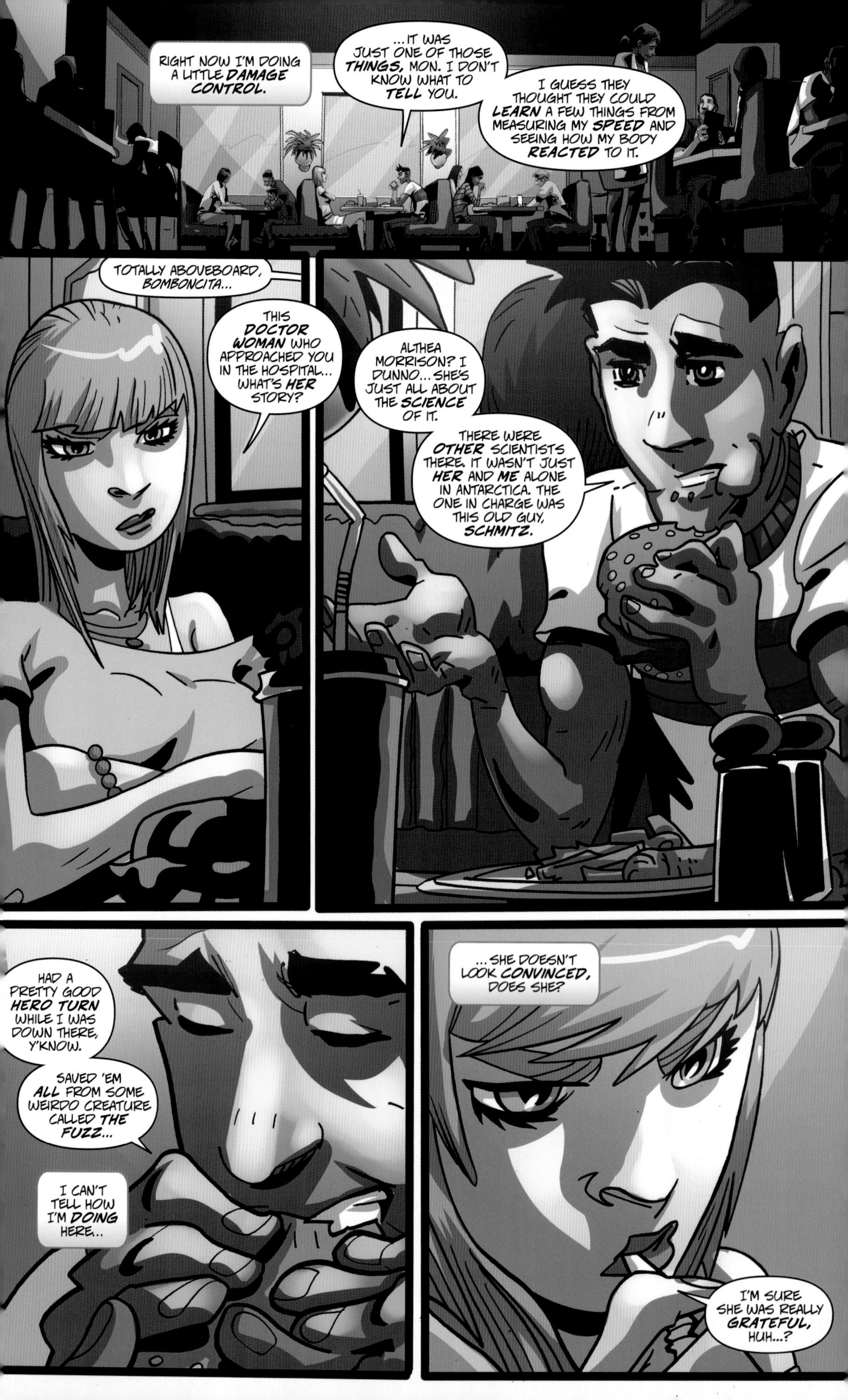
RIGHT NOW I'M DOING A LITTLE DAMAGE CONTROL.
...IT WAS JUST ONE OF THOSE THINGS, MON. I DON'T KNOW WHAT TO TELL YOU.
I GUESS THEY THOUGHT THEY COULD LEARN A FEW THINGS FROM MEASURING MY SPEED AND SEEING HOW MY BODY REACTED TO IT.
TOTALLY ABOVEBOARD, BOMBONCITA...
THIS DOCTOR WOMAN WHO APPROACHED YOU IN THE HOSPITAL... WHAT'S HER STORY?
ALTHEA MORRISON? I DUNNO... SHE'S JUST ALL ABOUT THE SCIENCE OF IT.
THERE WERE OTHER SCIENTISTS THERE. IT WASN'T JUST HER AND ME ALONE IN ANTARCTICA. THE ONE IN CHARGE WAS THIS OLD GUY, SCHMITZ.
HAD A PRETTY GOOD HERO TURN WHILE I WAS DOWN THERE, Y'KNOW.
SAVED 'EM ALL FROM SOME WEIRDO CREATURE CALLED THE FUZZ...
I CAN'T TELL HOW I'M DOING HERE...
...SHE DOESN'T LOOK CONVINCED, DOES SHE?
I'M SURE SHE WAS REALLY GRATEFUL, HUH...?

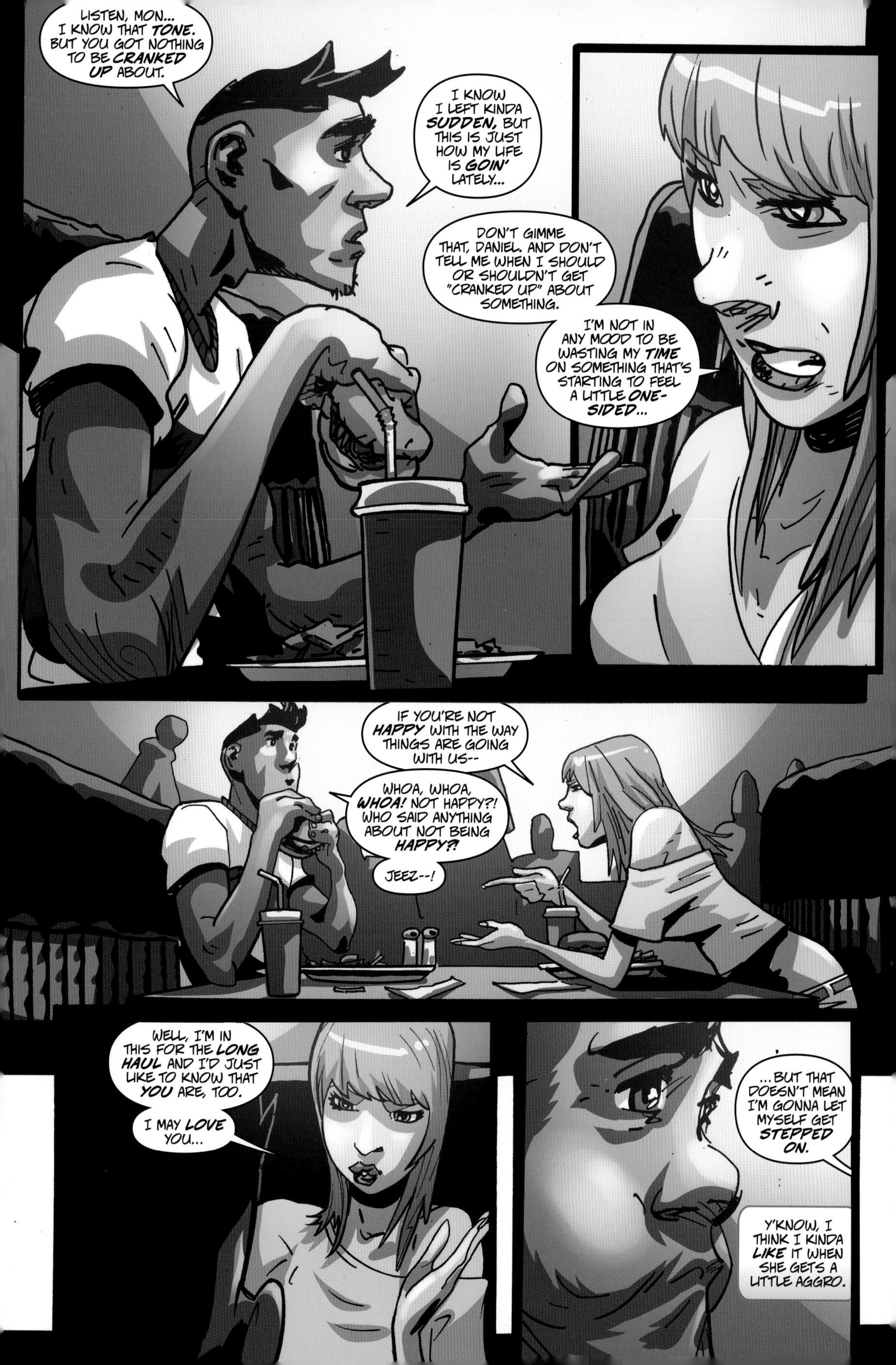
LISTEN, MON... I KNOW THAT TONE. BUT YOU GOT NOTHING TO BE CRANKED UP ABOUT.
I KNOW I LEFT KINDA SUDDEN, BUT THIS IS JUST HOW MY LIFE IS GOIN' LATELY...
DON'T GIMME THAT, DANIEL. AND DON'T TELL ME WHEN I SHOULD OR SHOULDN'T GET "CRANKED UP" ABOUT SOMETHING.
I'M NOT IN ANY MOOD TO BE WASTING MY TIME ON SOMETHING THAT'S STARTING TO FEEL A LITTLE ONE-SIDED...
IF YOU'RE NOT HAPPY WITH THE WAY THINGS ARE GOING WITH US--
WHOA, WHOA, WHOA! NOT HAPPY?! WHO SAID ANYTHING ABOUT NOT BEING HAPPY?!
JEEZ--!
WELL, I'M IN THIS FOR THE LONG HAUL AND I'D JUST LIKE TO KNOW THAT YOU ARE, TOO.
I MAY LOVE YOU...
...BUT THAT DOESN'T MEAN I'M GONNA LET MYSELF GET STEPPED ON.
Y'KNOW, I THINK I KINDA LIKE IT WHEN SHE GETS A LITTLE AGGRO.

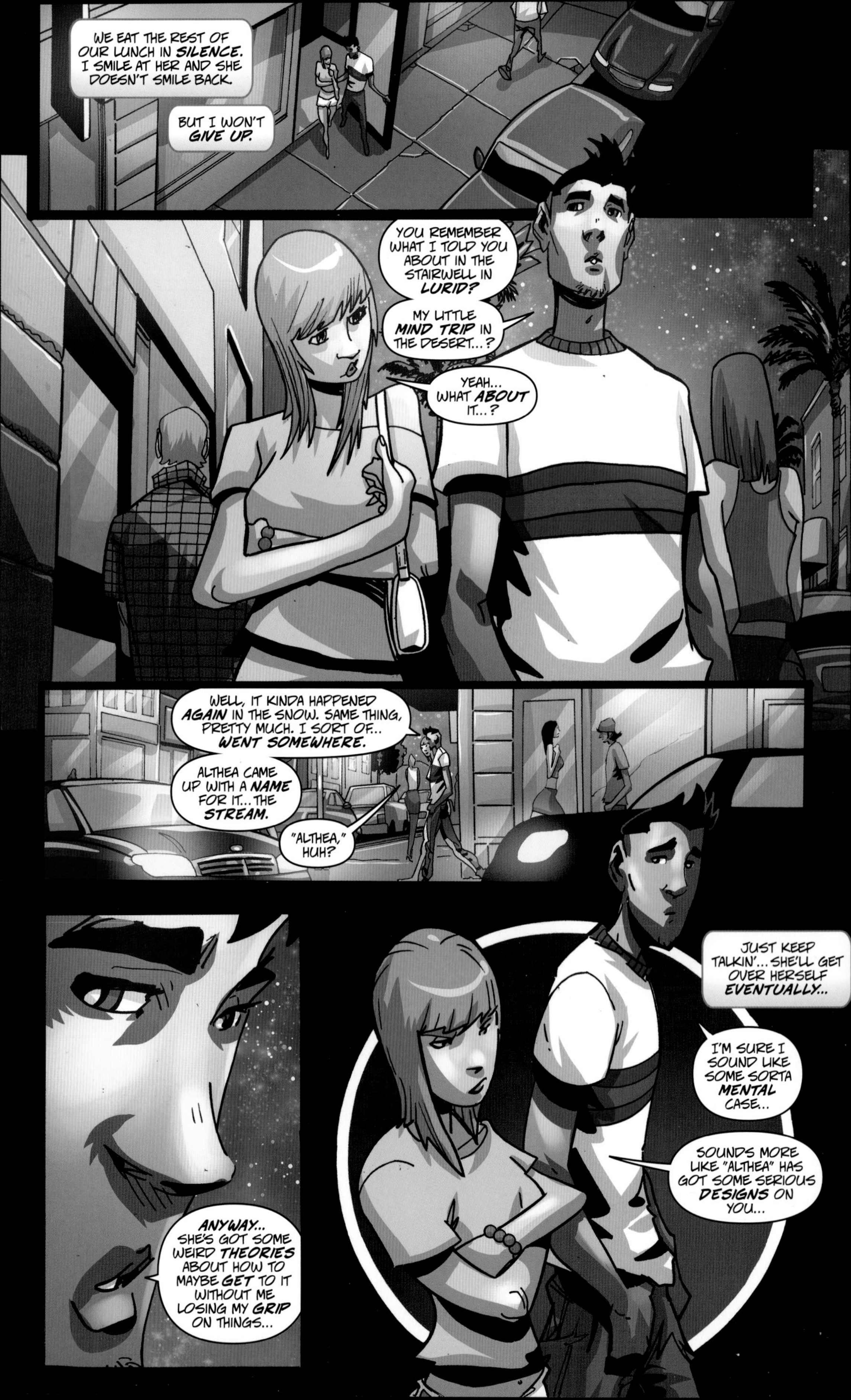
WE EAT THE REST OF OUR LUNCH IN SILENCE. I SMILE AT HER AND SHE DOESN'T SMILE BACK.
BUT I WON'T GIVE UP.
YOU REMEMBER WHAT I TOLD YOU ABOUT IN THE STAIRWELL IN LURID?
MY LITTLE MIND TRIP IN THE DESERT...?
YEAH... WHAT ABOUT IT...?
WELL, IT KINDA HAPPENED AGAIN IN THE SNOW. SAME THING, PRETTY MUCH. I SORT OF... WENT SOMEWHERE.
ALTHEA CAME UP WITH A NAME FOR IT... THE STREAM.
"ALTHEA," HUH?
JUST KEEP TALKIN'... SHE'LL GET OVER HERSELF EVENTUALLY...
I'M SURE I SOUND LIKE SOME SORTA MENTAL CASE...
SOUNDS MORE LIKE "ALTHEA" HAS GOT SOME SERIOUS DESIGNS ON YOU...
ANYWAY... SHE'S GOT SOME WEIRD THEORIES ABOUT HOW TO MAYBE GET TO IT WITHOUT ME LOSING MY GRIP ON THINGS...

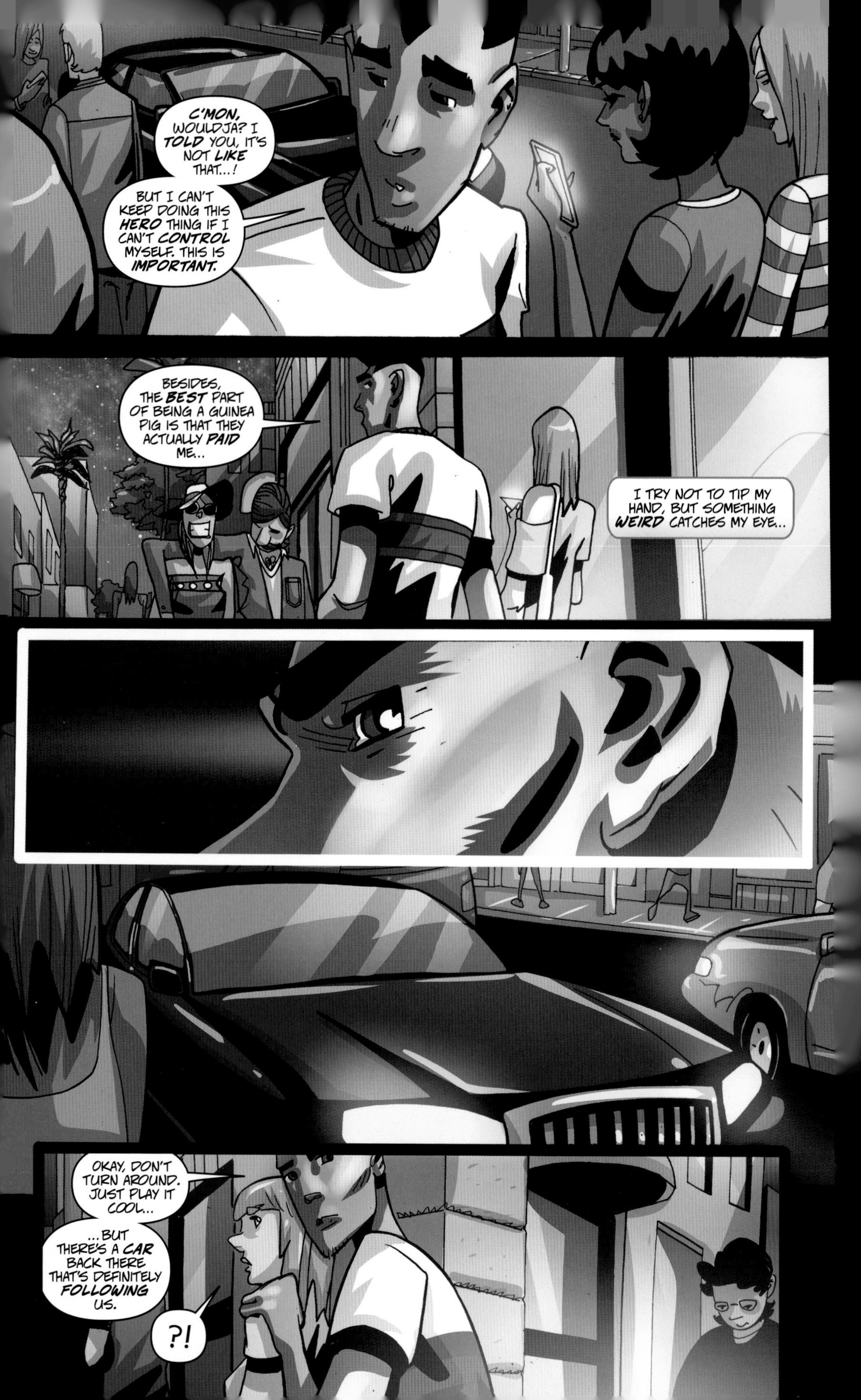
C'MON, WOULDJA? I TOLD YOU, IT'S NOT LIKE THAT...!
BUT I CAN'T KEEP DOING THIS HERO THING IF I CAN'T CONTROL MYSELF. THIS IS IMPORTANT.
BESIDES, THE BEST PART OF BEING A GUINEA PIG IS THAT THEY ACTUALLY PAID ME...
I TRY NOT TO TIP MY HAND, BUT SOMETHING WEIRD CATCHES MY EYE...
OKAY, DON'T TURN AROUND. JUST PLAY IT COOL...
...BUT THERE'S A CAR BACK THERE THAT'S DEFINITELY FOLLOWING US.
?!

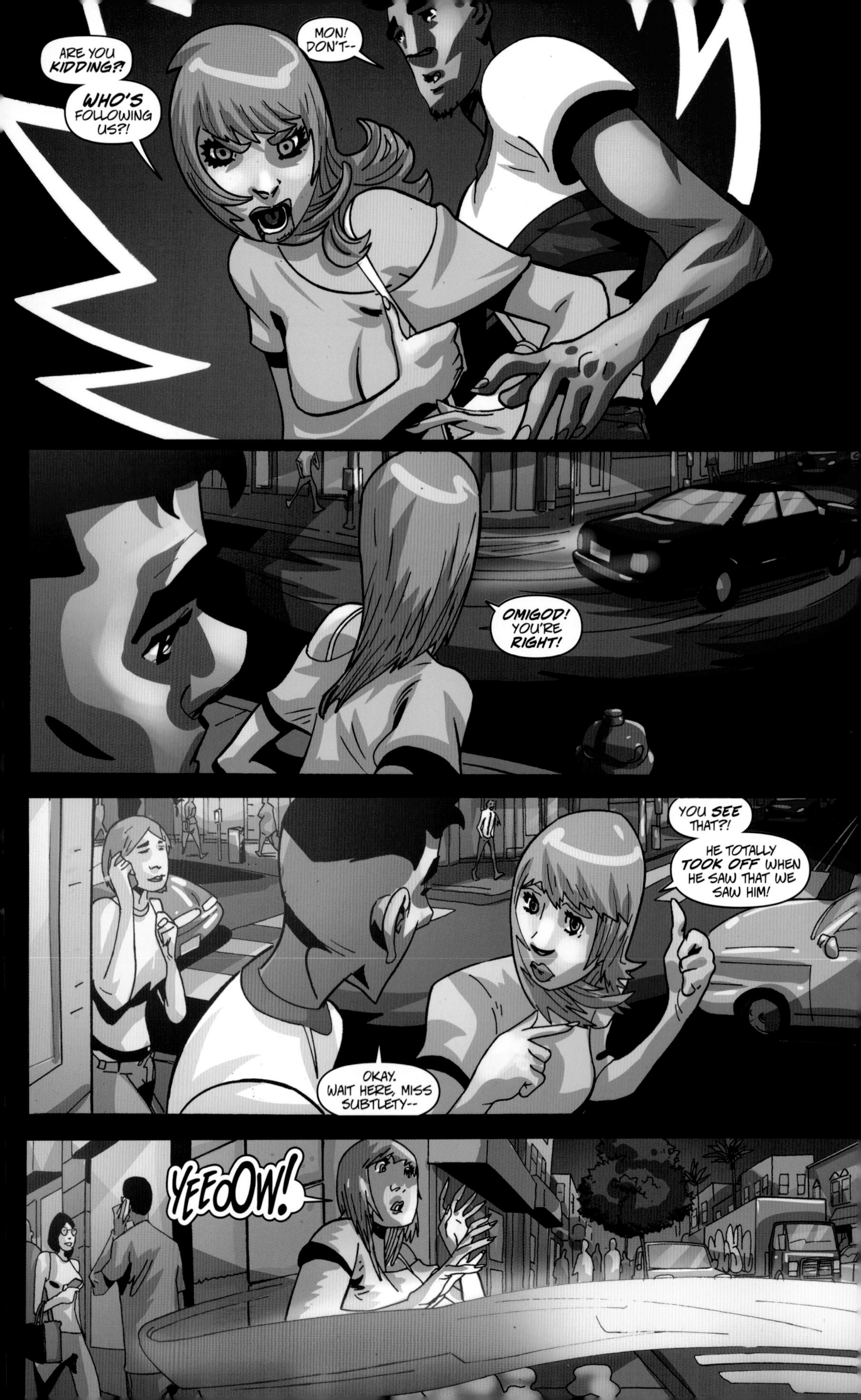
ARE YOU KIDDING?!
WHO'S FOLLOWING US?!
MON! DON'T--
OMIGOD! YOU'RE RIGHT!
YOU SEE THAT?!
HE TOTALLY TOOK OFF WHEN HE SAW THAT WE SAW HIM!
OKAY. WAIT HERE, MISS SUBTLETY--
YEEOOW!

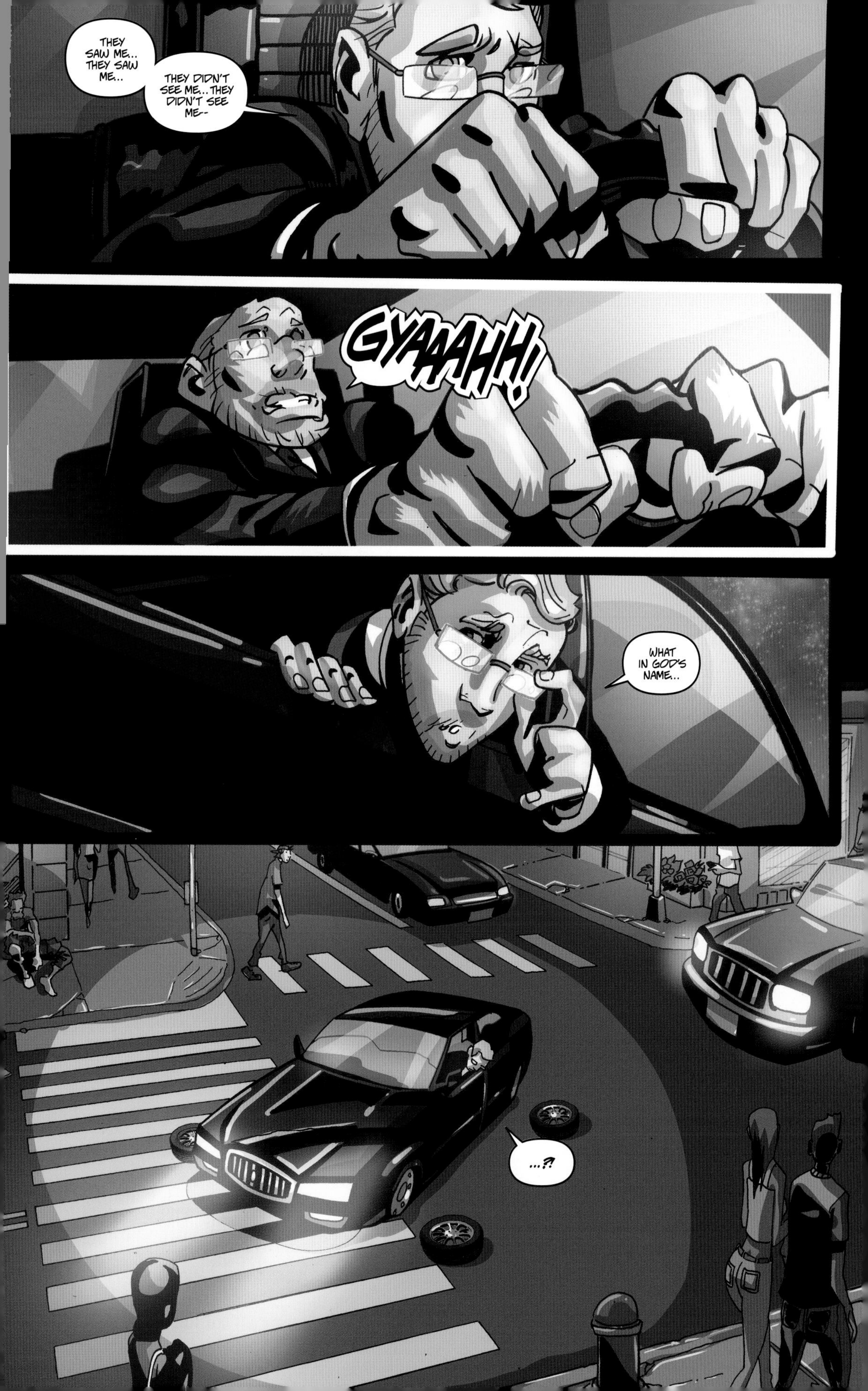
THEY SAW ME... THEY SAW ME...
THEY DIDN'T SEE ME...THEY DIDN'T SEE ME--
GYAAAHH!
WHAT IN GOD'S NAME...
...?

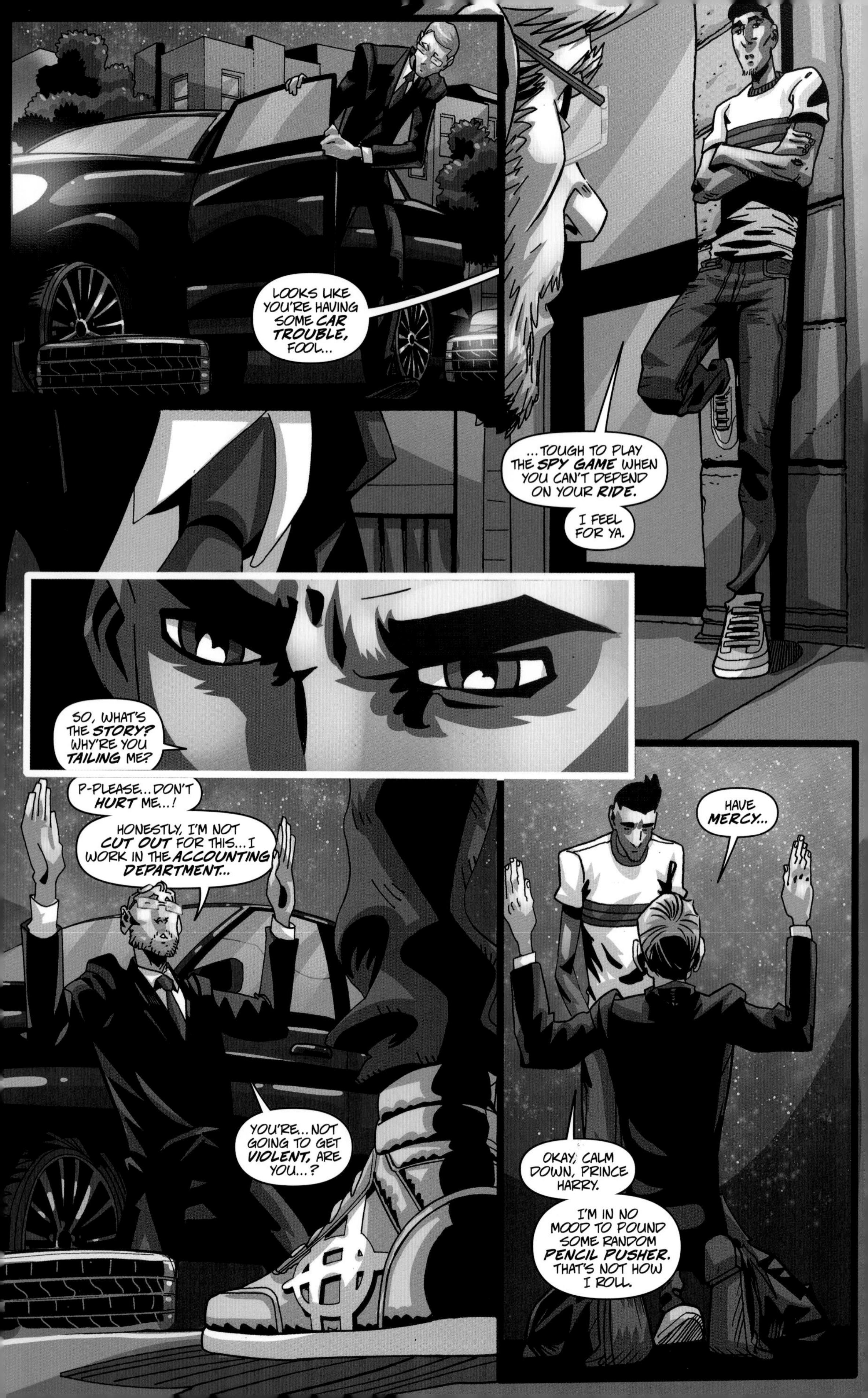
LOOKS LIKE YOU'RE HAVING SOME CAR TROUBLE, FOOL...
...TOUGH TO PLAY THE SPY GAME WHEN YOU CAN'T DEPEND ON YOUR RIDE.
I FEEL FOR YA.
SO, WHAT'S THE STORY? WHY'RE YOU TAILING ME?
P-PLEASE...DON'T HURT ME...!
HONESTLY, I'M NOT CUT OUT FOR THIS...I WORK IN THE ACCOUNTING DEPARTMENT...
YOU'RE...NOT GOING TO GET VIOLENT, ARE YOU...?
HAVE MERCY...
OKAY, CALM DOWN, PRINCE HARRY.
I'M IN NO MOOD TO POUND SOME RANDOM PENCIL PUSHER. THAT'S NOT HOW I ROLL.

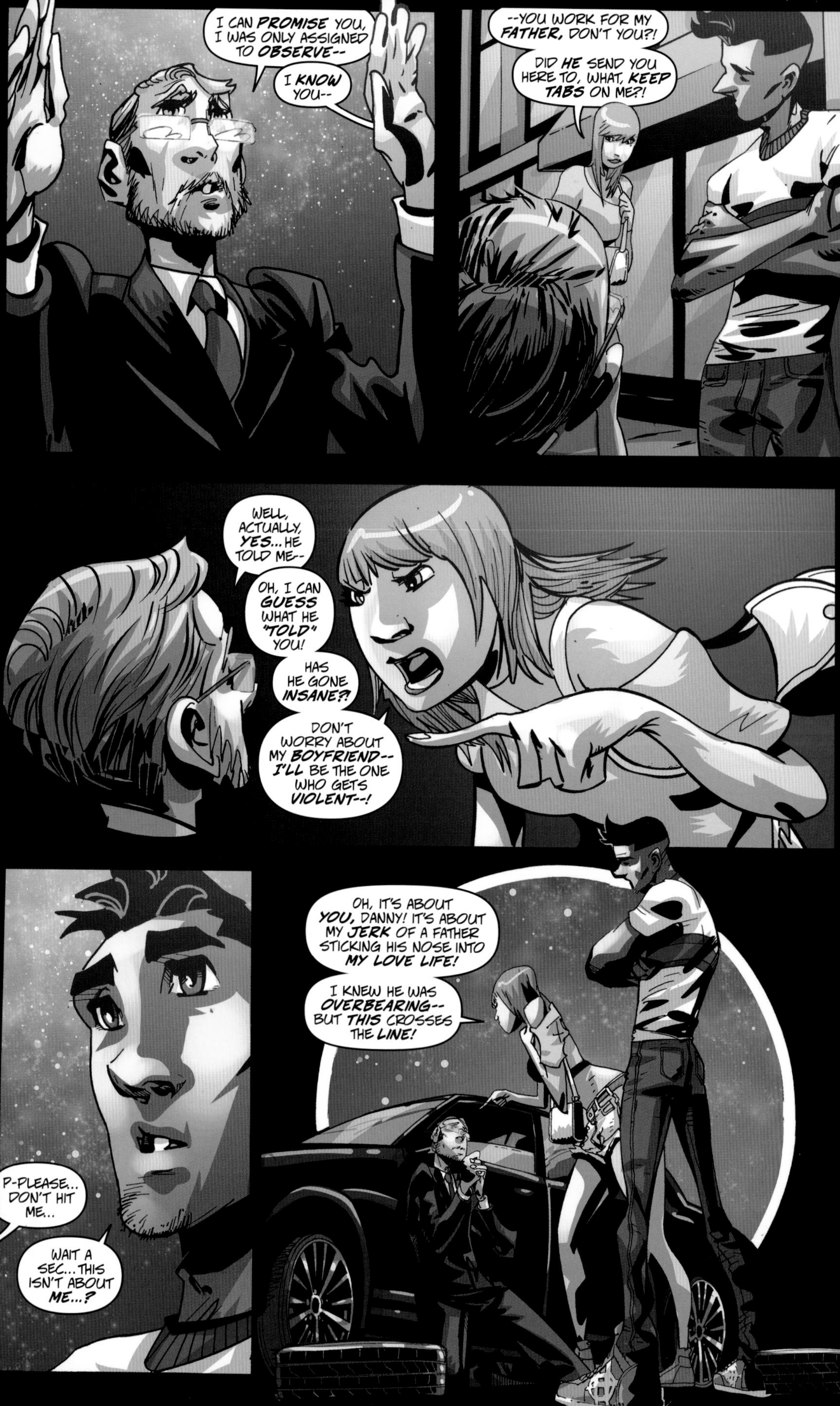
I CAN PROMISE YOU, I WAS ONLY ASSIGNED TO OBSERVE--
I KNOW YOU--
--YOU WORK FOR MY FATHER, DON'T YOU?!
DID HE SEND YOU HERE TO, WHAT, KEEP TABS ON ME?!
WELL, ACTUALLY, YES... HE TOLD ME--
OH, I CAN GUESS WHAT HE "TOLD" YOU!
HAS HE GONE INSANE?!
DON'T WORRY ABOUT MY BOYFRIEND-- I'LL BE THE ONE WHO GETS VIOLENT--!
P-PLEASE... DON'T HIT ME...
WAIT A SEC... THIS ISN'T ABOUT ME...?
OH, IT'S ABOUT YOU, DANNY! IT'S ABOUT MY JERK OF A FATHER STICKING HIS NOSE INTO MY LOVE LIFE!
I KNEW HE WAS OVERBEARING-- BUT THIS CROSSES THE LINE!

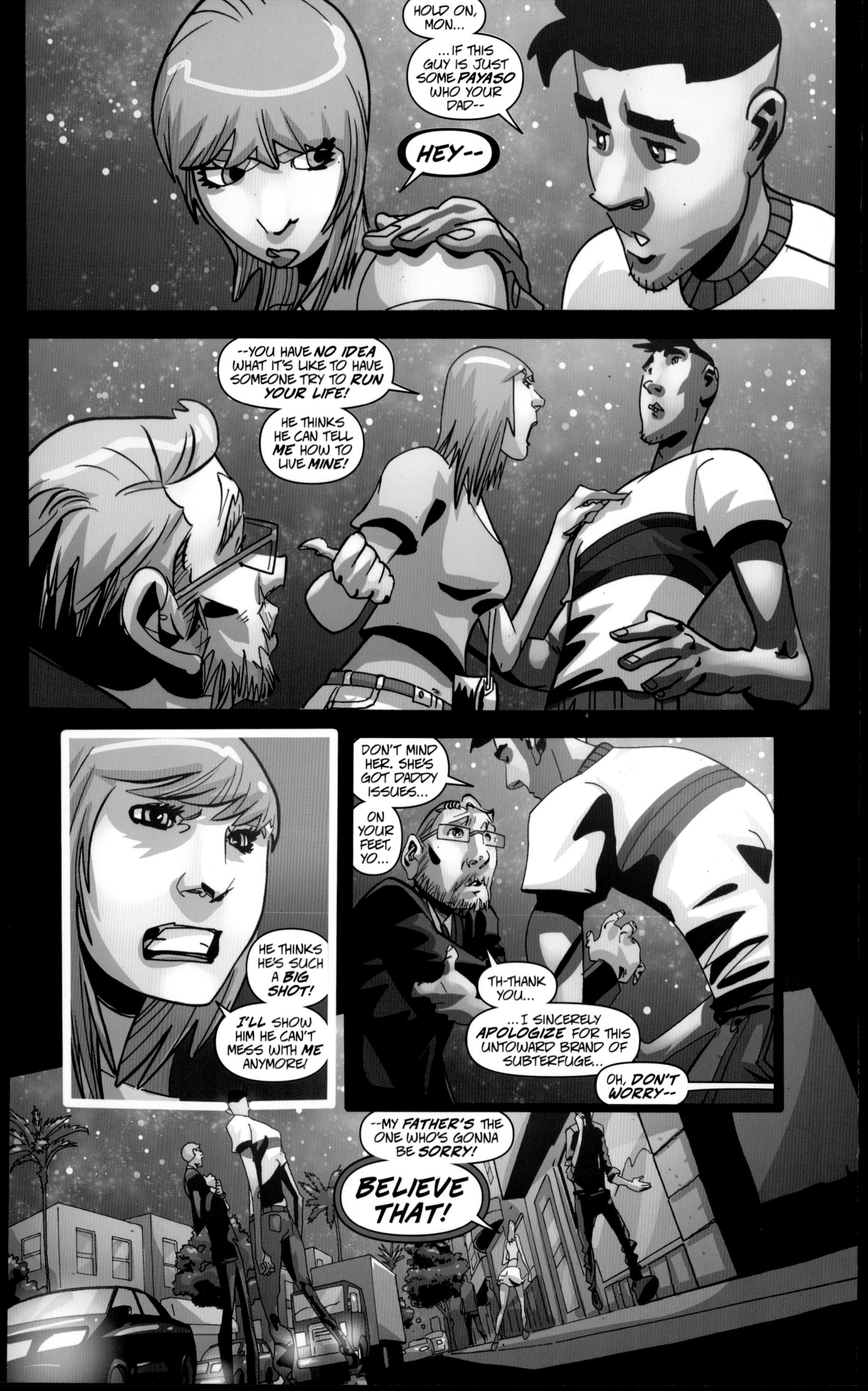
HOLD ON, MON...
...IF THIS GUY IS JUST SOME PAYASO WHO YOUR DAD--
HEY--
--YOU HAVE NO IDEA WHAT IT'S LIKE TO HAVE SOMEONE TRY TO RUN YOUR LIFE!
HE THINKS HE CAN TELL ME HOW TO LIVE MINE!
HE THINKS HE'S SUCH A BIG SHOT!
I'LL SHOW HIM HE CAN'T MESS WITH ME ANYMORE!
DON'T MIND HER. SHE'S GOT DADDY ISSUES...
ON YOUR FEET, YO...
TH-THANK YOU...
...I SINCERELY APOLOGIZE FOR THIS UNTOWARD BRAND OF SUBTERFUGE...
OH, DON'T WORRY--
--MY FATHER'S THE ONE WHO'S GONNA BE SORRY!
BELIEVE THAT!

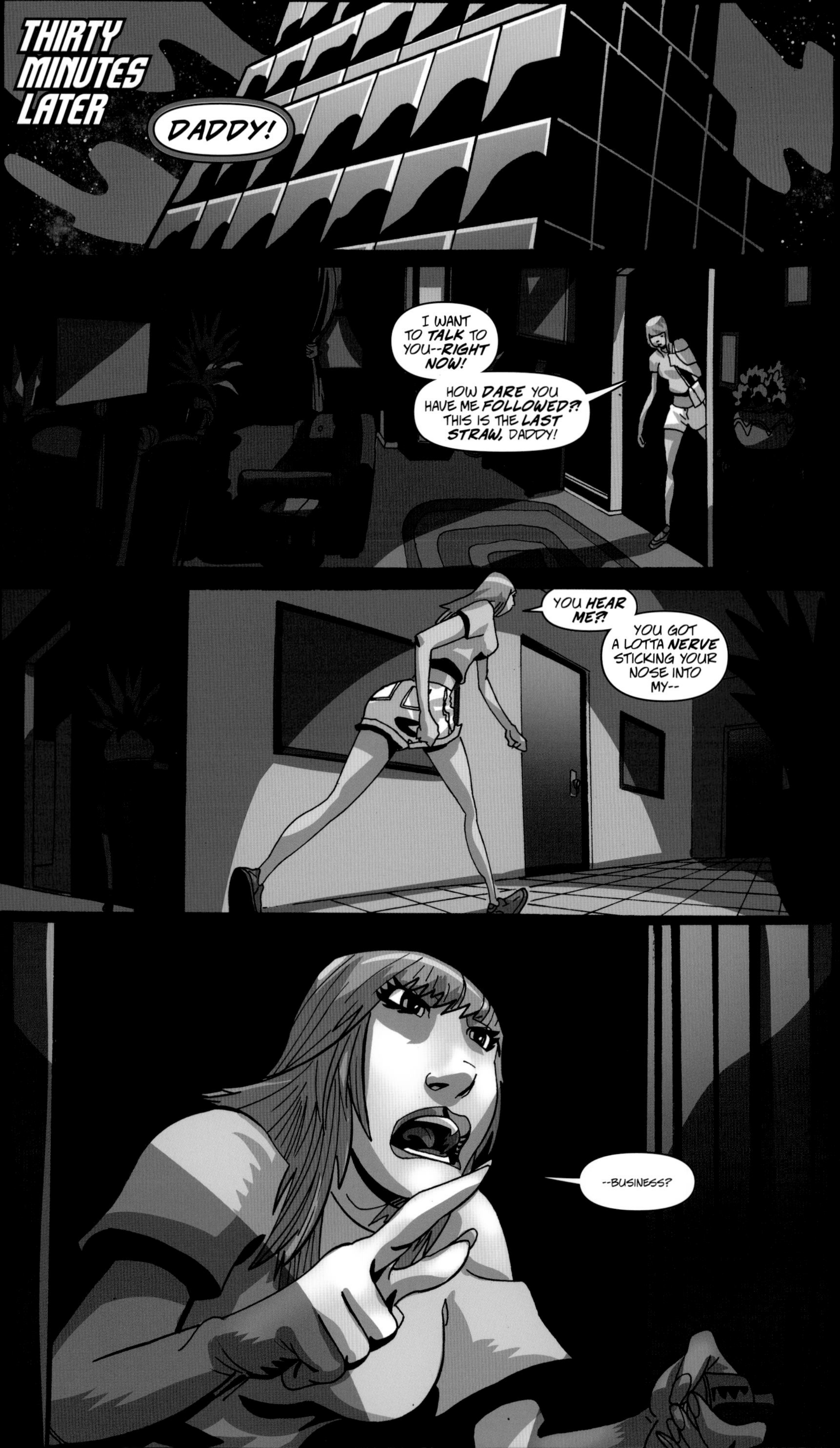
THIRTY MINUTES LATER
DADDY!
I WANT TO TALK TO YOU--RIGHT NOW!
HOW DARE YOU HAVE ME FOLLOWED?! THIS IS THE LAST STRAW, DADDY!
YOU HEAR ME?!
YOU GOT A LOTTA NERVE STICKING YOUR NOSE INTO MY--
--BUSINESS?

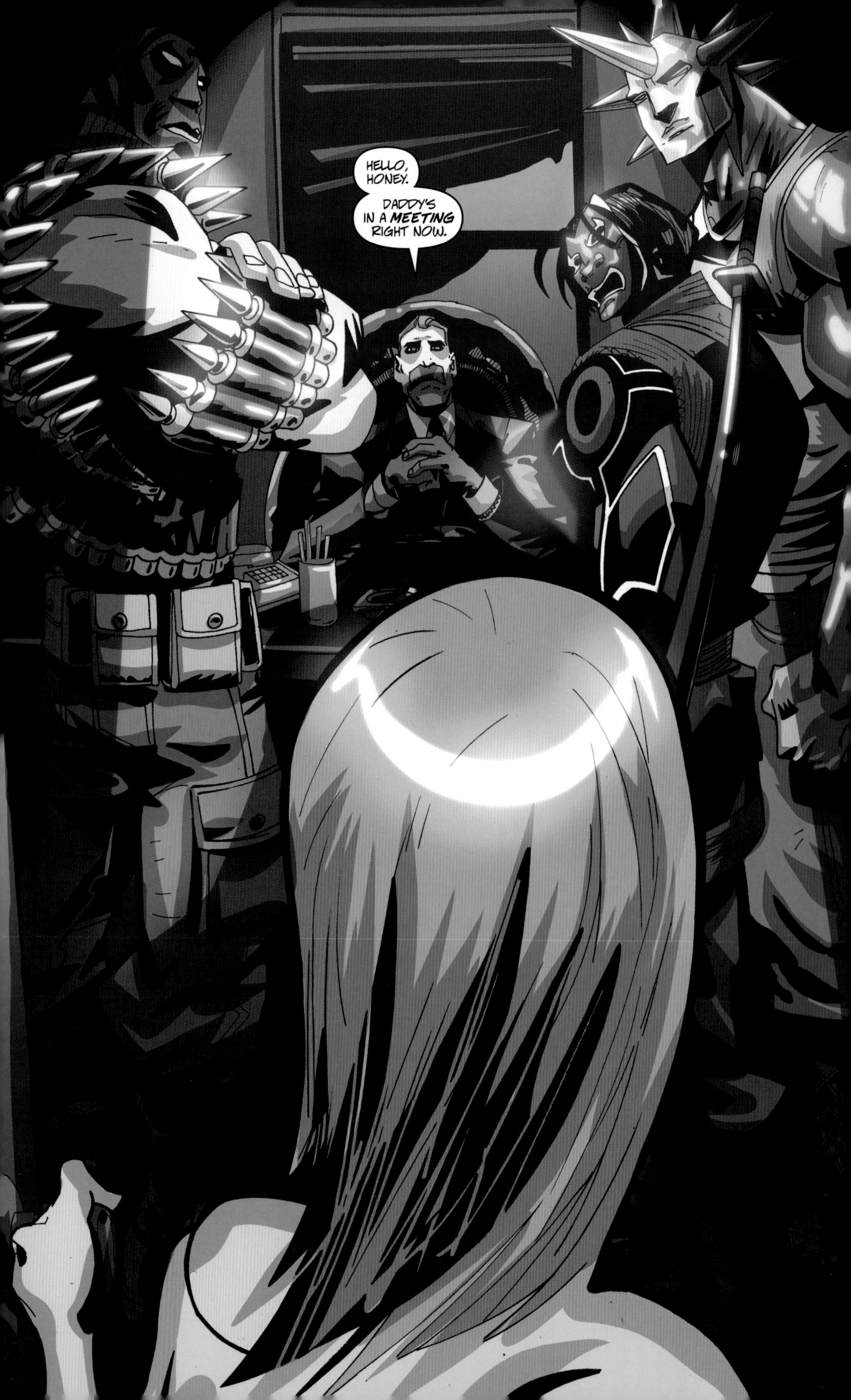
HELLO, HONEY.
DADDY'S IN A MEETING RIGHT NOW.

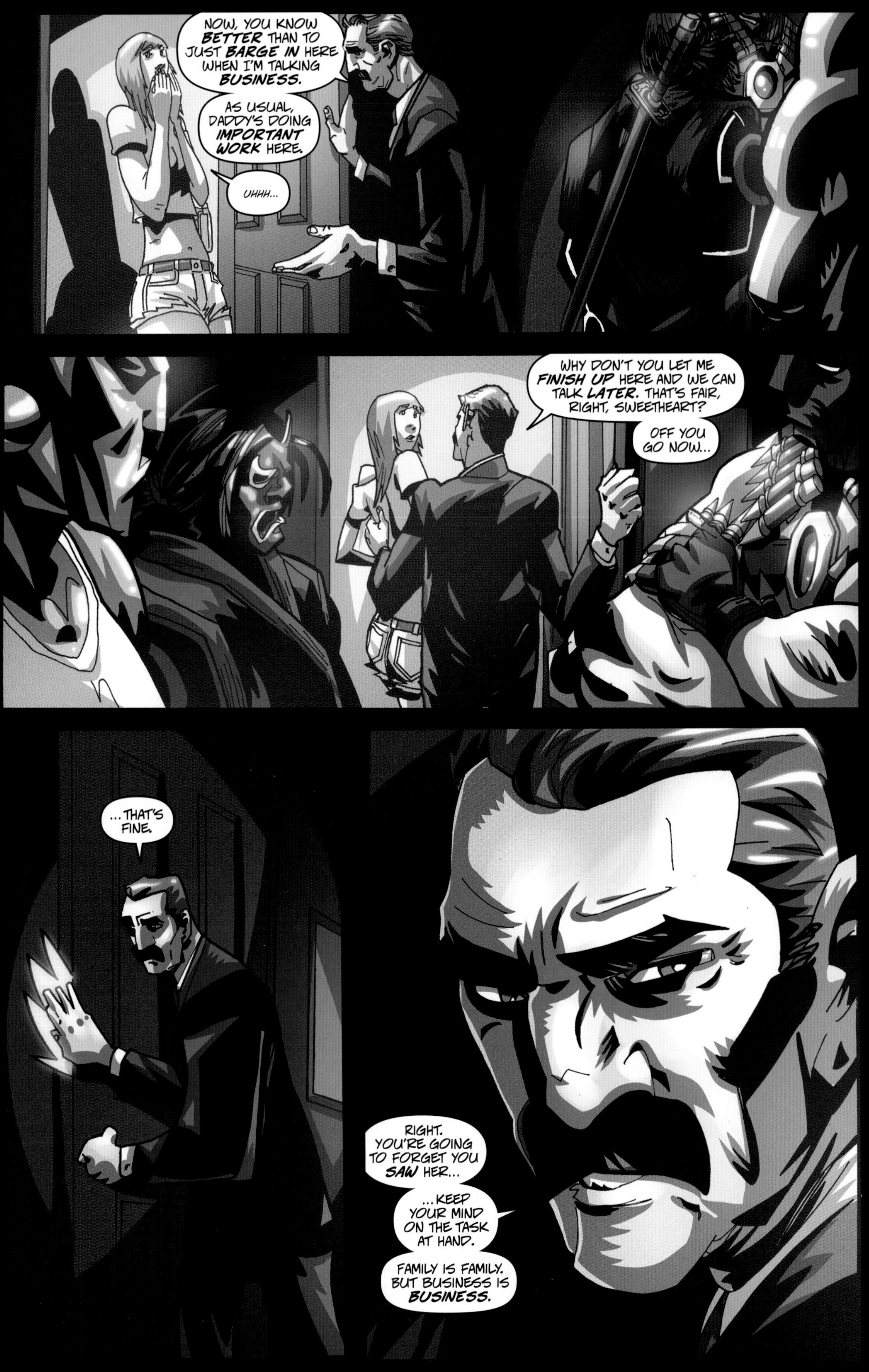

NOW, YOU KNOW BETTER THAN TO JUST BARGE IN HERE WHEN I'M TALKING BUSINESS.
AS USUAL, DADDY'S DOING IMPORTANT WORK HERE.
UHHH...
WHY DON'T YOU LET ME FINISH UP HERE AND WE CAN TALK LATER. THAT'S FAIR, RIGHT, SWEETHEART?
OFF YOU GO NOW...
...THAT'S FINE.
RIGHT. YOU'RE GOING TO FORGET YOU SAW HER...
...KEEP YOUR MIND ON THE TASK AT HAND.
FAMILY IS FAMILY. BUT BUSINESS IS BUSINESS.

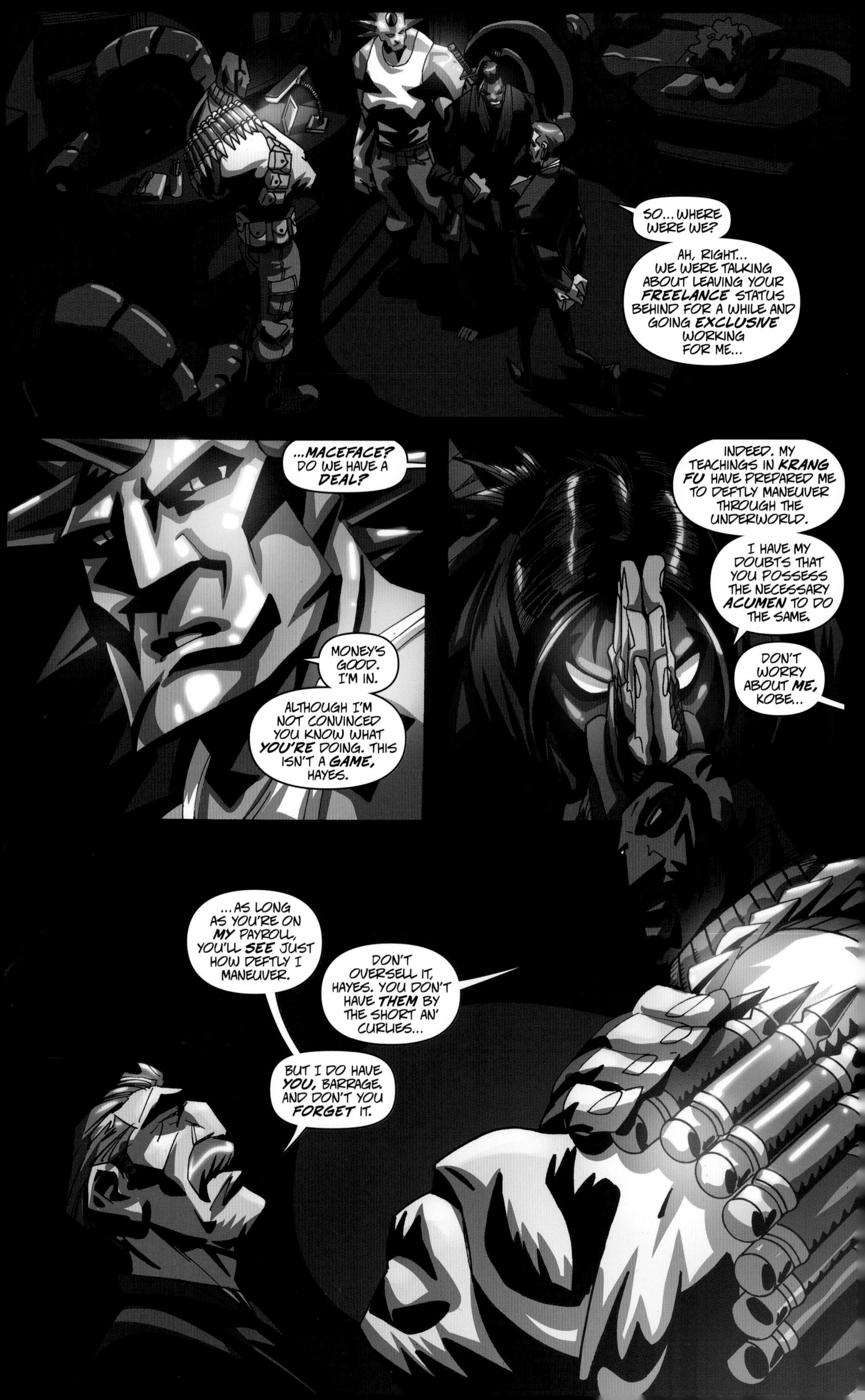
SO... WHERE WERE WE?
AH, RIGHT... WE WERE TALKING ABOUT LEAVING YOUR FREELANCE STATUS BEHIND FOR A WHILE AND GOING EXCLUSIVE WORKING FOR ME...
...MACEFACE? DO WE HAVE A DEAL?
MONEY'S GOOD. I'M IN.
ALTHOUGH I'M NOT CONVINCED YOU KNOW WHAT YOU'RE DOING. THIS ISN'T A GAME, HAYES.
INDEED. MY TEACHINGS IN KRANG FU HAVE PREPARED ME TO DEFTLY MANEUVER THROUGH THE UNDERWORLD.
I HAVE MY DOUBTS THAT YOU POSSESS THE NECESSARY ACUMEN TO DO THE SAME.
DON'T WORRY ABOUT ME, KOBE...
...AS LONG AS YOU'RE ON MY PAYROLL, YOU'LL SEE JUST HOW DEFTLY I MANEUVER.
DON'T OVERSELL IT, HAYES. YOU DON'T HAVE THEM BY THE SHORT AN' CURLIES...
BUT I DO HAVE YOU, BARRAGE. AND DON'T YOU FORGET IT.

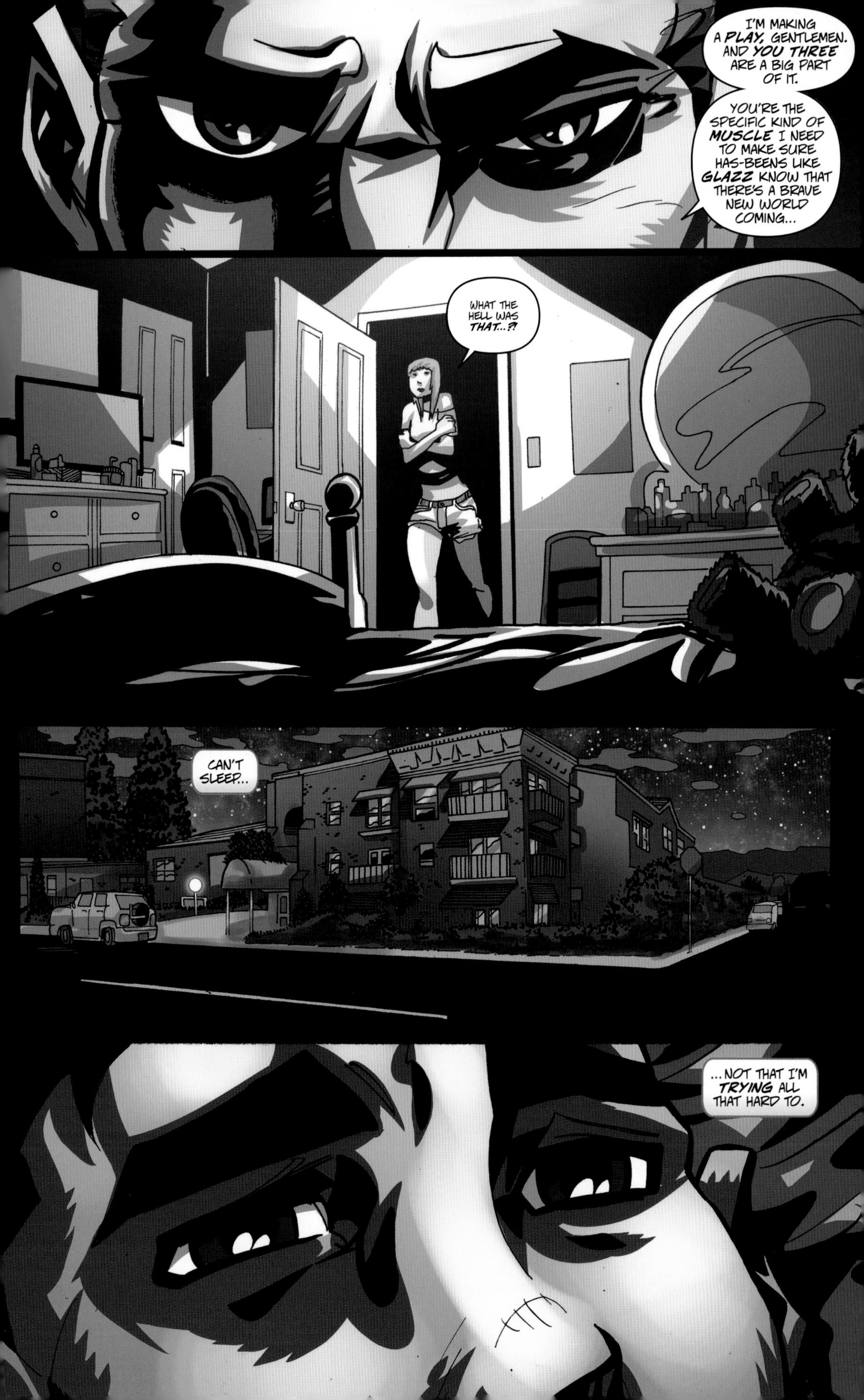
I'M MAKING A PLAY, GENTLEMEN. AND YOU THREE ARE A BIG PART OF IT.
YOU'RE THE SPECIFIC KIND OF MUSCLE I NEED TO MAKE SURE HAS-BEENS LIKE GLAZZ KNOW THAT THERE'S A BRAVE NEW WORLD COMING...
WHAT THE HELL WAS THAT...?!
CAN'T SLEEP...
...NOT THAT I'M TRYING ALL THAT HARD TO.

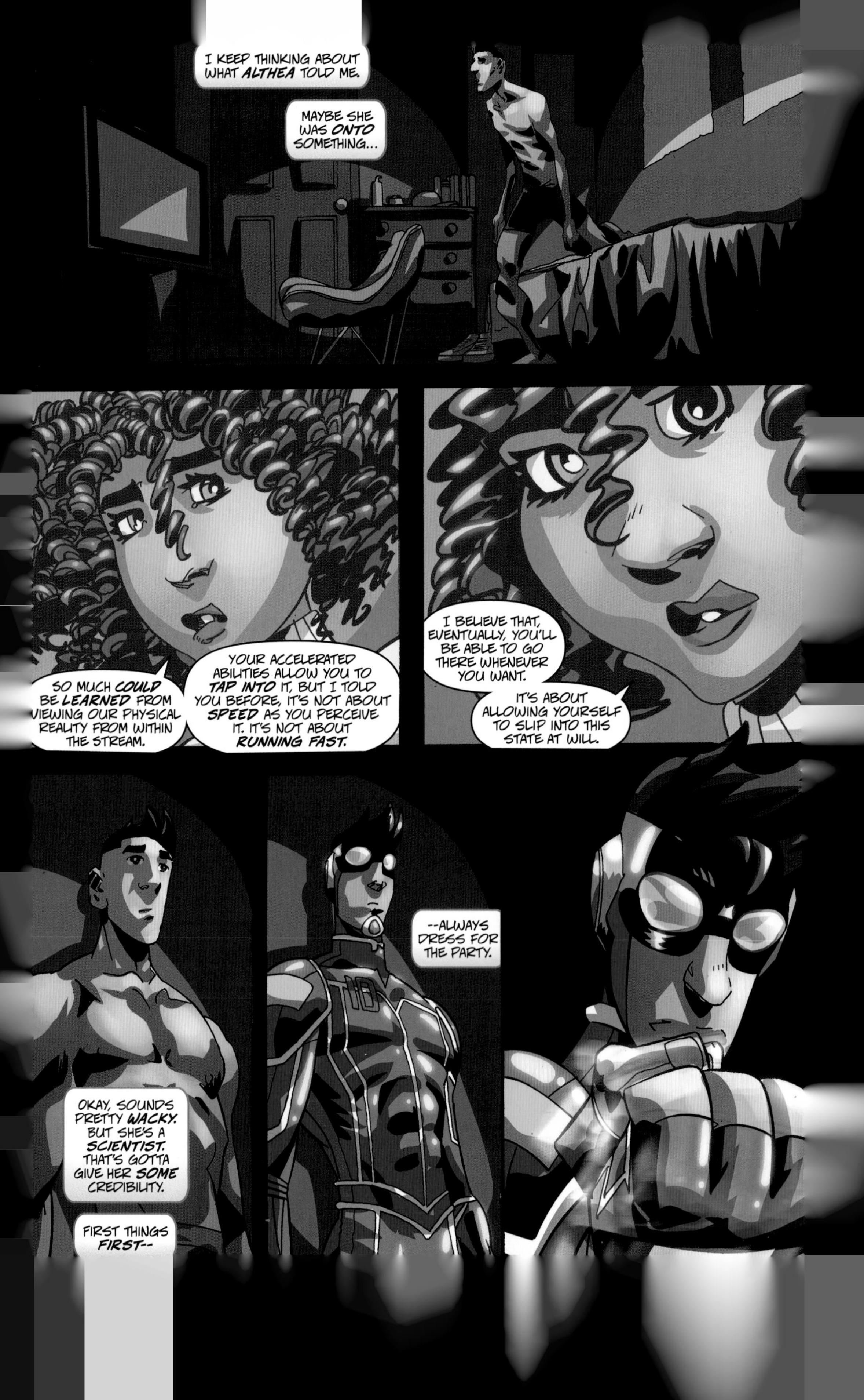
I KEEP THINKING ABOUT WHAT ALTHEA TOLD ME.
MAYBE SHE WAS ONTO SOMETHING...
SO MUCH COULD BE LEARNED FROM VIEWING OUR PHYSICAL REALITY FROM WITHIN THE STREAM.
YOUR ACCELERATED ABILITIES ALLOW YOU TO TAP INTO IT, BUT I TOLD YOU BEFORE, IT'S NOT ABOUT SPEED AS YOU PERCEIVE IT. IT'S NOT ABOUT RUNNING FAST.
I BELIEVE THAT, EVENTUALLY, YOU'LL BE ABLE TO GO THERE WHENEVER YOU WANT.
IT'S ABOUT ALLOWING YOURSELF TO SLIP INTO THIS STATE AT WILL.
OKAY, SOUNDS PRETTY WACKY. BUT SHE'S A SCIENTIST. THAT'S GOTTA GIVE HER SOME CREDIBILITY.
FIRST THINGS FIRST--
--ALWAYS DRESS FOR THE PARTY.

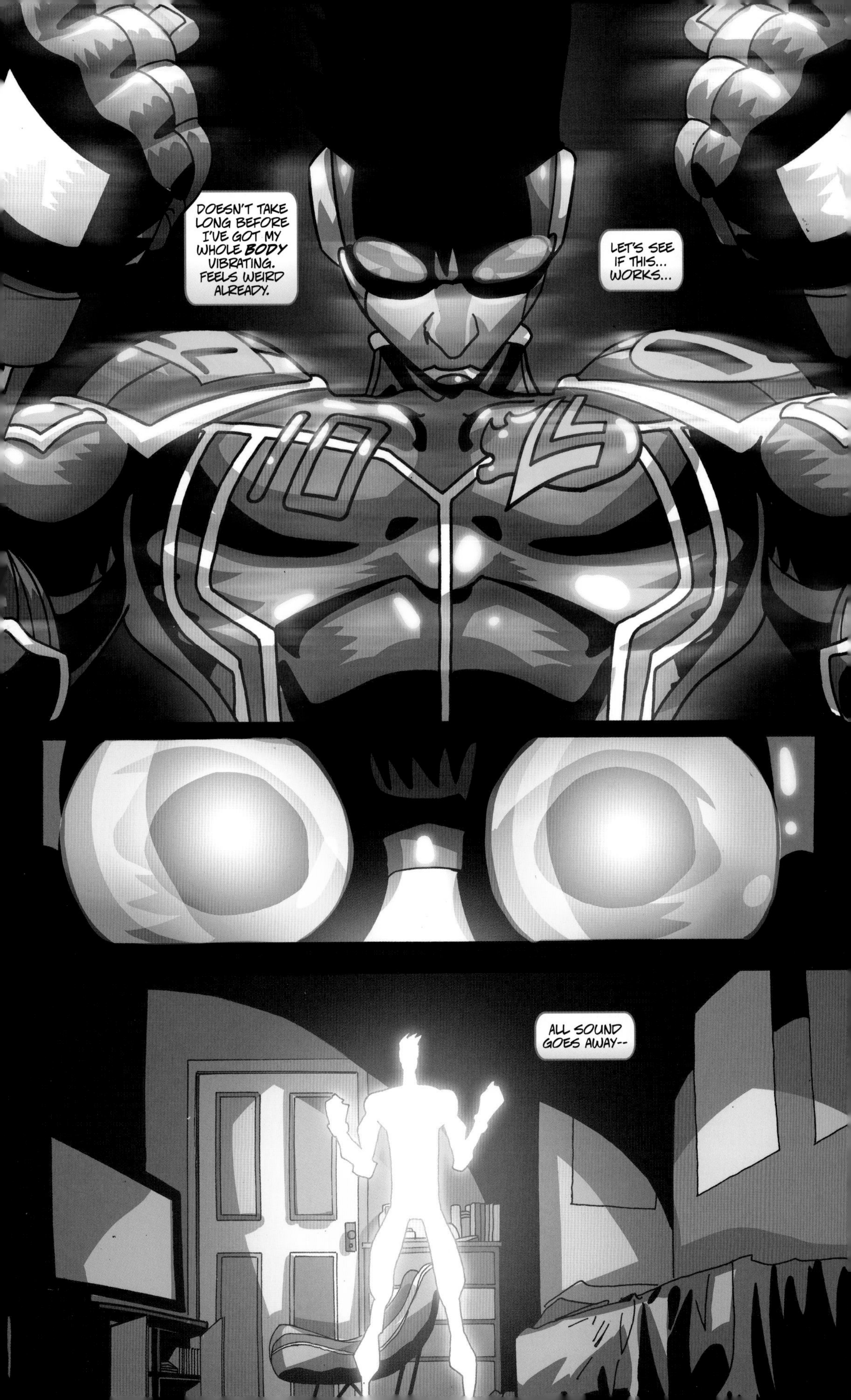
DOESN'T TAKE LONG BEFORE I'VE GOT MY WHOLE **BODY** VIBRATING. FEELS WEIRD ALREADY.
LET'S SEE IF THIS... WORKS...
ALL SOUND GOES AWAY--

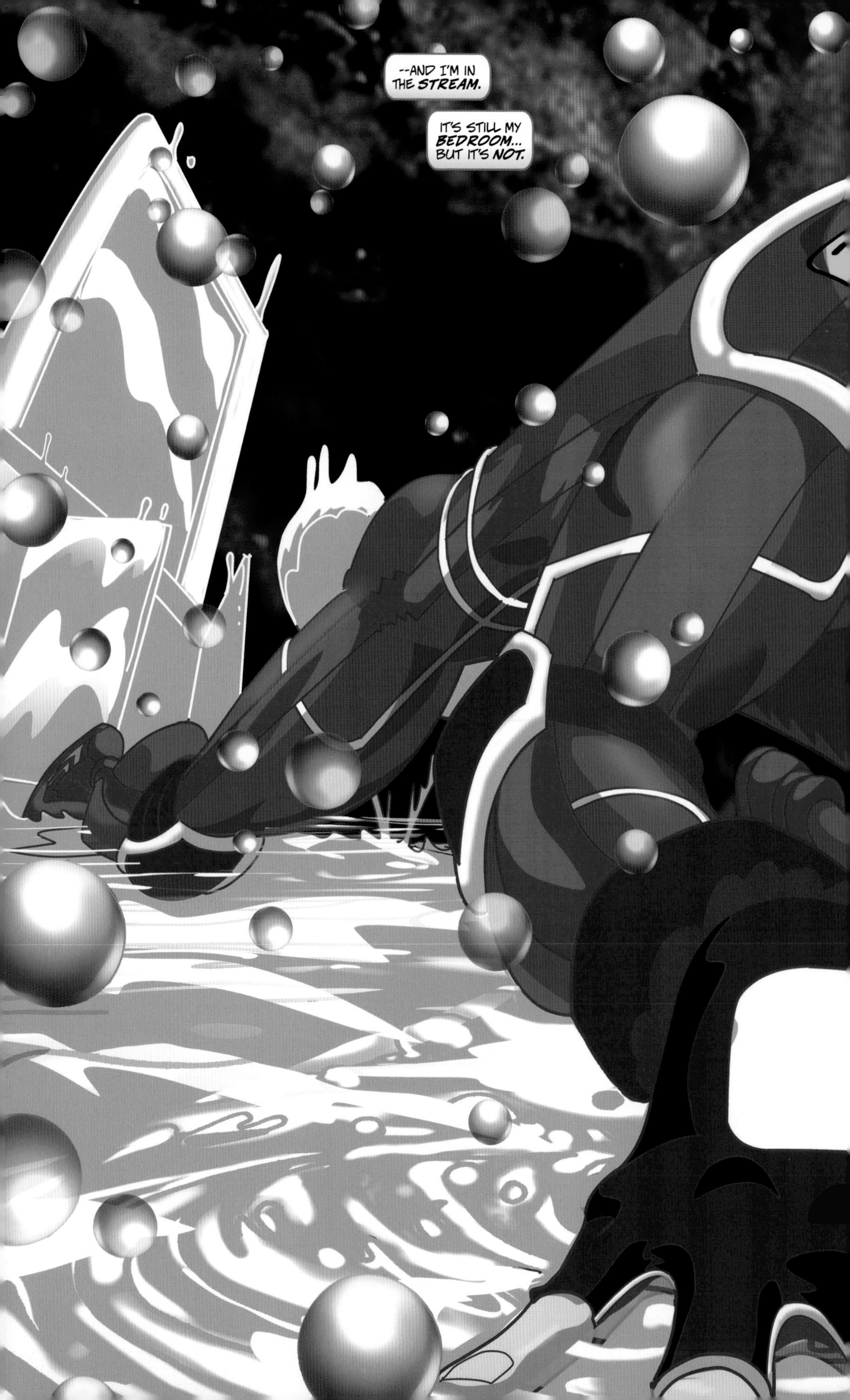
--AND I'M IN THE STREAM.
IT'S STILL MY BEDROOM... BUT IT'S NOT.

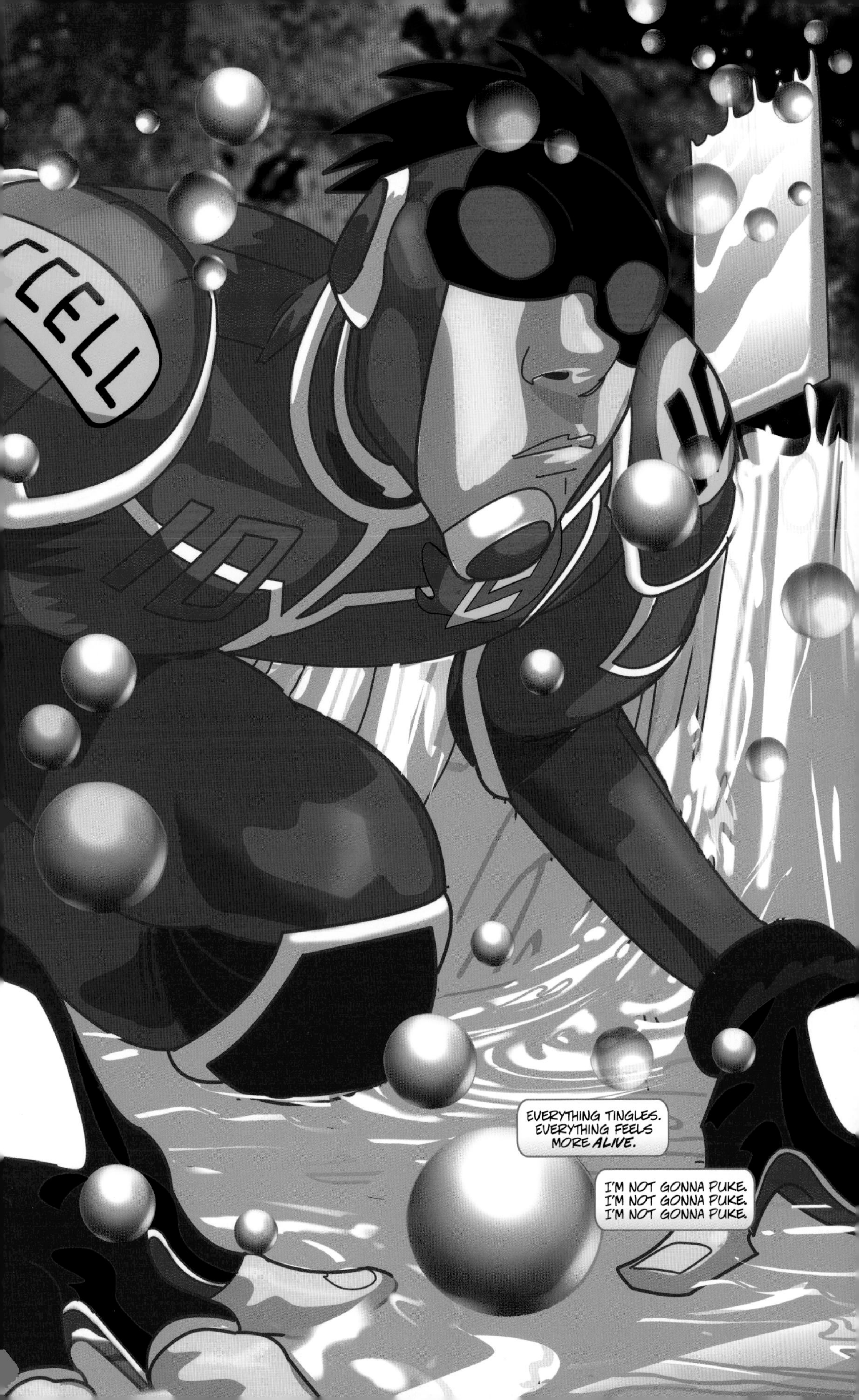
CCELL
EVERYTHING TINGLES. EVERYTHING FEELS MORE ALIVE.
I'M NOT GONNA PUKE. I'M NOT GONNA PUKE. I'M NOT GONNA PUKE.

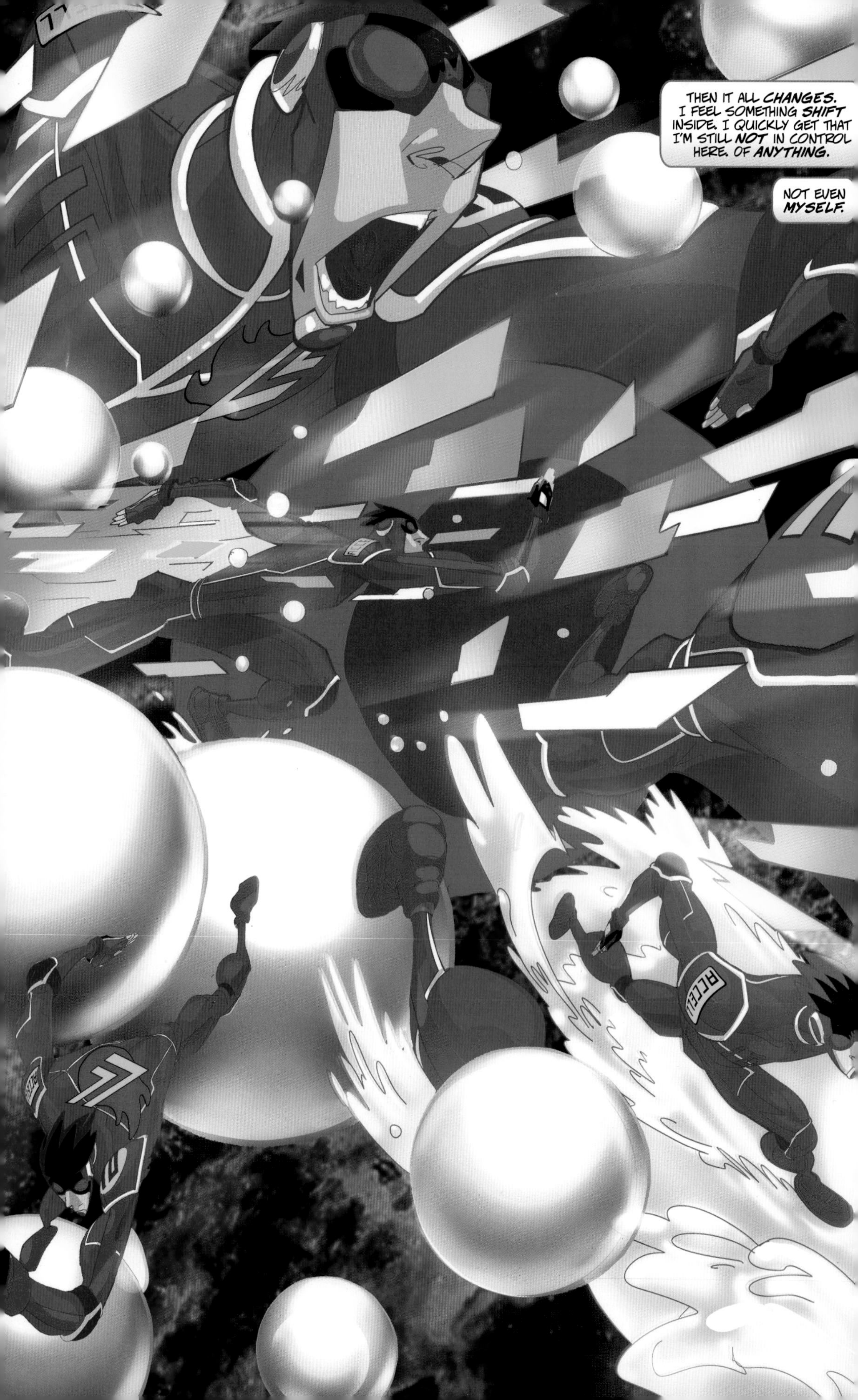
THEN IT ALL **CHANGES.** I FEEL SOMETHING **SHIFT** INSIDE. I QUICKLY GET THAT I'M STILL **NOT** IN CONTROL HERE. OF **ANYTHING.**
NOT EVEN **MYSELF.**
ACCEL
ACCEL

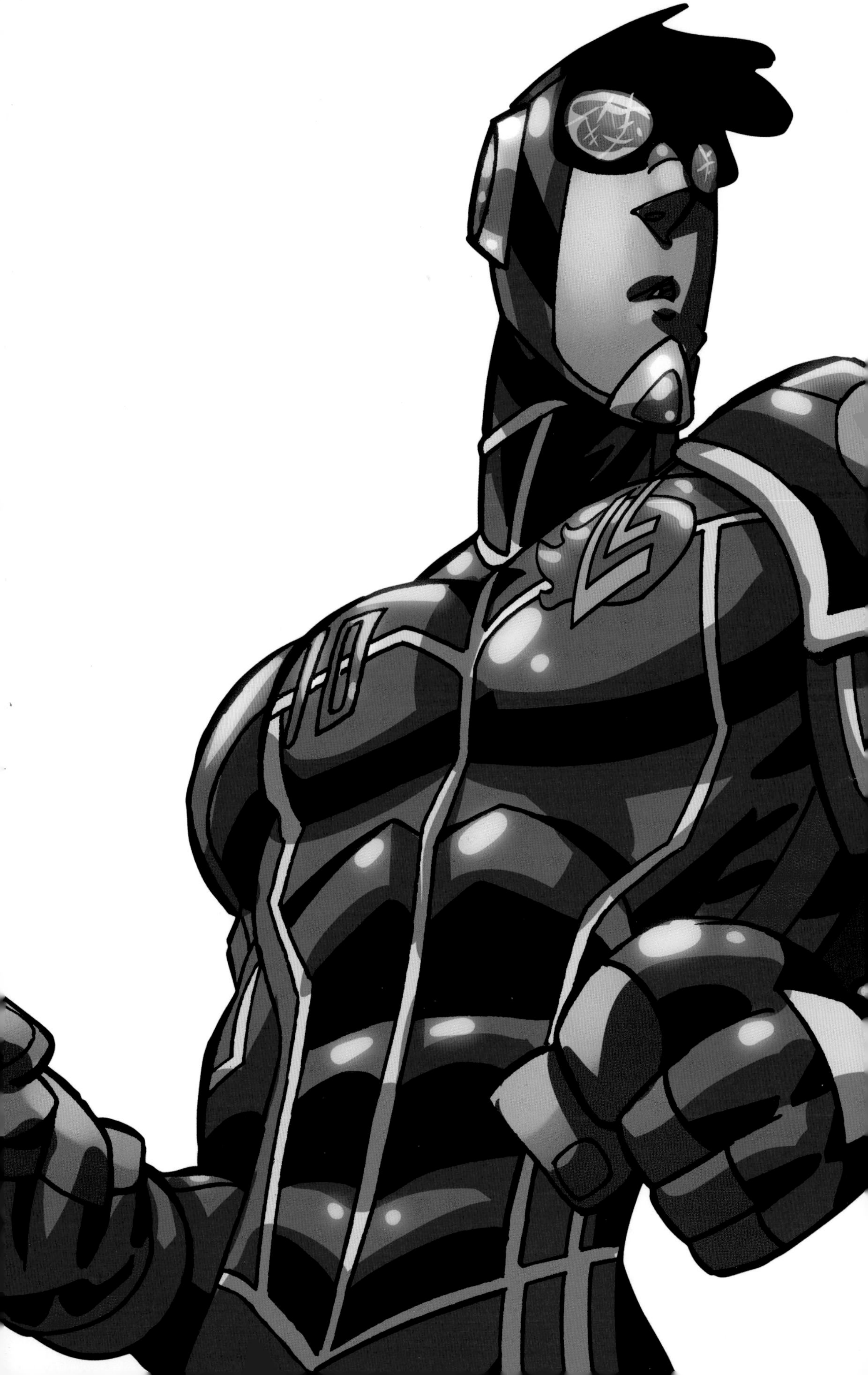

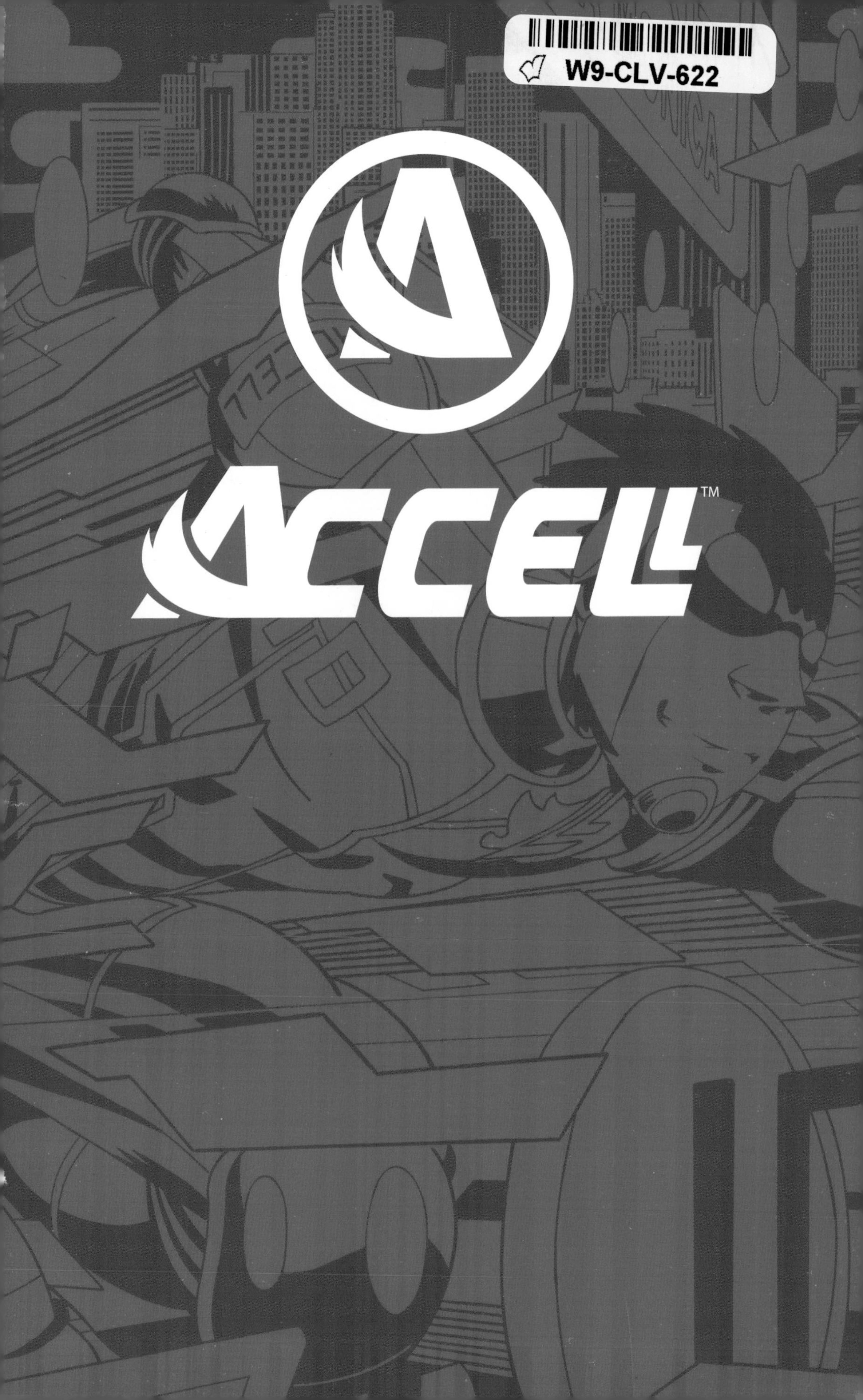

ACCELL™

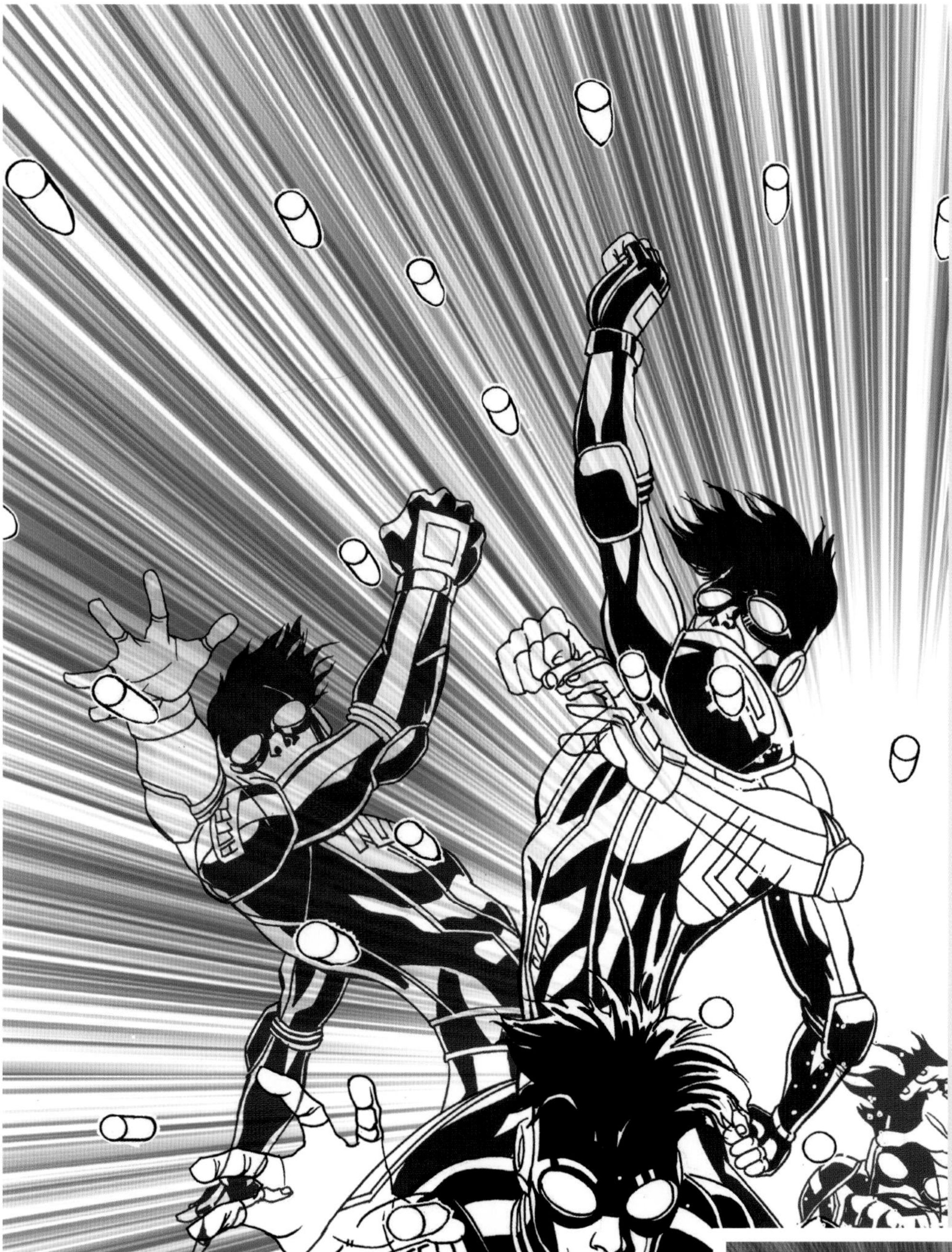
ACCELL
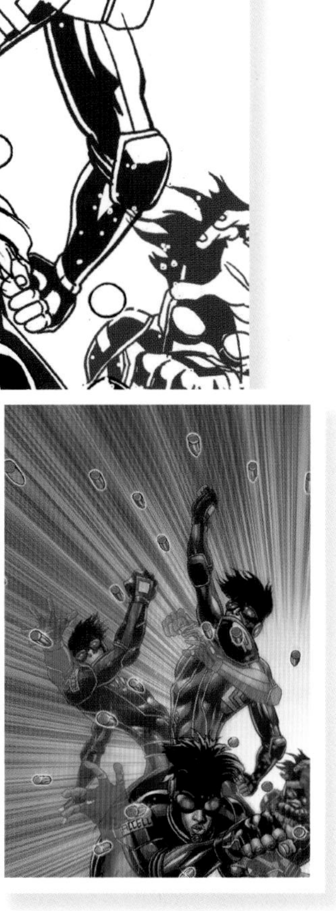

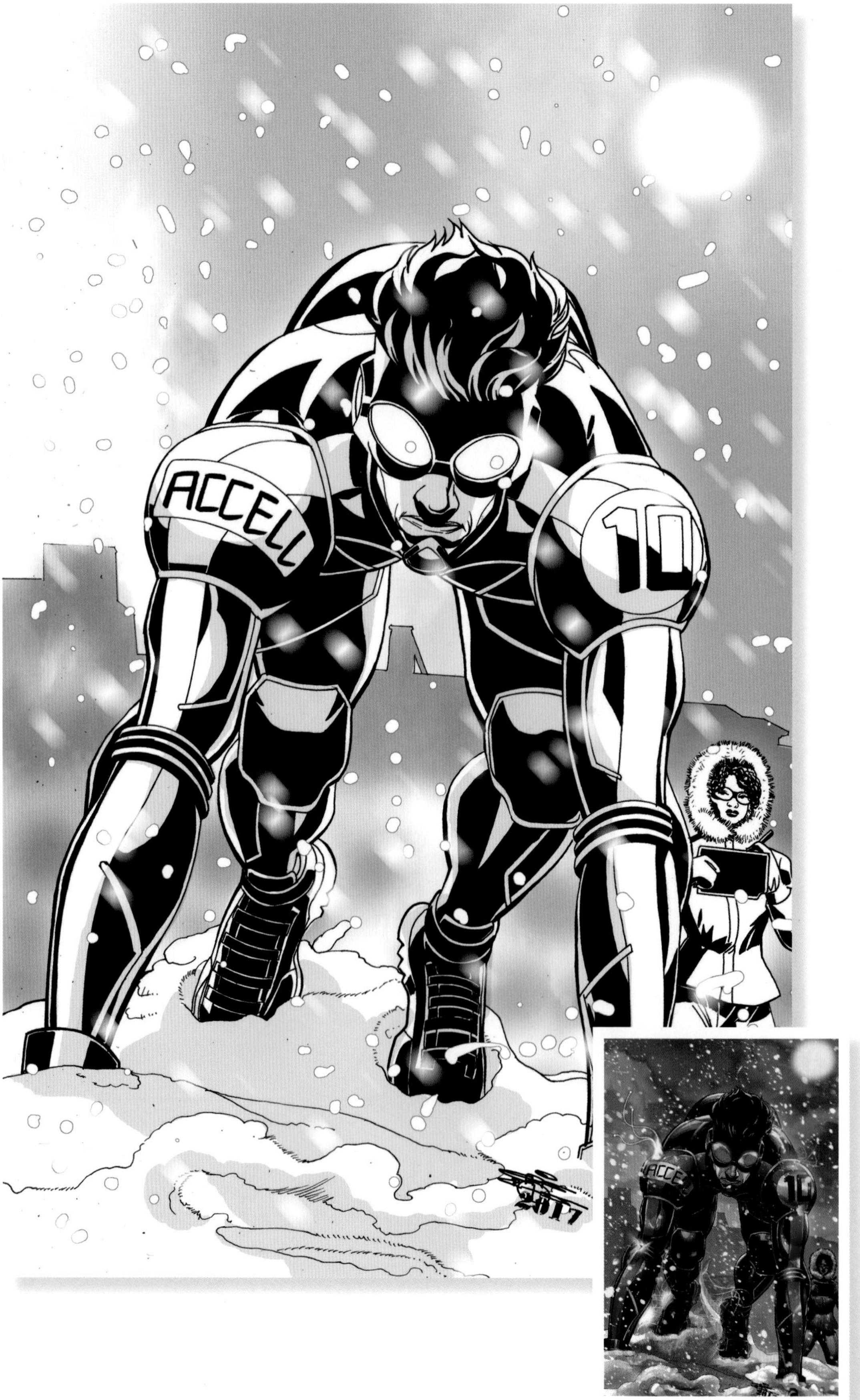
ACCELL
10
2017

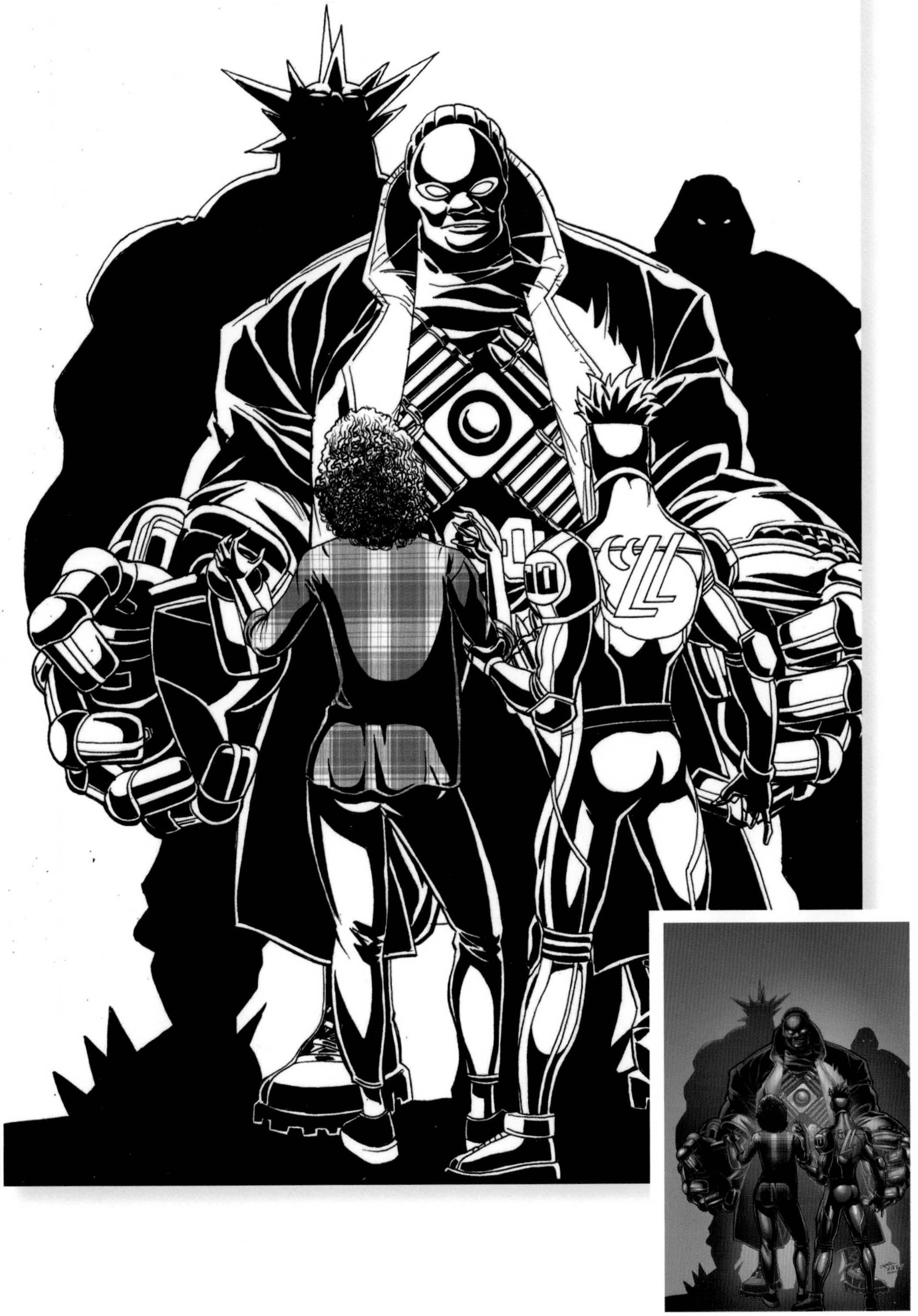

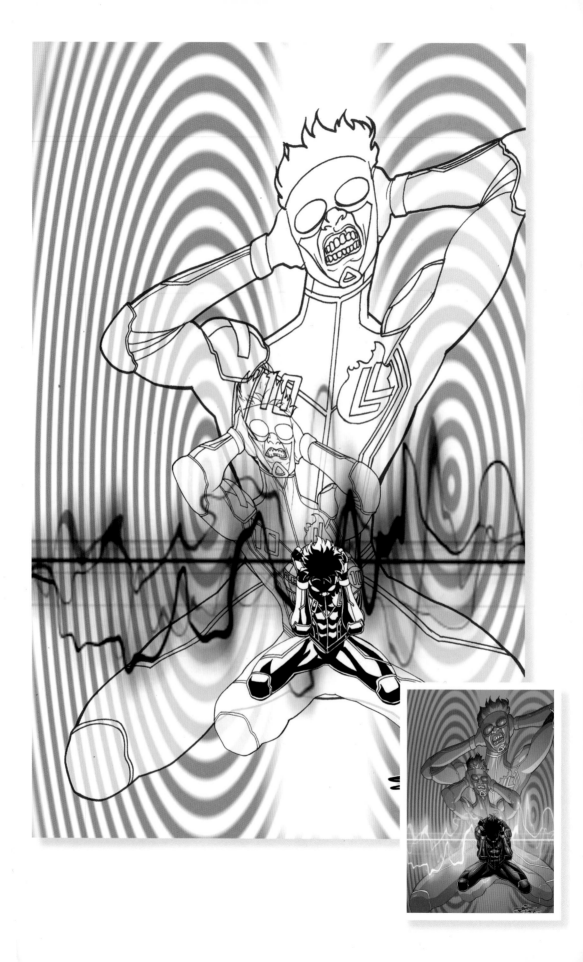